WITHDRAWN
UTSA Libraries

The Ethiopian Transformation

The Ethiopian Transformation

The Quest for the Post-Imperial State

John W. Harbeson

Westview Press
BOULDER & LONDON

Westview Special Studies on Africa

All rights reserved. No part of this publication may be reproduced or transmitted in any form or by any means, electronic or mechanical, including photocopy, recording, or any information storage and retrieval system, without permission in writing from the publisher.

Copyright © 1988 by Westview Press, Inc.

Published in 1988 in the United States of America by Westview Press, Inc., 5500 Central Avenue, Boulder, Colorado 80301

Library of Congress Cataloging-in-Publication Data
Harbeson, John W. (John Willis), 1938- .
  The Ethiopian transformation:the quest for the post-imperial state
by John Harbeson
    p. cm.—(Westview special studies on Africa)
  Bibliography: p.
  Includes index.
  ISBN 0-8133-7418-9
  1. Ethiopia—Politics and government—1974- . 2. Ethiopia—Social conditions—1974- . I. Title. II. Series.
DT387.95.H37 1988
963'.07—dc19   87-20134
                                                                                  CIP

Printed and bound in the United States of America

∞ The paper used in this publication meets the requirements of the American National Standard for Permanence of Paper for Printed Library Materials Z39.48-1984.

10 9 8 7 6 5 4 3 2 1

For my father
and
to the memory of my mother

Contents

Preface ix
Acknowledgments xi

1 Introduction: The Dimensions of Controversy 1

Three Revolutions, Three Phases, 2
Theoretical Dimensions, 9
Conclusion, 17
Notes, 17

2 The Historical Foundations of the Ethiopian State 22

The Legacy of the Ancient Empire, 23
The Birth of the Modern Empire, 30
The Consolidation of the Twentieth-Century Empire, 38
Foundations of the Modern Ethiopian State:
  An Interim Appraisal, 41
The Political Economy of Haile Selassie's
  Postwar Empire, 43
Conclusion, 57
Notes, 59

3 Ethiopia on the Eve of the Transformation 66

Geography, 66
Societies and Cultures, 68
Political Economy, 71
Conclusion, 80
Notes, 80

4 The Beginnings of Change 82

Causes, 82
Reform, Revolution, or Creeping Coup? 94

Conclusion, 115
Notes, 115

5 The Crisis of the Post-Imperial State — 117

The Troubled Legacy, 118
Revolutionary Policies, 126
The Politics of State Transformation, 144
Conclusion, 164
Notes, 164

6 Military Rule and the Transformation of State and Society — 168

Toward a Command Economy, 170
Political Development from Above, 179
Military Rule and Socioeconomic Transformation, 191
Conclusion, 215
Notes, 215

7 Conclusions — 220

The State of the Ethiopian Transformation, 220
Lessons of the Ethiopian Transformation, 226
Notes, 230

Select Bibliography — 231
Index — 234

Preface

The plan of this book is as follows. Chapter 1 will introduce the major outlines of the Ethiopian transformation. It will identify the sources of violent contention over the direction of the country since the overthrow of Emperor Haile Selassie I. A major point of the chapter is that imbedded in these controversies are issues of considerable significance for theories of revolution and of the political economies of developing nations. Finally, the chapter will suggest the existence of a prima facie lack of "fit" between the nature of the Ethiopian struggles and the manner in which some prevailing theoretical positions have been formulated. But it will also suggest that the Ethiopian case may not be simply deviant but rather one that could assist in the further refinement of such theories. The chapters that follow will address the Ethiopian transformation from these perspectives.

Chapter 2 will place the Ethiopian transformation in the context of the country's long and tumultuous history. The central question to be addressed is in what senses a degree of political community emerged that was not dependent for its legitimacy upon the existence of imperial institutions and thus might survive their demise. The chapter argues that while such a historical basis for an Ethiopian state did emerge as the Mengistu government has maintained, it was more decentralized in accepted practice than the post-1974 government has insisted it must be. Chapter 3 will appraise the condition of Ethiopia's economy and society on the eve of the beginning of the transformation. It will consider the socioeconomic and geographical roots of the Ethiopian state at the end of the imperial era.

Chapters 4, 5, and 6 will trace the course of the Ethiopian transformation since its inception in 1974. Chapter 4 will center upon the collapse of the empire and the emergence of a military regime in what has become known as the February Revolution, and Chapter 5 will examine the objectives, policies, and processes of the Mengistu government. These chapters will consider the bases and forms of opposition to the regime and the theoretical problems of state definition and transformation and of social revolution that those controversies have engendered. Chapter 6 will examine the course of the Ethiopian transformation since 1979 after the military regime survived the challenges of its opponents sufficiently to turn more of its attention to other matters. Chief among these have been consolidating the political structure of the new order and promoting economic development based on the land reforms the regime has introduced. This chapter will give particular attention to the implications of the regime's management strategies for the theoretical concerns explored in preceding chapters. Finally, Chapter 7 will attempt to sum up the state of the transformation, assess its costs and benefits, identify its winners and losers, and offer a tentative assessment of its future prospects. It will apply these findings to the theoretical questions introduced at the beginning of the book.

John W. Harbeson
Croton-on-Hudson, New York

Acknowledgments

When I accepted a visiting professorship at what was then Haile Selassie I University for 1973–1975, I did not expect that a book on a revolution would be one of the outcomes of my research during that tour. Nevertheless, after a brief glimpse of Ethiopia under its last emperor, the old order passed and revolutionary changes unfolded, and I could not fail to study and write about them. I am greatly indebted to my colleagues at the University who, while being caught up in the turbulence of the times in very personal ways, taught me about their country and engaged me in their shared efforts to understand the course of events. I wish particularly to express my appreciation to my colleagues in the Department of Political Science and Public Administration, Negussay Ayele, Asmelash Beyene, Marilyn and Baissa Lemmu, the late Tefarraworq Beshah, and in the Institute for Development Research, Asseffa Mehretu and Teshome Mulat. I am also indebted for their support to three successive presidents of the university: Taye Gulilat, Duri Mohammed, and Abiy Kifle. For my students, revolutionary change in Ethiopia was an absorbing personal calling, and many were imprisoned, killed, or forced into exile as a consequence of the bitter, violent struggles considered in this book. Yet they were equally passionate in their quest for knowledge and in their belief that the classroom should be a place for understanding rather than for engaging in the momentous struggles in which they were absorbed.

This book has been more than a decade in the making both because of innumerable professional distractions and because events themselves and my understanding of them needed time to gel. In that time I have incurred numerous debts I can never fully repay to those who have encouraged me in this enterprise, read and commented on my work, and provided indispensable moral and material support. I could not have written the book without the contributions of Ethiopians in all walks of life who, in both formal interviews and informal conversations, have nurtured my understanding of their country. Nor could I have done so without the friendship and constructive criticism of a community of Ethiopian specialists within which competitiveness is understated and genuine professional collegiality the norm. A great many individuals have been particularly helpful to me in various stages of the development of the book. I wish especially to thank Arthur Berger, Aklog Birara, Paul Brietzke, Akalu Negewo, John Burns, John Cohen, Pat and Elaine Garland, Robert Hess, Harold Marcus, Robert Roundy, Edward Schten and his family, Barry Riley, Robert Armstrong, David and Marina Ottaway, Donald Rothchild, and Blair Thomson.

I am grateful for financial support to the Institute for Development Research at Addis Ababa University, the Johnson Foundation, David Johnson, the Wisconsin Alumni Research Foundation, the University of Wisconsin–Parkside, the City University of New York Research Foundation, and Universities Field Staff International. Begun before microcomputers were prevalent, early drafts of what was to become this book were typed by Terry Koehler and Phyllis Konikow. John Kranz prepared the index. This book was completed in the age of the microcomputer revolution, and my son and daughter, Eric and Kristen, put up with having their favorite toy monopolized by Dad and "the book." They and my wife, Ann, have shared my encounter with Ethiopia in every way, and it has been their moral support that has made writing this book important and possible.

All the errors of fact and interpretation that remain are mine alone.

J.W.H.

1

Introduction: The Dimensions of Controversy

Ethiopia officially became a people's democratic republic in September 1987. Arrival at this milestone completed, formally at least, the country's thirteen year transformation from a tradition-laden feudal imperial state with an overlay of bureaucracy and incipient capitalism to a new Ethiopian state publicly pledged to realizing the teachings of Marx and Lenin. A popular uprising early in 1974 prompted a military committee to dismantle the government of Emperor Haile Selassie I, institute fundamental social and economic reforms, establish a vanguard Communist party, and prepare a new constitution that was formally inaugurated six months after it received broad approval in a popular referendum.

A principal hypothesis of this book, however, is that ratification of the new constitution has signified a milestone primarily in the entrenchment of a once transitional regime rather than in the legitimization of a transformed, post-imperial Ethiopian state. The apparent fruition of the Ethiopian revolution, represented by electoral endorsement and inauguration of the constitution of the People's Democratic Republic, has camouflaged a reality of fundamental, unresolved, multifaceted conflicts concerning the validity, nature, and direction of a revolutionary Ethiopian state for which the military regime has claimed to be prophet, midwife, and architect. This often-tumultuous thirteen-year period of political change, civil war, regional conflict, far-reaching social and economic reforms, leadership struggles, and international realignment, bounded at either end by catastrophic famine relief and rehabilitation efforts, has centered on three fundamental and interrelated problems.

The first problem has been whether, in what form, and how to maintain the Ethiopian state after the demise of the imperial regime of Haile Selassie I and his predecessors. The second problem has been how, amidst the ruins of the *ancien regime,* to design and effect the transformation of the Ethiopian state. The third problem has been how to promote rapid economic development by and for some of the poorest people on earth within the framework of comprehensive measures inspired by a vision of social revolution. The formal inauguration of the new Ethiopian constitution consummates the emergence of seemingly established working, if profoundly controversial, answers to these questions.[1]

One principal purpose of this book is to examine the controversies surrounding the formation of the *nouveau regime* as both perpetrator and product of many profound struggles, and to examine evolving working answers to these controversies. A second major purpose of this work is to explore some of the larger theoretical issues these controversies have posed and their implications for the literature on revolution, political economy, the state, and management in developing countries. The remainder of this chapter will present, first, an overview of the Ethiopian transformation and, second, an outline of some of its more important theoretical implications.

Three Revolutions, Three Phases

The fall of Haile Selassie's government opened the way not to one but to three distinct and competing, yet overlapping, revolutionary movements that have warred with each other over three identifiable phases. These revolutionary movements may be identified as (1) *military-led socialism,* designed by the regime of the current ruler, Mengistu Haile Mariam; (2) *civilian socialism,* whose advocates have objected fundamentally to military leadership of the revolution and to the regime's manner of effecting the transformation, though they have also harbored other points of ideological disagreement with the regime and with each other; and (3) *separatist nationalism,* pledged to full independence or substantial autonomy for major regions of the former empire. The struggles of these competing revolutionary movements define three identifiable phases: (1) a transiton phase during which the old regime collapsed and was progressively dismantled by an emerging military cadre; (2) a reform phase between 1974 and 1979, during which the military regime sought to establish the bases of a socialist post-imperial Ethiopia and participated in a major international political realignment within the Horn of Africa; and (3) a development phase between 1979 and 1988 during which the primary objectives have been to realize the possibilities for economic development and improved standards of living the regime believed its reforms to portend and to formulate and establish a people's democratic republic signifying the official end of provisional military rule.

The Transition

The transition from the old regime to the new military order began with the resignation of Haile Selassie's cabinet in response to pressures from the military that were born of both the drought-famine syndrome and inflationary conditions that beset the country as a whole.[2] An unprecedented move in itself, the collective cabinet departure presaged a seven month interregnum within which a "reform" government appointed by Emperor Haile Selassie I was rendered almost totally impotent by strikes and demonstrations throughout the country in support of demands for a range of reforms. A committee of middle-ranking and junior officers from each of the armed forces divisions established a coordinating committee, which began the systematic but gradual arrest of officials of the old regime leading inexorably to the arrest of the emperor himself on September 12, 1974. Remarkably, almost all those arrested turned themselves in voluntarily upon being asked to do so by the military.

Many factors combined to create the impression that a change of government and in basic policies, rather than a fundamental reconstitution of the Ethiopian political order, were in prospect.[3] These factors included the docile submission of officials of the imperial regime to the military, the gradual process by which they were called upon to submit to arrest, the ceremonial fashion in which the emperor himself was finally removed from office, the military coordinating committee's stated loyalty to the emperor almost up to the point when it deposed him, the anonymity of the military committee members throughout this phase, and the tacit acquiescence in the military's leadership of the transition by most communities, including those who later were to oppose Mengistu's regime.

Reform

The execution of General Aman Andom, who replaced Haile Selassie as head of state, and of nearly sixty other arrested notables of the old regime in November 1974, shattered previously cultivated illusions of continuity between the new and old orders. Whereas the removal of Haile Selassie and his entourage constituted the substitution of one government for another, the executions called into question whether and in what senses an Ethiopian state survived the illusions of political and economic development cultivated by the emperor's regime. They provoked a continuing and still unresolved "constitutional" crisis between a military regime that has sought to establish a new foundation for the Ethiopian state, on the one hand, and civilian and separatist nationalist revolutionary movements pledged, respectively, to contrasting concepts and alternative boundaries for the post-imperial Ethiopian state, on the other hand.

While Eritrean and other insurgencies long predated the November executions and demands for civilian rule surfaced immediately after the emperor was deposed, the crisis of how to constitute a post-imperial Ethiopian state nonetheless commenced in earnest with the executions.[4] Mengistu Haile Mariam and his associates subsequently removed some of the ambiguity concerning their intentions. Eritrean liberation parties began a sustained drive for full independence, and since that date appear to have given only fleeting encouragement to negotiations with the government in Addis Ababa on any basis other than complete independence. This is the case despite reports that at least some cadres within the movement have at times seemed to recognize their military incapacity to expel completely the Ethiopian troops from the region. Demands for civilian and more participatory government plagued Mengistu's government, known as the *derg* ("committee" in Amharic), from within and from outside its ranks. These demands interfered with the implementation of the reforms that the military government sought to sponsor especially during the next five years. An ironic result of this conflict was Mengistu's emergence as undisputed leader of a military government within which there had initially been a broader degree of power sharing.

The *derg* moved quickly after the executions to establish its agenda for post-imperial Ethiopia. Within the next eighteen months, the military ushered in most of the major reforms of inherited socioeconomic institutions that it was to propose. Mengistu's regime ended its anonymity and proclaimed the achievement of Ethiopian socialism as its objective.[5] His government nationalized major industrial and commercial firms, promulgated reforms nationalizing all rural and urban land, restaffed and cursorily retrained personnel for reorganized governmental structures, launched crash programs to raise the country's extremely low literacy levels, reorganized the country's educational system, and launched *zemechas* (campaigns) in which high school and college students and teachers were sent to the countryside to mobilize revolutionary consciousness and help implement the reforms. Of all these measures, the rural land reform has been the centerpiece of the military regime's initiatives to eradicate the endemic poverty and inequality sustained under the emperors and to implant the foundations of a new socialist Ethiopia.[6] With the reform, the government addressed the grinding poverty and stark inequality of the sector, where over 80 percent of the population earned a living, 90 percent resided, 50 percent of the country's income was earned, and 90 percent of export income was derived.

The military regime introduced these reforms to establish new social and economic structures *before* it addressed directly the overarching issues it raised in seizing power concerning the structure of the post-imperial state. In effect, Mengistu's government appeared to argue that (1) formation of the structures of the new state should begin from the ground up and (2) the superstructure of the new Ethiopian state should be built upon the foundation of new socioeconomic institutions within which most people were to live and work. Implicitly, it claimed further that such grassroots structures should be established by central decree through a temporary military administration with responsibility for reconstituting the Ethiopian state on new foundations.

The military government's postponement of civilian and more democratic rule contributed to its apparent retreat into a counterrevolutionary posture. The Ethiopian Democratic Union, though perhaps not strictly a royalist party, opposed the *derg* from the right but never threatened its rule as seriously as did movements seeking the liberation of Eritrea from the Ethiopia of the emperors or as did the Ethiopian People's Revolutionary Party, which disputed the military government's claim to rule.[7] Had there been such opposition from the right, the military might have successfully cast itself as a centrist broker between left and right. In the absence of such strong rightist opposition, both the regime and its opponents were more able to portray each other as counterrevolutionary, thereby magnifying the controversy and the apparent stakes in their disputes.

The rejection by the *derg* of civilian and more democratic rule was one approach to a rather complicated strategic problem of state transformation. Had it chosen to admit civilians, many of those eligible might well have been among the considerable numbers who had been beholden previously to the emperor for status, occupation, and wealth. The military regime made a symbolic concession to such groups by establishing as a senior adviser a liberal son of the emperor's cousin who had been known as the "red *ras*" (prince) for disposing of his lands to his tenants. But the government's reorganization of the trade union movement, which had been in the forefront of demands for civilian rule, helped establish in the minds of the union's adherents that one form of authoritarian rule had been replaced with another.

The military government has consistently rejected public negotiations with the Eritrean liberation movements. It has refused to accept, at least officially, that the movements truly represent the will of the Eritrean peoples or that the "unity" of the Ethiopian polity can be a subject of negotiations. The *derg* has insisted on adopting the boundaries of the empire as those of the new Ethiopian state. While there have been serious conflicts among the Eritrean forces and at least some periodic divergences in their posture vis-à-vis the Addis Ababa regime, they have shared the position that the Ethiopian empire must be destroyed and the component nationalities liberated according to the pattern set by European empires elsewhere on the continent. Like the civilian opponents of the regime, who nonetheless wished to maintain the boundaries of Ethiopia as established by the emperors, Eritrean and other liberation movements have appeared to reject the military regime's strategy of rebuilding the social and economic foundations of the polity prior to the political reconstitution of the state. They have viewed its alleged authoritarianism as reminiscent of the emperor's regime.

The *derg* introduced a National Democratic Revolutionary Program in April 1976, which appeared to open the way both to popular civilian participation in the reconstitution of the state and to some autonomy for national groups within the new order.[8] The outcome, however, was nearly three years of open conflict, which blended subtle but significant ideological differences with long-standing personal and family feuds leading to near civil-war conditions in Addis Ababa and elsewhere. These conflicts spurred a series of purges and putsches within the military government itself, ending in a strengthening and consolidation of authoritarian rule: the emergence of Mengistu as the largely unchallenged ruler within a regime that had once been an association of more than one hundred members, the suppression of the newly surfaced political parties, and the strengthening of central government administrative authority within the land reform and other structures. These responses of the military government seemed to its opponents to confirm the existence of the old authoritarianism of the emperors in a new form.

In the midst of the "domestic" constitutional and political struggles, the long-simmering border dispute between Somalia and Ethiopia erupted into a full-scale war in 1977 in the Somali-inhabited Ogaden region of Ethiopia.[9] The war completed the two countries' exchange of great power sponsors. Soviet efforts to mediate on the basis of supposed ideological affinity between the two protagonists led to their expulsion from Somalia. Soviet and Cuban military assistance that poured into Ethiopia enabled the military regime to suppress a strong Somalia bid to detach the Ogaden from Ethiopia. The two powers remained to assist the Addis government in its Eritrean campaigns with more limited results— essentially the restoration of a stalemate that the Eritreans had begun to erode in their favor in the preceding two years. These campaigns, augmented by some ill-considered officially organized peasant militia forays against Eritrean insurgents, did much to reinforce the image and reality of the military regime, in the eyes of its detractors, as a permanent rather than transitional administration and as the embodiment of, rather than the liberating successor to, the regime of the emperor.

Development

The third and current phase of the Ethiopian transformation has been defined by the Mengistu regime's efforts to complete the formation of the new Ethiopian state, to extend reform processes begun earlier, and to promote processes of economic development within the framework of these new institutions. The government has pressed hard to advance the rural land reform, in which individual household usufruct has predominated, toward new stages wherein control of the land and equipment is to become increasingly collective in the hands of producer cooperatives.

With the most serious domestic and international military challenges to its authority under better control by 1979, Mengistu's government turned to establishing administrative machinery to influence and direct production efforts as well as other initiatives such as the literacy campaigns.[10] Under these initiatives, peasant associations increasingly became the instruments of centrally directed development campaigns. At the same time, however, a range of economic incentives were formulated to favor the numerous state farms or the more collectivized producer cooperatives at the expense of the preexisting peasant associations. Finally, the government redoubled its efforts to defend the country's territorial integrity by introducing compulsory and universal military service in 1983.[11]

The regime established a commission to form a single workers' party to which it nominally handed over authority on the tenth anniversary of the revolution though the transition reflected little change in top leadership. A commission was established to prepare a constitution for the reorganized state, taking into account its ethnic diversity, and a report was issued in mid-1986. After a period of discussion of the draft within the rural and urban associations that resulted in few major changes, 95 percent of the eligible voters turned out on February 1, 1987, to ratify the new constitution by an 81 percent majority. The new order was then formally inaugurated on the thirteenth anniversary of the deposing of the emperor, September 12, 1987.

Ecological and economic realities have severely tested not only the Mengistu regime's policies but the reforms it has proposed to institute and, most fundamentally, its designs for the formation of a scientific socialist post-imperial Ethiopian state. Any social and economic progress achieved since 1974 has been overshadowed not only by wars in the 1970s but also by the recurrence of severe drought and famine since the mid-1980s claiming thousands of lives and endangering not just the health but the very survival of a generation of Ethiopians.[12] More than the famine of the early 1970s, which precipitated the fall of the emperor's government, this renewed plague at least periodically brought hardship to residents of Addis Ababa and other urban areas as well as catastrophe to thousands of rural households.

The massive relief efforts that international agencies have mounted, however, have been hindered by the very circumstances that contributed to the crisis in the first place. The poverty of the country has been reflected in the limited port facilities at Assab for receipt of imported grain and in the poor roads in the areas hardest hit. Grain shipments have been placed in competition with arms imports with which the country's "constitutional debate" has in reality been in large part waged. Attempted massive resettlement of families from overpopulated, heavily eroded, soil-fragile northern areas to southern precincts has floundered for lack of resources to establish these families in the new areas, and the relocation efforts thus have been heavily in need of foreign assistance. Ironically, some donors accused the *derg* of resettling for the political purpose of scattering its opponents when officially sponsored resettlement had long occurred and had been advocated by expatriate advisers.[13]

Problems in conveying relief supplies to the famine-stricken areas have demonstrated the thin line between "national" and "international" activity in the Horn of Africa. Relief agencies have wrestled with the problem of "safe passage" for goods between the Ethiopian capital and the afflicted districts, many of which are intermittently or wholly under the influence of secessionist forces that now embrace much of Tigre and parts of other northern provinces as well as Eritrea. Terms such as "safe passage" have suggested conflict between more than one sovereign entity, the confirmation of which would powerfully influence the on-going "constitutional debate" in favor of some of the regime's opponents. The same merging of domestic and regional international politics has been evident in relief agencies' reliance on cross-border shipments of supplies from Sudan into famine stricken zones of northwestern Ethiopia. This occurred at a time when Sudan and Ethiopia were accusing each other of giving sanctuary to secessionist groups bent on redrawing the borders of the two states, even as peoples of Bete Israel (the Falasha) were being airlifted from Ethiopia to Israel through Sudan.

Ethiopia in 1988 was a country visibly reorganized in political terms. It featured a central government with significantly increased capacity to govern at the grass roots levels, but the sphere within which its writ ran had shrunk compared with that exercised by Haile Selassie's government as a result of extended liberation movement activity. Access to educational opportunity has greatly expanded though education resources have not expanded, at a corresponding rate. The transformation has left the country no less vulnerable to ecological catastrophe than before, though the regime has made determined efforts to arrest deforestation. And the harsh economic reality is that the country is as poor in 1988 as it was in 1974, monumental efforts at social revolution and force-paced economic development notwithstanding. Unlike most other African countries, including some staunchly socialist ones, Ethiopia under the Mengistu regime has not only resisted policy reform in the face of economic stagnation but has redoubled commitments to its existing strategy.

Theoretical Dimensions

The controversies outlined in the foregoing account pose fundamentally important theoretical questions for the study of (1) social revolutions, (2) class formation in developing country contexts, (3) state transformation, and (4) management of social transformations with a view to achieving commensurate economic development. These questions will be introduced in the remainder of this chapter and reconsidered in the concluding chapter on the basis of the full account of the Ethiopian transformation that follows.

Ethiopia and the Comparative Study of Social Revolutions

Theoretical interest in events in Ethiopia since 1974 arises in the first instance because it is not yet clear whether, or in what senses, it is appropriate to speak of them as constituting a "revolution." The problem is not primarily the consequence of a multiplicity of extant analytical frameworks for identifying and classifying revolutions. Rather, definitions that may well be helpful in other contexts beg essential questions in the case of Ethiopia. For just one example, Skocpol in her classic study of three social revolutions relies on a definition of revolutions as "rapid, basic transformations of a society's state and class structures accompanied and carried through by class-based revolts from below."[14] But whether such social revolution has occurred, or is in the process of occurring, in Ethiopia is very much at issue. Protagonists in the Ethiopia arena have profoundly, even violently, disagreed on which of two possible meanings of the term "transformation" is appropriate.

The military regime of Mengistu Haile Mariam believes it has wrought a transformation, meriting designation as a "revolution," in the sense that it considers Ethiopia's political, economic, and social goals, structures, and policies to be fundamentally different from and very much better than those existing prior to 1974. It believes these changed institutions and values to be the basis for eventual realization of much-improved standards of living for ordinary Ethiopians if only they can be preserved against challenges from internal and external detractors.

The regime's opponents, however, view the work of Mengistu's government as a transformation in the more mathematical sense of the term, as a conversion of the traditional imperial Ethiopian political equation from one form to another without change of meaning. They believe the changes wrought by the regime to be superficial, concealing a present-day and likely future continuity in the underlying socioeconomic and political realities in the country. These they characterize as authoritarian rule and continued socioeconomic subjection of the majority of the country's primarily rural households rather than their liberation.

The choice of the term "transformation" in this book is an appropriate term for characterizing events in Ethiopia, by contrast to others such as "revolution," precisely because its dual meaning renders it relatively neutral as between alternative interpretations of events in the country since 1974. It represents a provisional means of distinguishing Ethiopian events from other types and patterns of change elsewhere, without begging the fundamental questions about those events that remain at issue. The term is also appropriate to the conclusions of the book which are that the Ethiopian transformation in some respects does, and in others does not, merit designation as a revolution with the normative connotations the term carries for Skocpol as for others.

Beyond the problem of applying definitions of revolution to Ethiopian events lies a fundamental issue concerning the components of successful social transformations. In *States and Social Revolutions,* one of the most important recent examinations of the subject, Skocpol finds the extent to which the state is an autonomous actor vis-à-vis the roles of dominant classes and/or popular disaffection rallying under ideological banners to have been understated as a key element in the "success" of the French, Russian, and Chinese revolutions.[15] Noting mass mobilization by the military regime against the legacies of the *ancien regime* and external threats and strong influence by the great powers, Skocpol (in a footnote) considers Ethiopia to have conformed to "classic social-revolutionary patterns."[16] Implicitly, her analysis leads her to deny the claims of the regime's opponents that precisely because of its asserted autonomy from dominant classes, the regime has stolen, preempted, or betrayed the revolution that was to have been and has in fact reinforced many of the most despised features of the old order. Curiously, by contrast, it is the ideological vision and quest for modernity through structural reforms, which Skocpol considers less fundamental, upon which the military regime appears to base its claims to revolutionary legitimacy. Ethiopian data suggest that the regime's assertion of autonomy in its difficult quest for survival, far from facilitating a successful social revolution, may indeed have been a prominent factor impeding its realization.

A fundamental problem with the "relative autonomy" thesis may be that it fails to account for revolutions that purport to transform the *state* itself, not merely social relations within the state. This in turn results from a tendency to reduce the concept of the state to the institutions of government (a problem to be discussed shortly), even as the same tendency attacks reduction of the "state" to underlying patterns of social relations. The Ethiopian case suggests that in the course of revolution a *government's* assertion of autonomy vis-à-vis dominant social forces may undermine an *interdependence* between them necessary to realize and legitimize a revolution in the nature of the state.

State, Class, Development, and the Lessons of Ethiopian History

Continuing economic stagnation on the African continent has spurred an academic debate over the causes.[17] Of central importance in the debate has been the continuing dependence of more than 70 percent of the African people on agriculture for their livelihood. Goren Hyden's *Beyond Ujamaa* suggested not only the autonomy of the state vis-à-vis these small producers, at least in Tanzania, but its near irrelevance to such a largely precapitalist peasant sector enmeshed in its economy of affection.[18] He argues again in his later *No Shortcuts to Progress* that the promotion of capitalism is essential to the economic liberation of the peasant sector and the development of African agriculture.[19] Hyden never quite makes clear, however, whether it is the state itself, the *socialism* of the state, or the state's *management* of development that creates the gap. *No Shortcuts* suggests the value of nongovernmental organizations in promoting rural development, but without indicating the relative importance of anticipated improved management, decentralization, and economic restructuring in achieving higher levels of development. He also gives little attention to the role of government per se in promoting the capitalism he believes to be essential.

The subsequent debate over state and class in emergent African political economies has moved toward the view both that the state has in fact been an important element in class formation and that the state is an important theater itself within which class formation occurs.[20] But this debate has continued to obscure the question of whether and/or how the state should influence the *kind* of class structures that emerge in developing economies. There has been broad recognition concerning the importance of smallholder agriculture to the health and development of African economies.[21] However, the controversy over the relationship of state and class in the continent has left unclear whether and/or how the state can or should shape emerging class structures to the benefit of such economically essential but politically peripheralized small producers. At a policy level, moreover, the widespread recognition that official prices should favor agricultural producers as distinct from urban food consumers does not normally reach the question of whether "getting the prices right" can, should, or is likely to strengthen the position of small producers as against larger ones.

The normative question of whether as well as how the state can influence the shape of class formation in developing economies is of critical importance in the Ethiopian case. The Ethiopian data suggest the inextricability of state, regime, and class formation in processes of economic change. More fundamentally, the Ethiopian case illustrates a basic definitional problem in the debate over state and class, i.e., the definitions of class employed. Both the regime *and* many of its opponents have viewed themselves as the exponents of a class-based, or at least mass-based, revolution against what both sides consider to have been an oppressive feudal oligarchy under the *ancien regime*. Rather than either the regime or its opponents being wrong or engaging in self-delusion, it is at least possible that both sides have intermixed economic power with political power, nationality, ethnicity, and/or regionalism in their working definitions of the movements they purport to lead. The Ethiopian case thus suggests the possibility that more complex, context-sensitive definitions of "class" must be introduced into the theoretical debate if the term is to have meaning and validity in particular contexts.

The normative question concerning the role of the state in class formation and the problem of contextuality in defining "class" may be important in addressing a fundamental historical issue posed by Hyden that has a direct bearing on the Ethiopian case. Much of the policy debate on the revitalization of African economies tacitly assumes that the many forms of socialism are collectively *intrinsically* inappropriate to the task of promoting economic development. Hyden, on the other hand, has argued that socialist strategies have been historically *premature* in Africa, a position with which orthodox Marxists might be expected to concur.

The argument between the military regime and its opponents, however, has recognized no such historical guidelines for political and socioeconomic transformation, notwithstanding the professed scientific socialist commitment of the regime as well as many of its opponents. Thus, at least two fundamental questions arise for the more theoretical debate. First, to what extent do African countries have sufficiently unique historical patterns of development that the lessons of such history cannot be deduced from general theory? Perhaps, at most, developing countries' historical patterns can only be grouped in categories through more empirically oriented comparative analysis. Second, each side has accused the other of being historically regressive, thus posing for the theoretical debate the often overlooked problem of developmental decay recognized by Huntington more than two decades ago but seldom considered in specific situations.[22]

The Ethiopian data suggest that working definitions of class have centered upon the *political* credentials of the contending "classes" to lead in the formation of a successor state, credentials which were significantly affected by their possibly distinctive relationships to the imperial government. Chapter 2 explores the historical foundations of the Ethiopian polity that may survive the demise of the imperial regime. It considers the evolution of class and regime relationships especially during the reign of Haile Selassie I and considers their implications for the formation of a successor state.

Ethiopia, Policy Reform, and the Problem of State Transformation

The debate on policy reform has centered upon (1) the shrinkage but also the decentralization and reorientation of the public sector, and (2) a public sector that nevertheless remains omnipresent enough to influence price structures in the interests of agricultural producers (small-scale ones in some formulations).[23] Opponents have centered on the importance of international as opposed to domestic factors emphasized by the World Bank and others in explaining the continent's continued stagnation.[24] They have called for more horizontal economic cooperation among poor countries as opposed to interdependence with industrialized states, and/or they have advocated interdependence on more favorable terms than some industrialized countries have been prepared to accept. More important for this book, however, is an assumption by both "sides" that the state retains sufficient autonomy to be able to change the character of the economies and societies they seek to regulate. This assumption is opened to serious question by the many accounts, by Hyden and many others, of the weakness or "softness" of states in developing countries.[25] How successfully can even strengthened governments within still weak states decentralize and still retain their authority, liquidate governmental structures and still be able to cause their writ to run broadly among their constituents, and reorient themselves internally in favor of planning agencies without seriously enlarging crippling internal divisions? The feasibility and processes of state transformation are thus a critical and largely unaddressed dimension of the policy debate.

The Ethiopian data suggest the underlying if weakly articulated strength of the foundations of the Ethiopian state. The evidence suggests further that regimes may weaken both themselves and those underlying foundations of statehood by persistent actions considered illegitimate within the framework of those foundations. For all sides in the Ethiopian arena, the question of state transformation is also fundamental. The general issue is what course of state transformation will strengthen rather than weaken the historical foundations of the state. The specific issue is how the processes and the results of reordering the relationship of government toward specific sectors of the economy in fact tax and/or strengthen the underlying bases of statehood. Both sides seek to erect a post-imperial order radically different from the *ancien regime,* yet each side considers that the other in political terms *represents* the old order in a new form, in fact if not by purpose. Both sides thus have a great deal invested in the problem of *how* states get transformed, if at all.

The nature of the problem of state transformation turns critically upon the working definition of the state that is employed. A predominant tendency in the literature implicitly has been to equate the state with the institutions of government. Rothchild, for example, in a recent review of literature on the state in African development observes a prevailing tendency of analysts to conceive of the state as a "group of institutions which allocate social values authoritatively" and as "a bounded core of hierarchically organized public officials."[26] Skocpol's autonomous state consists of "a set of administrative, policing, and military organizations headed, and more or less well coordinated by, an executive authority."[27] Possibly a quite different conception of the state is indicated by Max Weber, who defined the state as a "compulsory association with a territorial basis."[28] Weber's definition suggests that governmental institutions may not be *synonymous* with the state but rather *derivative* from an underlying generally recognized basis for political community—in other words, a "constitution" even if not formally codified or rooted in long-established common law. Rothchild, in the same review, argues for the importance of this more fundamental aspect of the state as "a set of organizing principles." This book argues that the Ethiopian transformation cannot be understood in either theoretical or practical terms except on the basis of this larger conception of the state.

Control of the institutions of government has been the *object* of the struggles between the Ethiopian military regime and its opponents. Now that the empire has been dismantled, however, the *bases* of their dispute, however, have been (1) whether or on what basis an Ethiopian state, in the more Weberian sense of the term, existed or continues to exist; and (2) how and by what means the revolution should achieve the transformation of any residual basis of such statehood. For all sides in the Ethiopian drama, the focus of concern has been the use of governmental institutions to define or redefine the underlying basis of an Ethiopian polity from which those institutions must derive their legitimacy. The military regime has considered itself the midwife of revolutionary change not only in social and economic structures but in the very constitution of the Ethiopian polity from an empire to a socialist republic. The regime's opponents have been united in rejecting the role the military government has arrogated to itself. Some have seen the military regime as attempting to entrench itself and thus betray the revolutionary transformation of the state. Others have challenged not only the military's vision of the new order but whether a basis for an Ethiopian community, as it has been geographically defined during the twentieth century, continues to exist. Such exponents of liberation for the former empire's component nationalities have reacted to the facts both that the empire has been dismantled and that the successor military regime has afforded such nationalities scant recognition of their identity or their quest for measures of self-determination.

The contention of this book is that historical foundations for the Ethiopian state have existed that are more durable than the institutions of the imperial regime. However, despite the professed objectives of the participants, the post-imperial Ethiopian transformation has taken a course that has seriously undermined instead of strengthening those *state* foundations. This has occurred even as *government* under Mengistu's leadership has asserted more direct control over the lives of more people than occured under any of the preceding emperors, as Clapham among others has noted.[29] Indeed, such expanded governmental scope may be a consequence as well as a cause of weakened state foundations. In any event weakened state foundations have impeded the process of their transformation as well as implementation of the socioeconomic revolution upon the basis of which they were in turn to be reconstituted.

The Management of Social Transformations

The preceding debates have rarely incorporated the implications of a revolution in management theory and practice that has occurred in two dissimilar theaters, one centered on improving the management of large corporations in industrial democracies, the other based on analysis of causes of success and failure in the implementation of development projects in less developed countries. The fundamental premises of this management "revolution" have been the importance of informal processes over formal structures, of matrix over hierarchical organizational governance, of participatory over command-based decision making, and of bureaucracies "learning" from as well as acting upon the constituencies they are to serve.[30] The evidence that such "new" managment works is to be found in both industrialized and developing country contexts.[31]

Consideration of new management theory in the context of the study of the Ethiopian transformation suggests potential insights pointing to the possible advancement of both the theory and the transformation itself. On the one hand, the Ethiopian context poses a fundamental issue for a new management theory for which sensitivity to the cultural context of those being managed is axiomatic. That issue is whether and to what extent political and cultural parameters of the contexts within which managers themselves operate may be prevented from impeding or, alternatively, manipulated to encourage their sensitivity to the contexts of those they serve. This book will argue that the Mengistu regime's long struggle to surive, sustain its power, and demonstrate legitimacy for itself and its definition of the revolution-to-be have been dominant influences on the way in which the reforms it has promulgated, especially the rural land reform, have been managed in fact. At the same time, such management methods appear to have undermined the regime's pursuit of these very objectives. Not only have the economic results been discouraging, but the regime's methods have increased its exposure to opponents' charges that its authoritarianism replicates or exceeds that of the emperors whose legacies it seeks to eradicate. In this sense, opponents' opposition to the regime has helped to make their charges against it self-fulfilling.

On the other hand, the existence of the new management further sharpens the issue of the relative influence of state form, ideology, policy, and management practices in contributing to continuing development stagnation and failure to realize the promise of socioeconomic revolution in Ethiopia, particularly in the countryside. It may not necessarily be the case that the shortcomings of socialist development in countries like Tanzania and Ethiopia are necessarily derivative from particularly ideological or policy formulations or theory about the historical contexts within which they are advanced.[32] Rather, preliminary Ethiopian evidence from responses to the land reform suggests that implementation failure may result primarily from the use of management practices that are less appropriate to realizing self-reliant socialism in practice than are those associated with "new" management concepts that may have been codified a little too late for the critical phases of both countries' initial planning. If the realities of the political and cultural context within which the regime's managers' authoritarian practices have evolved were to change or be manipulated to favor newer management practices, the possibility remains that its application might yet bear very different fruit.

The preliminary evidence from responses to the Ethiopian rural land reform appears to sustain the argument that management may indeed be a most significant variable affecting not only rural development progress but the de facto character of the revolutionary policies and structures the regime has sought to implant in the countryside. To be sure, revolutionary visions inspired by adherence to Marxist-Leninist ideology have clearly and heavily influenced the reform policies and the organizational structures of the Ethiopian transformation. But ideology, policy, and structure may not necessarily be the sole or even the primary influences upon how management takes place within the frameworks they establish. Indeed, the Ethiopian evidence suggests that the struggle for power and to survive in power—more generally, the struggle to shape the character of the post-independence state—and the military rulers' own professional backgrounds have been the greater influences on measures taken to implement and manage the regime's economic reforms.

Conclusion

This book examines the interrelationships between state, class, development, and development management within the framework of political and socio-economic transformation. These themes are considered against the background of Ethiopia's distinctive historical evolution and violent conflict over the processes of its contemporary transformation.

Notes

1. Numerous analyses and commentaries appeared in the first years of the Ethiopian transformation, but there have been fewer studies in recent years partly because civil war has increased the difficulty of doing research in rural areas. The depth of the controversy has been such that many commentaries have reflected the same deeply held partisanship as the protagonists. Among the most important contributions have been the following: Michael Chege, "The Revolution Betrayed: Ethiopia 1974-9," 14 *Journal of Modern African Studies*, 3, 1979, pp. 359-80; John M. Cohen, "Agrarian Reform in Ethiopia: The Situation on the Eve of the Revolution's 10th Anniversary," Development Discussion Paper No. 164. Boston: Harvard Institute for International Development, April 1984; Tom J. Farer, *War Clouds on the Horn of Africa: A Crisis for Detente*. New York: Carnegie Endowment for International Peace, 1976; Fred Halliday and Maxine Molyneux, *The Ethiopian Revolution*. London: Verso, 1981; Marilyn Hall, "The Ethiopian Revolution: Group Interaction and Civil-Military Relations" (unpublished Ph.D. dissertation). Washington: The George Washington University, 1977; John W. Harbeson, "Whither the Revolution," 21 *Africa Report*, 4, July-August 1976, pp. 48-50; John W. Harbeson, "Socialist Politics in Revolutionary Ethiopia," in Carl Rosberg and Thomas Callaghy (eds.), *Socialism in Sub-Saharan Africa: A New Assessment*. Berkeley: Institute for International Studies, University of California, 1979, pp. 345-417; John W. Harbeson, "Socialism, Traditions, and Revolutionary Politics in Contemporary Ethiopia," 11 *Canadian Journal of African Studies*, 2, 1977, pp. 217-35; Addis Hiwet, *Ethiopia: From Autocracy to Revolution*.

London: Review of African Political Economy, 1975; Edmond Keller, "State, Party and Revolution in Ethiopia," 28 *African Studies Review,* 1, March 1985, pp. 1–19; John Markakis and Nega Ayele, *Class and Revolution in Ethiopia.* Nottingham, England: Spokesman Books, 1978; Marina Ottaway, "Democracy and New Democracy: The Ideological Debate in the Ethiopian Revolution," 21 *African Studies Review,* 1, April 1978, pp. 19–31; Marina Ottaway, "Social Classes and Corporate Interests in the Ethiopian Revolution," 14 *Journal of Modern African Studies,* 3, September 1976, pp. 469–87; David and Marina Ottaway, *Ethiopia: Empire in Revolution.* New York: Africana Publishing Co., 1978; Dessalegn Rahmato, *Agrarian Reform in Ethiopia.* Trenton, N.J.: Red Sea Press, 1984; Berekhet Habte Selassie, *Conflict and Intervention in the Horn of Africa.* London: Monthly Review Press, 1980; Jack Shepherd, *The Politics of Starvation.* New York: Carnegie Endowment for International Peace, 1975; John M. Cohen and Dov Weintraub, *Land and Peasants in Imperial Ethiopia: The Social Background to Revolution.* Assen, Netherlands: Van Gorcum, 1975.

2. Among the early studies see Peter Koehn, "Ethiopian Politics: Military Intervention and Prospects for Further Change," 20 *Africa Today,* 2, 1975, pp. 7–21; W. A. E. Skurnik, "Revolution and Change in Ethiopia," 68 *Current History,* No. 405, 1975, pp. 206–10, 230–1, 240; John W. Harbeson, "Politics and Reform in Revolutionary Ethiopia," paper presented at the eighteenth annual meetings of the African Studies Association, 1975; John W. Harbeson, "Whither Ethiopia," *op. cit.*; Marina Ottaway, "Social Classes and Corporate Interests in the Ethiopian Revolution, *op. cit.*; and David and Marina Ottaway, *Empire in Revolution, op. cit.*

3. Harbeson, "Politics and Reform," *op. cit.*

4. Background on the Eritrean problem, which has not been widely researched, is to be found in Berekhet Habte Selassie, *op. cit.*; Tom Farer, *op. cit.*; J. Bell, "Endemic Insurgency and International Order: The Eritrean Experience," 18 *Orbis,* 2, Summer 1974, pp. 427–50; Berekhet Habte Selassie, "The Evolution of the Principle of Self-Determination," 1 *Horn of Africa,* No. 4, October-December 1978, pp. 3–9; John Campbell, "Background to the Eritrean Conflict," 16 *Africa Report,* 5, May 1971, pp. 19–25; G. K. N. Trevaskis, *Eritrea: A Colony in Transition.* London: Oxford University Press, 1960; Yesus Gebre Medhin, "Eritrea: Background to Revolution," 28 *Monthly Review,* 1976, pp. 52–61; and L. Ellingson, "The Origins and Development of the Eritrean Liberation Movement," in Robert L. Hess (ed.), *Proceedings of the Fifth International Conference on Ethiopian Studies.* Chicago: University of Illinois Press, 1979, pp. 613–28.

5. Declaration that "Ethiopia Tikdem" (Ethiopia First) meant Ethiopian socialism or *hebrettesebawinet* appeared first in the *Ethiopian Herald* on December 21, 1974. It was followed a few weeks later by the *Declaration of Economic Policy for Socialist Ethiopia.* Addis Ababa, Government Printer, 1974.

6. Addis Ababa, Ethiopia: Proclamation No. 31 of 1975. Government Printer.

7. The Ethiopian Democratic Union was formed in March 1975. The leaders included Ras Mengesha Seyoum of Tigre, a descendant of Emperor Johannes; General Nega Tegegne, formerly commander of the third division and governor of Gondar region for a brief time before his defection; and General Iyassu

Mengesha, who had been ambassador to Britain. The EDU's policy statement specifically denied that it sought restoration of the imperial house. Many EDU followers opposed the old regime, but appeared to seek a more conservative and democratic change than the military regime portended.

8. Addis Ababa, Ethiopia: Government Printer, April 1976.

9. For background on the Ogaden conflict, see Farer, *op. cit.*; A. A. Castagno, "The Horn of Africa and the Competition for Power," in A. J. Cottrell and R. M. Burrell (eds.), *The Indian Ocean: Its Political, Economic, and Military Importance.* New York: Praeger, 1972; John Drysdale, *Somalia Frontier Dispute.* New York: Praeger, 1964; Negussay Ayele, "The 1952-1957 Ethio-Italian Boundary Negotiations: An Exercise in Diplomatic Futility," *Journal of Ethiopian Studies,* July 1971, pp. 127–48; Negussay Ayele, "The Politics of the Somali-Ethiopia Boundary Problem: 1960-1967" (unpublished Ph.D. dissertation). University of California, Los Angeles, 1969; Sven Rubenson, "The Genesis of the Ethio-Somali Conflict," in Robert L. Hess (ed.), *Proceedings, op. cit.*; and John W. Harbeson, "Multilateral Approaches to Multidimensional Conflict Resolution: Lessons from the Horn of Africa," in Arthur R. Day and Michael W. Doyle (eds.), *Escalation and Intervention: Multilateral Security and Its Alternatives.* Boulder, Colorado: Westview, 1986.

10. Addis Ababa, Ethiopia: Proclamation No. 156 of 1978. Government Printer.

11. Addis Ababa, Ethiopia: Proclamation No. 286 of 1983. Government Printer.

12. Background on the imperial politics of drought and famine in 1973 is provided by Jack Shepherd, *op. cit.*; on the drought itself see also Abdul M. Hussein, *Drought and Famine in Ethiopia.* London: International African Institute, 1976. Reporting on the drought and famine conditions in the mid-1980s has been largely by the press, but see Jack Shepherd, "The Politics of Food Aid," 30 *Africa Report,* 2, March-April 1985, pp. 51–55; and an interview with Ethiopian relief officials conducted by Margaret Novicki, "Ethiopia's Drought and Famine Crisis," 30 *Africa Report,* 1, January-February 1985, pp. 47–50.

13. An analysis of imperial era settlement schemes is to be found in Gail Simpson, "Socio-Political Aspects of Settlement Schemes in Ethiopia and Their Contribution to Development," *Land Reform, Land Settlement, and Cooperatives,* No. 2, 1976, pp. 22–40.

14. Theda Skocpol, *States and Social Revolutions.* Cambridge: Cambridge University Press, 1979. For comparison see Harry Eckstein, *Internal War.* New York: Free Press, 1964. Eckstein employs a more inclusive term, which he took to mean "any resort to violence within a political order to change its constitution, rules, or policies" in his "On the Etiology of Internal War," 4 *History and Theory,* No. 2, 1965, p. 133. Ted Gurr defined revolution as "highly organized political violence with widespread popular participation, designed to overthrow the regime or dissolve the state and accompanied by extensive violence" in his *Why Men Rebel.* Princeton, New Jersey: Princeton University Press, 1970, p. 11; Chalmers Johnson in his *Revolutionary Change* (Boston: Little Brown, 1966, p. 1) says "revolutions are social change" and Hannah Arendt defined them in

terms of the values pursued, i.e., freedom and social justice, in *On Revolution.* New York: Viking, 1963, p. 21. These definitions, broader and less specific than Skocpol's, partly for that reason do not help to establish at least in the Ethiopian context which movements if any are genuinely revolutionary and/or have achieved revolutionary outcomes.

15. *op. cit.*
16. *Ibid.*, p. 350.
17. See note 21.
18. Goren Hyden, *Beyond Ujamaa in Tanzania: Underdevelopment and an Uncaptured Peasantry.* Berkeley: University of California, 1980.
19. Goren Hyden, *No Shortcuts to Progress: African Development Management in Perspective.* London: Heinemann, 1983.
20. See note 2.
21. The literature on smallholder agriculture is voluminous. Representative of this literature is Uma Lele, *The Design of Rural Development.* Baltimore: The Johns Hopkins University Press, 1975; Robert Chambers, *Managing Rural Development: Ideas and Experience from East Africa.* Uppsala: Scandinavian Institute of African Studies, 1974; Milton Esman and Norman Uphoff, *Local Organizations: Intermediaries in Rural Development.* Ithaca: Cornell University Press, 1984; David Korten and Norman Uphoff, *Bureaucratic Reorientation for Participatory Development.* NASPAA Working paper No. 1. Washington: National Association of Schools of Public Affairs and Administration, 1981; Bruce Johnson and William Clay, *Redesigning Rural Development: A Strategic Perspective.* Baltimore: The Johns Hopkins University Press, 1982; E. H. Gilbert, D. Norman, and F. E. Winch, *Farming Systems Approach: A Critical Appraisal.* East Lansing, Michigan: Michigan State University, Department of Economics, 1980; Peggy Barlett (ed.), *Agricultural Decision-Making: Anthropological Contributions to Development.* New York: Academic Press, 1980; and David Leonard, *Reaching the Peasant Farmer: Organization Theory and Practice in Kenya.* Chicago: University of Chicago Press, 1977.
22. Samuel Huntington, *Political Order in Changing Societies.* New Haven: Yale University Press, 1968; and Samuel Huntington, "Political Development and Political Decay," 17 *World Politics,* April 1965, pp. 386-430.
23. See note 21.
24. Organization of African Unity, *The Lagos Plan of Action for the Development of Africa 1980-2000.* Geneva: International Institute of Labor Studies, 1981.
25. The term was first used extensively by Gunnar Myrdal in *Asian Drama: An Inquiry into the Poverty of Nations.* New York: Twentieth Century Fund/ Parthenon Books, 1968.
26. Donald Rothchild, "Hegemony and State Softness: Some Variations in Elite Responses," in Zaki Ergas (ed.), *The African State in Transition.* New York and London: Macmillan, forthcoming.
27. Skocpol, *op. cit.*, p. 4-5.
28. *The Theory of Social and Economic Organization.* trans. by Talcott Parsons. Glencoe, Illinois: The Free Press, 1947, p. 156.
29. Christopher Clapham, "The Ethiopian Government: Character, Capability, and Responsiveness," a paper prepared for the Wilson Center conference on the

Horn of Africa, Washington, D.C., June 1987. The paper exemplifies a tendency to focus on the capabilities implicit in governmental structures as though they were synonymous with the state.

30. See note 5.

31. The success stories are often buried within the internal reports of donor agencies such as the Agency for International Development. The studies divison of the Office of Policy Planning and Program Coordination has produced a long series of special impact evaluations that detail instances of the success of participatory, flexible management strategies in particular projects. Some of these, focusing on participation through local organizations, are identified in Esman and Uphoff, 1984, *op. cit.*

32. This "nontraditional" perspective is expressed in my "Tanzanian Socialism in Transition: Agricultural Crisis and Policy Reform," Hanover, New Hampshire: Universities Field Staff International, *Reports,* No. 30, 1983.

2

The Historical Foundations of the Ethiopian State

The struggles over the direction, character, and achievements of Ethiopia since the fall of Haile Selassie I center on the nature and meaning of the historical context in which they have been fought. The purpose of this chapter is, therefore, to outline the historical evolution of Ethiopia's socioeconomic and political contours over the century and a quarter of the "modern" empire preceding the present transformation in order to address two fundamental issues.[1]

First, to what extent was the historically evolving Ethiopian state synonymous with traditional institutions of imperial rule? Alternatively, to what extent was it based on some fundamental sense of political association more durable than the structures of any given regime? To the extent that peoples were brought into the empire involuntarily by conquest or intimidation, one might expect them to assert independence when political structures of the empire fall into disarray or dissolve.[2] On the other hand, peoples incorporated into an empire may evolve some sense of common political and cultural identity akin to nationhood, as well as bonds of economic interdependence.[3] Such ties may also lead to generally recognized and genuine bases of political association more fundamental than the authority of the regimes by which they are actually governed.

Second, to what extent and in what ways have complex relationships between state and class evolving over the country's long history confused the claims of alternative groups to leadership in a post-imperial state, thus helping to produce the bitter struggles that have dominated the country's politics since the end of Haile Selassie's rule? The Ethiopian case may in turn help to shed light on more general theoretical questions of political economy in developing countries. On the one hand, the state is variously conceived as theater, prize, and instrument for the struggles of emerging classes. On the other hand, definitions of class may be impeded by what Kasfir has termed the "plasticity" of class formation in developing countries and the influence of political and cultural parameters on the working meaning of "class" to those within such formations.[4] A hypothesis of this study is that theoretical ambiguities such as these have been reflected in the specific Ethiopian context and help to explain the complexity, intensity, and durability of the struggle for leadership of the state after the emperors.

The Legacy of the Ancient Empire

The historical development of contemporary Ethiopia has been distinctive among African and other Third World states. Until its demise in 1974, the Ethiopian monarchy symbolized political continuity stretching over nearly two thousand years, notwithstanding periods of grave weakness. Virtually alone among Third World nations, Ethiopia was only partially colonized, though severely tested by Italian occupation in World War II and persistent contests with movements of Islamic expansion. Ethiopia's history, however, has been one of endemic competition and military struggle among diverse constituent political entities and ethnic groupings included within its present boundaries. Thus, Ethiopia's present international boundaries did not result from the actions of European powers but from persistent local territorial expansion within the northwestern highlands of the ancient kingdom and, in the late nineteenth century, to the areas now internationally recognized as included within the country. Yet these struggles and simultaneous dealings of various Ethiopian potentates with foreign powers permitted a degree of political cohesion requisite to the maintenance of Ethiopia's essential independence during the period of European expansion in Africa.[5]

How and why did Ethiopia succeed in maintaining its essential independence, and what has the basis of this independence signified in terms of the current struggle to maintain and/or redefine the Ethiopian state? Rubenson's important study, *The Survival of Ethiopian Independence* details the politics of Ethiopian independence during the nineteenth century. This period embraced much of the *zamena mesafint* ("the era of princes"), a time of great political disunity and near collapse of central government institutions that was followed by restoration and strengthening of the monarchy through the exertions of the four emperors of the "modern" period: Tewodros, Johannes, Menelik II, and Haile Selassie I.[6] Rubenson attacks the Toynbee thesis that Ethiopia's survival resulted from a mountainous terrain forbidding to foreign armies. Instead he finds the source of Ethiopia's ability to defend its independence in "the awareness of a spiritual and national identity [more than] in material resources." This consciousness, he says, "was a part of the heritage from earlier centuries." He finds as elements of that consciouness "awareness of and attachment to the monarchy, directly or through the hierarchy of feudal lords," the fact that it was "a Christian monarchy with a long history," and the development of this consciousness to meet new challenges.[7]

Rubenson's argument centers on the symbols of national identity as the crucial foundation for Ethiopia's survival as a state during the *zamena mesafint*. These symbols included the monarchy, Christianity, and a political hierarchy linking people to their monarch. He suggests that these were living symbols strengthened by testing in the faces of challenges, among which external designs on the country were clearly of central importance. Left out of this assessment, however, were at least two other potentially important elements that might either contribute to, or detract from, the cultivation of a sense of Ethiopian statehood. First were expectations concerning how rulers intervened in the socio-economic life of the people; second were understandings concerning rights and obligations of subjects within the political order. Both elements were to become increasingly important in the subsequent development of the empire state. This brief examination of the ancient empire considers the following five five variables: (1) underlying political values, (2) institutions such as the church, the army, and the nobility, (3) the role of emperors and nobility in the economic life of the country, (4) rights and obligations of the citizenry, and (5) relations with foreign powers.

1. The historical record of the ancient kingdom to which Rubenson refers, the period prior to Menelik's expansion, is to a large extent the chronicle of kings and emperors.[8] This record suggests a basis for Rubenson's observations for it centers on the initiatives of strong kings to maintain religious orthodoxy, expand the state by military means, and acquire technologies possessed by Western visitors with those purposes in mind. Some of Ethiopia's most successful emperors have been those who have sought diplomatic relations with the Western world, quested for recognition by fellow Christian heads of state, and/or undertaken to attract Western equipment and craftsmen for building churches or strengthening the army.

Students of Ethiopian history have centered on the importance of the Solomonic legend as the basis of imperial legitimacy. Cultivated by rulers since the thirteenth century, the legend roots the origin of Haile Selassie's dynasty in Menelik, the offspring of Solomon and Sheba, who brought the Ark of the Covenant to his mother's native land, Ethiopia. Menelik's descendants thus acquired a "divine right" to rule and claimed membership in the House of David and consanguinity with Christ.[9] Markakis has observed that the legend has been used not only to sanctify the ruling dynasty of Ethiopia (while not making the rulers themselves divine) but the Ethiopian peoples as well, to deify Ethiopian nationality.[10] The legend lent justification to early kings' quest for empire by conquering and incorporating pagan and Muslim peoples while the realm's Christian underpinnings became a rallying point in resistance to Islamic expansion. Curiously, the Ethiopian rulers have used Christianity as a justification in their quest for empire while the Ethiopian Church itself appears to have been less aggressive in expanding its spiritual kingdom.

2. The primary institutions of the realm included the monarchy, the church, and the nobility. If the rule of the monarch was absolute in theory and the source of law, it was less so in practice. Ethiopian emperors practiced divide-and-rule tactics among the nobility to preserve their supremacy, raised commoners and even slaves to positions of importance to counteract the power of the great lords, struggled to subordinate to their ends nobles for whom separatism and rebellion were a way of life, labored continually to maintain the boundaries of their realms by preventing outlying provinces from seceding or becoming bases of opposition, and resisted the efforts of nobility to make their offices and holdings hereditary.[11] For these reasons the effective boundaries of the empire were often changing and uncertain. Emperors, moreover, were dependent upon the greater and lesser nobility for collection of taxes and for the mobilization of troops in time of war to supplement their own quite limited personal bodyguard. The late Richard Caulk argued that the size of the imperial army at any point in time was in large part a function of the emperor's ability to weave bonds of personal loyalty to his authority among provincial elites.[12] Finally, emperor and lords alike were not immune from challenges by those lacking royal blood and high status, for the practice of brigandage often led commoners to positions of power. Emperor Tewodros, for example, forced his way to power by this route.[13]

The ancient empire, even its power structure, was historically polyethnic. The superior theological roots claimed by the Christian Ethiopians, especially Amhara and Tigre peoples, did not prevent assimilation of Muslim peoples into the empire nor acceptance of their chiefs as local potentates in return for payment of tribute, notwithstanding the great sixteenth century jihad of Gran that nearly eclipsed independent Ethiopia. The subsequent wars with and invasions by Oromo (or Galla) peoples likewise did not prevent political marriages to cement Oromo-Amhara alliances, the establishment of powerful Oromo princes, the formation of alliances with Oromo chieftains to exploit divisions among them, or the assimilation by Oromo to the language and religion of the Amhara— this despite the near collapse of the empire during the *zamena mesafint* largely as a result of Oromo invasions.[14] Markakis claims, however, that such processes left the assimilated as subordinate, second class citizens.[15]

3. Emperors and the nobility ruled their peoples through what many have considered a feudal system, though not necessarily reminiscent of any one European system.[16] The classical elements of feudalism were approximated but not precisely replicated in Ethiopia.[17] The nobility exercised an array of military and judicial functions as well as economic power through extensive landholdings, but Ethiopian emperors often successfully exercised the power to rescind and reassign such powers more than many of their European counterparts. The nobility received their offices and authority in return for military, tax-collecting, and judicial services to the emperor, though their effective subordination was often problematical. The lords of the realm made great demands on their subjects. Tamrat has suggested that even the peasantry's Christian spiritual life was conceived in feudal terms.[18]

Levine has argued, however, that patron-client ties in traditional Ethiopia were more voluntaristic and instrumental than in parts of medieval Europe, for he claims that they were less ceremonially enshrined and notes that the obligations of the lord's subjects were not for life but could be terminated. He also found a higher degree of individualism in Ethiopian than in French feudalism in that family ties and obligations were far looser and of a more voluntaristic nature.[19] And, as previously noted, subjects of humble status might occasionally improve their status through brigandage.

4. How did the ordinary folk participate in this postulated Ethiopian national consciousness? In the deeper recesses of Ethiopian history, as in more recent times, the ordinary subject peoples were characteristically pawns in the continual power struggles among their various overlords: emperors, kings, and local governors.[20] They were to varying, though always substantial, degrees beholden to these elites for the means of their survival. Conversely, relatively little is recorded of Ethiopian emperors deploying new technologies so as to promote beneficial social and economic change broadly among their subjects. The demands of governors, the church, perceived cultural norms and parameters, and the physical environment were such as to largely circumscribe the opportunities for subjects to achieve a degree of prosperity or mobility. In an empire peopled overwhelmingly by households scratching out a subsistence livelihood, elites and peasants alike were heavily dependent on a single economic resource: land. For most rural Ethiopians, access to and tenure upon land was very insecure.

The institutionalized insecurities of land tenure systems for ordinary subsistence cultivators were accompanied by substantial burdens upon their time and resources.[21] Important among these were the depredations of the physical environment. Ethiopian history is replete with evidence of recurrent natural disasters: locusts, drought, famine, and epidemics.

Almost every generation seems to have experienced at least one such visitation.[22] In addition, like the plagues of nature, the armies of princes and emperors quartered themselves upon peasant communities and often pillaged as well, both practices sanctioned by tradition and reinforced by peasant dependence upon elites for their tenure on the land. Even modern emperors more sensitive to the burden of armies upon the rural populace were unable or unwilling substantially to lift this burden from the backs of ordinary Ethiopians.[23] Service in the army was expected of grass roots proprietors of the land, taking them away from their plots but providing an opportunity to participate in the military exactions they otherwise suffered. But the depredations of armies and of nature forced some peasants off the land, not into cities but into armies of their overlords.

Even in the interstices between the ravages of war and of nature, the impositions upon the peasantry appear to have been suffocating economically. Political elites dependent for their own status upon higher overlords appear to have exacted excessive tributes from peasants to recover their investment in obtaining their position and to provide for a rainy day when they would no longer be in official favor. Compulsory hospitality for political elites and for priests of the church and participation in innumerable holiday celebrations distracted small cultivators from the task of coaxing a subsistence living out of frequently impoverished land. Compulsory service on the lands of the nobility survived even Haile Selassie's early official attempts to stamp it out. The varieties of taxes upon the characteristically slim earnings of small producers stifled entrepreneurial instincts and rendered more precarious the survival of a peasantry in a land whose considerable agricultural potential nonetheless survived even centuries of abusive and primitive cultivation technologies.

An important dimension of the traditional empire appears to have been the absence of established centers of political and economic power. Ethiopian capitals followed their peripatetic rulers until the time of Menelik II late in the nineteenth century. What long-distance trade occurred was not accompanied by the emergence of central market towns. Moreover, horizontal economic mobility was limited by the feudal structure itself as well as by topological barriers. There was therefore little migration within the empire before the end of the nineteenth century.[24] The contempt of the Ethiopian Church for all nonagricultural labor and its resistance to change in consumption patterns, e.g., coffee drinking and smoking, combined to discourage the emergence of nonagricultural mercantile groups and other forms of economic specialization. The exceptions were among Muslims whom the Church in general kept from attaining any real economic and political power within the empire. Ethiopian rulers, however, did show interest in foreign goods and technologies, particularly insofar as they were useful in building churches and strengthening armies.

The perpetually competitive, contingent character of Ethiopian political institutions may have enabled individual peasants to attack or escape those who burdened them (and sometimes to improve their station), but those same characteristics may also help explain why mass uprisings were rare.[25] Why? There are several extant hypotheses. Donald Levine and his most incisive critic, Gedamu Abraha, agree that even twentieth-century northern Ethiopian heirs of this ancient civilization exhibited marked ambivalence when faced with such fundamental choices, inclining them to passivity more than resistance.[26] Others have argued that the impositions of authority upon the peasantry emphasized and were accompanied by a propensity on the part of the peasantry to vicarious individualism.[27] Bound by vertical relationships to authority, the argument goes, Ethiopian peasants expressed this individualism not so much in relationship to each other as through vicarious participation in the exploits of their respective liege lords.[28] This argument might suggest that the fragmentation of a feudal society preempted the formation of horizontal solidarities that might in turn have led to resistance and, perhaps more fundamentally, to any basis for political identity independent of the imperial structures.

By contrast, evidence of "national" collective resistance did appear, notably in popular resistance to efforts of the Spanish Jesuit, Alphonzo Mendez, to Romanize the Ethiopian Church in the seventeenth century.[29] Such evidence partially qualifies the basic thesis that the struggle for survival, the exactions of the secular and ecclesiastical authorities, and the perpetual contests among elites combined to reinforce and reflect interpersonal distrust and hostility tempered by profound fatalism rooted in the acceptance of a vengeful God.

At local levels of the political structure of the empire, the hypothesized extreme individualism of Ethiopian society did not cause Ethiopian subjects to live their austere and penurious lives in total isolation from one another. The converse of obligatory hospitality seems to have been an internalized disposition to generosity. Social organization at the most local levels institutionalized cooperation at the high and low points of the biological cycle: birth, mating, and death.[30] Gamst has argued that the individual task of garnering a living did not prevent the development of local markets and of limited occupational specialization and interdependence between adjacent communities, forbidding terrain notwithstanding.[31]

There is little evidence, however, that such economic relationships significantly changed the basic political power and social status relationships of the kingdom. Authoritarianism in the family appears to have expressed itself in succoring and protecting of the very young to an unusual degree.³² Within these parameters of exploitation, conflict, and penury, some evidence of at least embryonic political and economic community did appear. It would be surprising if service in the army did not produce some sense of camaraderie among the ordinary foot soldiers and some cultural cross-fertilization within the context of a traditional Ethiopia of much diversity.³³ Shared, profound commitment to the Orthodox Church and the common obligation to participate in repelling military threats representing alien faiths would appear to have contributed to some sense of broader community.³⁴ In some regions, land tenure systems emphasized competition among kinfolk for usufructuary rights, but the eligibility to participate in such competition helped to reinforce genealogically based solidarities, however hierarchical the status relationships within such groups.³⁵ Thus, if the lives of the emperors' subjects were ones of comprehensive deprivation, such deprivations appear to a substantial degree to have been shared and survived together through local social institutions.

5. Medieval Ethiopia was isolated from broad contact with the Arab and European world through control of the Red Sea coast by Turkey, then Egypt, and later Italy, but such isolation did not prevent contacts with Europeans, however frustrating and unfortunate these contacts may have turned out to be. The Portuguese came to the aid of Ethiopia in its struggle with Gran, and Portuguese missionaries remained to counsel, proselytize, and eventually overextend their welcome in the courts of subsequent emperors.³⁶ Nor did such *international* isolation extend to *regional* isolation from alien and often antagonistic peoples whom the emperors sought to contain or incorporate with varying degrees of success. Enhanced definition of the empire through distinguishing it from its "enemies" long preceded the arrival of serious European intrusion in the area in the nineteenth century. One function of Christianity may in fact have been to preserve Ethiopian identity in a regional setting wherein the shifting effective boundaries of the empire rendered inexact any distinction between internal and external politics, a phenomenon preserved in the twentieth-century Horn of Africa.

A major and still largely unresolved historical question concerns the extent to which the Oromo wars and invasions of Amhara regions in the sixteenth and seventeenth centuries and the expansion of the empire under Menelik to incorporate these and other peoples changed the basis of the "national consciousness" of which Rubenson speaks. Levine postulates that Amhara and Oromo cultures, culturally antithetical to one another, began to synthesize and establish the basis for what he terms a greater Ethiopian culture.³⁷ But it remains unclear to what extent Oromo civilization, which he considers to have been somewhat more democratic and egalitarian, in fact exerted a leavening influence on the more hierarchical propensities of the Amhara or vice versa. Neither is it known to what extent any such cultural cross-fertilization contributed to a broader national consciousness that in turn may have helped to sustain the country's political integrity during the *zamena mesafint*.

The survival of the Ethiopian empire during the *zamena mesafint* is prima facie evidence of at least embryonic political consciousness not dependent for its continuation solely on the basis of imperial structures themselves. The *content* of that consciousness remains in the realm of speculation. However, existing scholarship suggests at least two important possibilities concerning the character of an evolving Ethiopian state as part of that consciousness. First, acceptance of de facto autonomy of constituent peoples based on "negotiated settlements" may have emerged in association with de jure recognition of emperors' absolute authority. Second, perhaps because of the somewhat fluid and contingent nature of Ethiopian politics in practice, there was more room within Ethiopian than in European feudalism for some individualism and local community to emerge within an overall framework of exploitation, inequality, and frequent conflict.

The Birth of the Modern Empire

The reemergence of strong imperial rule after nearly a century of disintegration during the *zamena mesafint* represented a watershed in the political history of modern Ethiopia. Four strong emperors over the 120-year period termed the "modern" empire not only restored and maintained vigorous imperial rule but redefined the structure of the empire itself. These were Tewodros (1855–68), Johannes (1868–86), Menelik (1889–1913), and Haile Selassie (1930–74). They defended the empire and established its relationship to the political and economic interests of advancing European empire, and they greatly influenced the country's response to broad and intensified patterns of socioeconomic change that paralleled European expansion. At the same time, these rulers' very different styles also carried important consequences for the other variables considered in the previous section that bear on this chapter's central questions: the relationship of the Ethiopian state to the institutions of empire and the bearing of both on political leadership during and after the regimes of the emperors. These variables are the underlying political values, the political institutions, the role of emperors and nobility in the country's evolving political economy, and the rights and obligations of citizens.

Tewodros

Tewodros was a militant nationalist and a zealous, even revolutionary, reformer of the country's social and political institutions.[38] His rise to power was unexpected and not foreordained by his possession of any royal pedigree. Indeed, his was a dramatic instance of the successful quest for and subsequent legitimation of power and status through brigandage.[39] Born in the remote border village of Quara, Kassa (as he was known before he became emperor) distinguished himself as a warrior. He gained power by building a military force sufficient to compel the submission of the country's nominal ruler, Ras Ali of Gondar, and to quell repeated uprisings against his rule. Tewodros is pictured in scholarship on nineteenth century Ethiopia as a man captivated by a secular vision of an Ethiopia once more united under strong central authority and as a secular prophet born to rejuvenate his country's political institutions.[40]

His reforms included seeking to lift the yoke of marauding armies from the backs of peasants by decreeing that armies were to be compensated from the royal treasury rather than through pillaging during expeditions. He did not seek to eliminate provincial authorities but to compel their recognition of his imperial authority. He sought to have the governors of provinces paid salaries from the royal treasury to secure their loyalty and reduce their exactions upon their subjects, though the elites of the Amhara and Tigre regions blocked this initiative.[41] Similarly, he sought to purify the Orthodox Church by ending priestly corruption, to unify it by ending doctrinal differences within its ranks, and to establish its obligations to the state by curtailing its tax exemption, a measure again blocked by the nobility. Tewodros encouraged technological emulation of Western countries. Crummey contends that in this he broke with his precedessors, who thought of Western technology as exotica to be toyed with.[42] Among the populace at large he campaigned to polygamy and to attach dignity to manual labor, which, except for agricultural work, the church held in contempt. He also condemned the institution of slavery but appears to have taken few steps, if any, to abolish it.

In the end he was unable to preserve the unchallenged imperial rule that was for a time within his grasp. He appears never to have fully consolidated his rule in the provinces.[43] As his wars to obtain and secure this elusive objective continued, he gradually lost support because the suppression of these local rebellions exhausted both his political and military resources. Though he is reported to have treated leniently those vanquished in his campaigns, his perpetual campaigns appear to have eventually undermined the very legitimacy he sought.[44] He launched his reforms and ordinances not from a secure position as an unchallengeable ruler but as rallying points in a continuing struggle to capture as well as reintegrate and reform the realm.

The fate of his reforms paralleled the course of his military campaigns. The more he was obliged to employ military force to suppress recurring rebellions, the more he lacked the resources to prevent the pillaging of the populace by his and his rivals' overworked armies, to enforce doctrinal unity within the church, or to establish direct financial and political accountability of local potentates to the crown. His domestic troubles were magnified by frustrations in international diplomacy: Rulers of foreign countries whose technologies he wished Ethiopia to emulate and from whom he sought recognition as a fellow Christian king responded by refusing to allow their consuls to accept local Ethiopian jurisdiction. His suicide when faced with imminent defeat at the hands of a British expeditionary force given encouragement by his disgruntled subjects epitomized his self-destructive pursuit of a noble vision.

Johannes

A period of disunity and civil war ensued between the death of Tewodros and Johannes's successful claim to the throne. If Tewodros was a visonary nationalist, Johannes IV was more a pragmatist sensitive to strategic and tactical problems of pursuing objectives he and Tewodros shared.[45] Despite his acknowledged military capabilities and the strength of his army, Jonannes confronted strong domestic and foreign challenges to his regime, requiring the most prudent use of his military and political resources. Teklehaimanot of Gojjam and Menelik of Shoa were strong enough to challenge Johannes's authority by acting independently of him. Indeed, having escaped capture by Tewodros, Menelik became King of Shoa, promptly declared Shoa's independence in 1865, and subsequently claimed the imperial throne upon the death of Tewodros.[46] However, Menelik was prevailed upon to withdraw his claim to the throne and to settle for a measure of de facto Shoan autonomy through a marital link between the Tigrean and Shoan lines and a recognition of Menelik as Johannes's successor over his son—a commitment he reportedly adhered to on his battlefield deathbed. While Johannes IV may have authorized and approved of Menelik's extension of Shoan authority to the south, west, and east, there is little evidence that Johannes could have prevented such expansion should he have chosen to try. Menelik continued a policy of expansion begun during the *zamena mesafint* under Sahle Selassie, developed his own access route to the Red Sea coast through the lands of the Afar, and sought the modernization of his kingdom. Shoan military and economic strength may have equaled or surpassed that of Johannes IV, partly for that reason, by the end of Johannes's reign in 1886.

Johannes IV engaged in almost continuous diplomatic and military struggle to maintain the country's boundaries against incursions from Sudan, to regain unrestricted access to the Red Sea port of Massawa, and in the process to maintain his own strength. At considerable cost, he proved to be an effective warrior in repelling Egyptian and Mahdist incursions on the country's western border, but he entered into protracted negotiations with the British in order to achieve by treaty the substitution of Ethiopian for waning Egyptian authority in the Red Sea port area of Massawa. Britain embarrassed its own consul in Massawa and undermined Johannes IV's patient diplomacy by encouraging Italy to seize territory it had seemingly ceded to Ethiopia by negotiation. Unlike Tewodros, Johannes took care not to antagonize the British permanently, even though the result was the beginning of an Italian colony in Eritrea and the foundation of a conflict that was to bedevil both future emperors and the current military regime. Meanwhile, Menelik cooperated actively with Italy, reached a modus vivendi with Teklehaimanot, and may have reached some understanding with Sudanese Mahdists—all measures that potentially threatened Johannes's position. The Italians gained a potential southern ally against Johannes, whose empire they coveted as part of their own. Menelik assisted Teklehaimanot against the Mahdists when Johannes could not. The Mahdists, like the Italians, coveted an alliance with Menelik in order to weaken and eventually conquer Johannes, after which they might have turned on Menelik and brought all Ethiopia into an empire reaching from Sudan to the Red Sea.

Domestically, Johannes shared Tewodros's objectives of extending and reforming the empire, converting Muslims to Christianity, and checking foreign incursions. But he pursued his objectives in a more pragmatic fashion. He wished to purge the Ethiopian Church of heretical doctrines, but he preferred to reconcile rather than punish the religious dissidents. While he held an aversion to the Roman Catholic missionaries, he found them useful as emissaries to European capitals. For some mixture of diplomatic and idealistic reasons, the first steps were taken under his regime to curtail the slave trade. Finally, while Johannes may or may not have been militarily stronger than Menelik in Shoa for most of his reign, he preferred accommodation to the prospect of a costly civil war, even one that might have established his authority and the unity of the empire more securely.

While Johannes's domestic and foreign challenges denied him the opportunity to undertake domestic reforms as Tewodros had attempted to do, there is evidence that Johannes was sensitive to the effects of prolonged military campaigns upon the populace on whom he relied to sustain his warring armies.[47] He tried to limit his marches in order to overtax neither his army nor the resident peoples. He appears to have accepted on at least a de facto basis the idea that the empire, though united under one emperor, nevertheless perpetuated a considerable degree of autonomy with regard to regional potentates. Greenfield suggests, however, that in accommodating his regime to the power especially of the two kings, Johannes undermined the struggle of both his predecessors and successors to curb the power of the nobility in the interests of a stronger, centralized empire.[48]

In blending military with diplomatic leadership and in ruling but also moderating his demands upon his people, Johannes's concept of the empire and of his office seems to have differed markedly from that of his predecessor. Tewodros's pursuit of a rejuvenated Ethiopia proved self-destructive and ended in an apparent loss of a requisite level of domestic legitimacy as well as military defeat. Johannes IV, by contrast, died a hero on the battlefield, his leadership respected and legitimate if not without competitors. However, the price of his more restrained and pragmatic leadership included major diplomatic setbacks though not military defeat, and he had to suffer the pursuit of somewhat conflicting "foreign policies" by his domestic rivals though neither directly of them challenged the legitimacy of his rule.

Two hypotheses emerge from this cursory review of the reigns of these two modern emperors: (1) recognition of the existence of an Ethiopian polity did not rest on the presence of a strong imperial regime, and (2) the "constitution" of this polity was sufficiently plastic to admit two quite different definitions under the first two "modern" emperors. The ignominy of Tewodros's personal and military defeat did not prevent Johannes's eventual succession, and competition between Johannes and his rivals did not result in civil war. Both emperors were able for at least a time to rally support for very contrasting models of the organization of the empire and the role of the imperial office, neither of which was without its costs as well as its virtues. The choice between the two approaches could not have been an easy one. On the one hand, Tewodros courted political bankruptcy through his zealous, militant pursuit of a noble vision. On the other hand, Johannes risked weakening the country's political integrity through diplomacy in foreign policy and moderation in domestic politics.

Menelik

Menelik redefined the empire. As emperor he completed a process of territorial expansion to the present boundaries of the country that was under way while he was king of Shoa. In so doing, he introduced economic relationships among his subjects and between them and the crown that were to change the face of the empire. He broadened and intensified much beyond that of his "modern" predecessors the realm's exposure to processes of technological and economic change that had long since begun to transform other African and Asian societies. In so doing, however, he opened up new and serious questions about the existence, nature, and validity of the Ethiopian polity that his predecessors had devoted their reigns to resurrecting.[49]

Menelik continued the policies of his "modern" predecessors, especially Tewodros, to centralize authority within the empire at the expense of the nobility. Like Tewodros and unlike Johannes, he did not bestow the title of *negus* (king) on any of the great nobility, though many sought it both in his reign and in Haile Selassie's as the ultimate recognition of their provincial power. He sought to neutralize the great families of the empire by creating many *rases* (commanders or, loosely, princes) from the ranks of commoners, including some Oromo. His encouragement of both the empire's modernization and its expansion reflected an asserted growth in the power and significance of the imperial *office*, not just of its incumbent.

In consolidating his conquests, Menelik imposed an imperial political economy upon his new subjects through his land distribution policies. The emperor became the possessor of the conquered lands, but he returned as much as one-third of this land to collaborating traditional authorities as *gult*, a form of tenure familiar in the north that permitted the holder to receive tribute from those working the land that might otherwise have been rendered directly to the crown as land taxes.[50] In addition, conquered land was assigned as *gult* or as private tenure, by grant or sale, to local administrators, those emigrating to the south from overcrowded regions of the ancient empire to the north, soldiers, and northern aristocrats. In this way Menelik gained assistance in consolidating his rule over the new dominions, financing his extended administration, dampening local opposition to the conquests through cooptation of local elites, compensating his soldiers, and rewarding loyal northern elites.[51]

Even as he extended the empire to the south, east, and west, he inherited Johannes's burden of defending the northern reaches of the old empire against foreign encroachment. Italy sought to enlarge the beachhead in Eritrea it acquired during Johannes's reign. Menelik, like Johannes, sought to negotiate limitations on the scope of the embryonic Italian colony, which the Italians for their part appeared to envison as the basis for an Italian protectorate over all of Ethiopia. In concluding the Treaty of Wichale with Menelik in 1889, Italy tried to establish that Menelik had accepted the right of Italy to act on Ethiopia's behalf with other European powers.[52] Italy's claims were rebuffed on the battlefield at Adwa in 1896.

At Adwa, Ethiopia's victory checked Italian pretensions in Ethiopia for two generations. Of still broader significance, it symbolized the successful assertion of Ethiopian national political identity and integrity against a would-be European imperial power. The victory gained Menelik recognition from the Mahdists, the French, and the British as well as the Italians, which had so eluded his predecessors. However, a historic and largely unaddressed question of considerable significance for post-imperial Ethiopia is why Menelik chose not to drive the Italians from Eritrea as well.[53] Were the reasons ones of military and political strategy involving a calculation about the prospects of success and the costs of failure, or did he in fact concede Italian claims to the region because he did not envisage Eritrea as an integral part of Ethiopia?

The increased importance of international trade within the region during the nineteenth century introduced changes in both lifestyles and power relationships. Pankhurst contends that imported textiles successfully competed with local products and that the Ethiopian Orthodox Church began to lose its battle against tobacco and coffee consumption. Western medicine made its appearance in the region early in the nineteenth century and appears to have affected the lives of rural as well as urban residents.[54] Maria Theresa thalers gained at least limited popular acceptance as a medium of exchange during the 19th century, supplementing salt. This transition to a monetized economy facilitated the arms trade, increased savings and investment possibilities, and led to the development of banking institutions during Menelik's reign.[55] Road construction advanced considerably under Tewodros, while telegraph development expanded Menelik's capacity to govern his much-enlarged realm. The construction of the Franco-Ethiopian railway between the port city of Djibouti and Addis Ababa during Menelik's reign multiplied the realm's linkages with the Red Sea coast and facilitated connections with European sources of capital. Labor migration became more significant, perhaps reflecting some changed economic expectations on the part of some Ethiopian subjects at the grass roots.[56]

Menelik expanded upon the efforts of his predecessors to increase utilization of Western technologies in the economic development of the country. He sought to build roads, develop industries, strengthen agriculture, expand education, fortify his army, develop waterworks, create banking institutions, and encourage introduction of a variety of technologies from abroad. So important were the purveyors of these crafts to Menelik that he demanded they be treated with special deference by his subjects. A foreign community, moreover, became much more in evidence in Ethiopia during Menelik's rule.[57] He sought to monopolize the most advanced weapons to strengthen his capacity to control and govern the realm, even as newer weapons came into the possession of ordinary Ethiopians.[58]

Among ordinary Ethiopians, some important innovations initially supplemented and only gradually displaced elements of the preexisting economy. For example, the introduction of thalers did not initiate either international trade or the use of a specialized currency but for some time they coexisted with salt for such purposes.[59] The Church's displeasure with smoking and drinking coffee began to exert less influence on the populace even before Menelik's reign, while Menelik undermined the restriction of certain forms of consumption, e.g., *tej,* a beerlike Ethiopian alcoholic drink.[60] Menelik appears to have been more adamant than his predecessors in inveighing against slavery and to have countered actively the Church's prejudice against nonagricultural labor.

Menelik's conquests and his receptivity to economic and social change—encouraged by new technologies and expanded international trade—posed new, fundamental, and still unresolved questions concerning underlying Ethiopian political identity and bases of state formation upon which the imperial structure may have rested. First, how were such identity and bases of state formation modified by the incorporation within the empire of so many new communities as a result of Menelik's conquests? Second, how did intensified European imperialism contribute to these newly subject communities' participation in whatever evolving Ethiopian political consciousness and sense of statehood may have been present? Third, was Menelik in a singularly favorable position to promote recognition of Ethiopian political identity and statehood because of the unique historical position of Shoa, his original power base? Earlier emperors had also often been kings of Shoa, creating a linkage to the regions of the older empire, yet Shoan kings appear to have had much stronger political and genealogical connections to the Oromo peoples than did other rulers within the original empire.[61] Fourth, the increasing pace of economic change in the empire by Menelik's time makes clear that Rubenson's dismissal of "material resources" as a factor in the political identity of the earlier empire was less plausible by the end of Menelik's rule early in the twentieth century. When and how, therefore, did evolving economic formations begin in fact, through the structures of empire, to influence the nature and extent of Ethiopian political identity and sense of statehood? These issues were to complicate at least implicitly the struggle to define and consolidate anew the nature of the Ethiopian polity during another period of prolonged political uncertainty stretching from the beginning of Menelik's terminal illness in 1906 to the establishment of a new imperial regime under Haile Selassie in the years just before the Italian invasion of 1936.

The Consolidation of the Twentieth-Century Empire

The quarter-century of political uncertainty in Ethiopia between the beginning of Menelik's decline and the enthronement of Haile Selassie included preparations for a succession in Menelik's last years, Iyasu's erratic rule, and the long regency of Haile Selassie during which time he successfully maneuvered his way to the imperial throne. This interregnum provided yet another test, analogous to that of the much longer *zamena mesafint*, of the proposition that even in the era of expanded dominions, the Ethiopian polity rested on foundations deeper than the institutions of the empire per se. The central issue is how these foundations were seemingly not only preserved but changed during this period of relative weakness of imperial rule.

Weakened by an initial serious illness in 1906, Menelik became intermittently and increasingly incapacitated, and he increasingly left the exercise of power to members of his entourage prior to his death in 1913.[62] Menelik used the circumstance of his illness for constitutional innovation by seeming to (1) place the rule of the empire at least for the interim on less personalistic terms, and (2) contemplate adaptation to the Ethiopian polity of foreign models of government. He provided for a cabinet, with specified positions for each minister, to assume the responsibilities he was increasingly unable to discharge. Pankhurst claims that he established a cabinet-like structure during the period of his decline out of a conscious desire to implant European customs.[63] This innovation may have been somewhat overshadowed by controversy over his successor, for not until 1909 did he name Iyasu as his imperial heir and a prominent *ras*, Tessema, as regent.[64]

On the death of Tessema, a consensus among the various *rases* emerged that Iyasu should succeed to the throne. His subsequent whimsical and erratic behavior led to his being deposed after little more than a year as ruler. The manner and bases for his removal provided important clues to the nature of the Ethiopian state as understood by the most powerful political figures. Notwithstanding his brief ascendancy, Iyasu managed to raise dramatically issues bearing directly on the definition of the Ethiopian polity. These included (1) how much influence foreign legations were to be allowed to exercise in Ethiopian politics, (2) how central Orthodox Christianity and the Ethiopian Church were to the definition of the empire, and (3) how Ethiopia should align itself vis-à-vis the forces of nationalism and colonialiam at work in the northeastern African region as a whole.

Iyasu chose to forsake the Orthodox Church for Islam, at one point making a gift to the Turkish consul that displayed a crescent and the inscription "there is no god but Allah"—this during the course of World

War I.[65] By converting to Islam, Iyasu opened vistas for possible further enlargement of the empire to include what is now Somalia, while in naming an ethnic Somali to rule the Ogaden, Iyasu helped to stimulate Somali nationalism within the empire. His actions thereby exposed at least one basic contradiction of the empire: the insufficiency of Orthodox Christianity as a basis for an extended imperial order in which a high proportion of the subjects followed Islam.

Iyasu's unorthodox departures united most of the lords of the realm and the Church against him. The Church released the empire's subjects from their vows of allegiance; and the nobility prevailed militarily, apparently not without difficulty, against Iyasu's father, Ras Mikael, whom Iyasu had crowned *negus* of much of the ancient empire.[66] Noteworthy in this struggle is the fact that it appears to have been principally the *Shoan* nobility who rallied to depose Iyasu, while it was the *Oromo* negus of Welo, Tigre, Gojjam, and Gondar who came to his defense. However, there appears to be little evidence that those principalities incorporated in the empire by Menelik took advantage of his decline or the deposing of Iyasu to seek to escape their fairly recently imposed imperial yoke.

By guile, manipulative skill, ruthlessness, and good fortune, Ras Tafari, as regent following Iyasu's removal, succeeded in overcoming a number of competitors and consolidating his power—ensuring that he would become *negusa negast* (king of kings) or emperor in 1930 following the death of Empress Zauditu, Menelik's daughter. In traditional dynastic terms, his succession preserved the supremacy of the Shoan line as against the scions of other houses of the traditional empire, principally those of Johannes IV in Tigre and of Teklehaimanot of Gojjam.

However, Haile Selassie also represented a degree of commitment to the forms and substance of economic and social change that distinguished him from his rivals. He showed an early interest, for example, in the political uses of the airplane and of education. These proclivities were to become among the defining—and also most problematic—features of his forty-four year reign. His regime's political investment in the *symbols* of development considerably exceeded its tangible commitment to real political and economic development and improved standards of living. As a result Haile Selassie's government blurred the outlines of resulting class formation, the extent to which the legitimacy of the regime rested on traditional versus "modern" foundations, and the power relationships within the imperial order. Most basic of all, his regime raised questions of whether and for whom the Ethiopian polity held a legitimacy resting upon more than simply imperial instruments of force.

Haile Selassie employed symbols and some tangible indicators of political and economic development along Western lines in consolidating his new regime. He placed particular emphasis on the development of educational institutions, making specific provision for educating the sons of the nobility.[67] Noting their disinterest, he recruited increasingly for his administration the sons of commoners and those who embraced western education. His regime sponsored some individuals for overseas education, including training at military academies such as Saint Cyr. In addition, he revised the customs bureau, an institution of great importance to a country dependent for publicly sponsored development upon indirect taxation. Road building commenced, including a link north from Addis Ababa to Dessie built by a joint Ethiopian-Italian concession established under the terms of the 1928 Treaty of Friendship between the two countries. The city of Addis Ababa became partially distinct from the imperial entourage with the appointment of a mayor and a separate police force for the city.[68] The emperor established a state bank, taking thereby the first cautious steps to distinguish it in form at least the treasury of the imperial government from that of the emperor himself. In promulgating the constitution of 1931, Haile Selassie I ratified his own consolidation of power, confirmed a largely unchanged imperial political structure, and presented these realities through the rhetoric of a Western-style constitution that connoted symbolic commitment to individual political rights and an embryonic parliament. It afforded the Ethiopian Church no constitutional status, the one possible concession to the sensitivities of those incorporated into the empire by Menelik's conquests.[69]

Ethiopia's participation in the Eurocentric world of international relations during the first years of Haile Selassie's reign was just sufficient to render the country a deployable pawn in European diplomatic struggles that were in reality peripheral to its interests. The emperor's years of diplomatic involvement with emissaries of the Western powers and his faith in collective security, described by a close adviser as "almost theological," were of no avail to Ethiopia when confronted by the offensive of Mussolini's Italy. Neither had been his courting of Italian economic cooperation by the 1928 Treaty of Friendship. The European powers for their part appeared reluctant to recognize the integrity of the Ethiopian empire. Though admitting it to the League of Nations in return for initiatives against slavery, European powers that contemplated Ethiopia's partition into spheres of influence in Menelik's time did so again shortly before Haile Selassie was crowned emperor through a 1928 tripartite agreement. They contemplated such partitioning of Ethiopia yet again in the infamous Hoare-Laval plan conceived on the eve of Italy's invasion in 1936.[71] Once the invasion took place, however, the great powers retreated to the position that the League of Nations should search for a settlement. Meanwhile, they promptly recognized Italy's conquest once it had occurred, rejecting Haile Selassie's famous appeal for activation of the League's collective security provisions on his country's behalf.

Insufficient research has been done on the long-term impact on the Ethiopian state formation and political identity, as well as on Haile Selassie's government itself, of the Italian invasion and occupation, Haile Selassie's decision to go into exile, and his restoration with the assistance of British expeditionary forces. The emperor went into exile with the apparent approval of his ministers, but how many patriots who remained behind to harass the Italians resented the emperor's decision not to join them?[72] How did the lack of well-coordinated "national" resistance affect the fabric of the Ethiopian polity over the long term? To what extent did the emperor's absence encourage among some patriots the concept of an Ethiopian polity not necessarily ruled by an emperor? The emperor took firm measures to excuse the British military and political presence following his return to the throne, but how much was his own rule and that of the imperial office itself compromised by restoration at the hands of a foreign army rather than directly as a result of resistance within the country itself?[73] What role did these factors play in post-restoration uprisings in Tigre and Gojjam? For example, at least one of the most prominent resistance leaders, Tekla Wolde Hawariat, was implicated in several post-restoration plots against the emperor, some of which appear to have been at least vaguely animated by republican sentiments.[74]

Foundations of the Modern Ethiopian State: An Interim Appraisal

The survival of the "modern" empire through crises of expansion, controversial rulers, regime succession, and external defense may be explained as the result of some combination of effective coercion, on the one hand, and an evolved shared sense of political identity and membership in a multiethnic state, on the other hand. Insofar as such a sense of political community has persisted and evolved, it may have been symbolized though not defined by the institutions of the empire *per se* or it may have come to rest upon some shared sense of common political destiny broader than the imperial structure itself. The evolving content of any such basis of Ethiopian statehood within the framework of the empire is, if anything, even more difficult to estimate in the twentieth century than it was for Rubenson in his analysis of nineteenth century Ethiopian political history. Yet, as stated earlier, these questions are central to an understanding of the contemporary struggle to define a post-imperial Ethiopia, and the Ethiopian case may be significant for underlying theoretical problems concerning the nature and evolution of African states and economies.

The absence of sustained secessionist movements, liberation movements, or prolonged civil wars during the first one hundred years of the modern empire testifies not only to the survival of the empire but to the likelihood that to a significant degree its survival was not attributable only to effective coercion by the imperial government. Tewodros's vision of an Ethiopian renaissance appears not to have been rejected; rather, it was his tactics that led to his downfall. The cohesion of the empire was sustained during Johannes's reign despite the destabilizing shift of power to Shoa, the presence of two formidable competitors, the expanded empire accomplished largely during Menelik's lifetime and held together during his decline, the erratic rule of Iyasu, and Tafari's prolonged maneuverings to reach the throne. The importance of the victory at Adwa to some fundamental sense of Ethiopian political association cannot easily be overestimated, while the dedication of the Ethiopian resistance to Italian occupation, some collaborators notwithstanding, is scarcely in doubt. Rebellions in Gojjam and Tigre, periodic coup attempts, and some murmurings of republicanism or constitutional monarchy following Haile Selassie's restoration suggested at least as much unhappiness with the *constitution* of the empire state as with its *existence*.

Levine's concept of historically evolving "Pan-Ethiopian" cultural patterns represents one explanation of the capacity of the twentieth century Ethiopian polity to survive the political uncertainties of a long succession struggle and foreign invasion.[75] One may question, however, the extent to which such evolving cultural commonalities have in fact helped to sustain the Ethiopian polity in practical terms, or to what extent such commonalities are recognizable to political elites themselves and facilitate their negotiations. Then, too, Levine's argument appears to treat Oromo culture as intrinsically weaker politically than that of the Amhara in its relative lack of motivation and capacity—the Oromo invasions notwithstanding—to subject other peoples permanently and its lack of an exportable culture with which to rationalize such expansionism. Finally, there are politically significant communities within the empire that would appear to identify themselves with neither culture.

An alternative assessment of the nature and durability of Ethiopian political association, plausible on the basis of the political history outlined above, may lie less in the realm of culture and more in the history of political and economic interaction per se among the communities of the empire. According to such a hypothesis, historically periods of conflict have been interspersed with ones of accommodation during which a sense of common political destiny may have emerged based on the attractions of trade, intermarriage, opportunities to exploit each other's internal divisions for domestic political advantage, and (increasingly later) resistance to common "external" enemies. On such foundations one may hypothesize the gradual emergence of a de facto political association whose tacitly recognized parameters were routinized competition and even conflict, expressed structurally in confederal terms, within the framework of a monarchy continually asserting its de jure absolute power over all its presumed subjects.

These alternative theses concerning the historical basis of political association within the empire are not antithetical to one another. They may have been less mutually exclusive of one another than opposite ends of a spectrum defining the limits of the acceptable. The one hypothesis seems to legitimize an Amhara-led empire as natural, while stopping short of implying a disposition of other peoples to accept complete political and economic subjugation. The other implies rejection of empire, but recognizes customary on-going competition and periodic conflict to establish power relationships among parties whose strength relative to each other may vary at different points in time. The one thesis implies the dominance of the Amhara theological worldview though not necessarily the conversion of all who fall under Amhara political domination, while the other implies cultural conflict on more equal terms while not excluding some cross-fertilization.

The implication of the foregoing analysis is that the sweep of Ethiopian political history established parameters of tolerance within which a basis for political association existed and outside of which political disintegration might ensue. Such parameters may, of course, broaden or narrow and change in content over time. If the parameters of tolerance for Ethiopian political association were as suggested above at about the time of Haile Selassie's restoration, then the question arises how the emperor's postwar regime affected these parameters. To what degree did the symbols and/or reality of the emperor's postwar centralization, bureaucratic reorganization, economic development, constitutional revisions, and international involvement with an African continent in the midst of decolonization preserve and/or modify those parameters of tolerance? Alternatively, to what extent did Haile Selassie's policies go beyond them and undermine not only his own regime but any underlying basis for an Ethiopian polity itself within the perimeters established by Menelik's conquests? To what degree did emerging patterns of class stratification associated with these postwar changes also have either of these effects? It is to such questions that we turn in the balance of this chapter.

The Political Economy of Haile Selassie's Postwar Empire

Haile Selassie's postwar reign from 1941 to 1974 encompassed significant measures to create the symbols and formal structures of centralized, embryonic constitutional monarchy together with bounded, compartmentalized economic development notably within agriculture. Though more symbolic than real, these measures (1) nonetheless carried real and negative consequences for development of Ethiopian statehood underlying the empire he inherited, (2) added new dimensions to extreme preexisting economic inequalities, and (3) confused class formation, which helped to sustain his own regime but prepared the ground for political conflict undermining the maintenance as well as the transformation of the Ethiopian state after his survival.

Bureaucratic Centralization and Personal Rule

After his return from exile, the emperor acted forthrightly to centralize and concentrate in his hands powers previously exercised by provincial noblemen, furthering an objective pursued by each of his predecessors in the "modern" era. In so doing, he acted at the same time to diminish the influence of British officials posted around the country as a result of Britain's temporary military occupation.[76] However, his initial 1942 edict appeared to restrict the independence and privileges of provincial governors without really circumscribing their local responsibilities or necessarily strengthening the hand of the central government. Whereas governors-general had previously reported directly to the emperor, they were now to be responsible for the implementation of directives issued them by cabinet ministers, especially the minister of interior. They were forbidden to raise armies on their own except as directed by the ministers and were forbidden to impose any taxes or dues of their own not legally fixed by the central government. Yet their responsibility for directing the legitimate administration of their provinces was general and comprehensive rather than defined and specific; they were empowered to exercise "all necessary care" to ensure "the proper and peaceful protection of the people of the provinces." Moreover, one subsequent analysis described the creation as an "unintegrated prefectoral system" preserving vaguely defined responsibilities, and imprecisely drawn district and provincial boundaries that exacerbated personal and community rivalries.[77] Moreover, the same decree made the emperor himself, not his ministers, the locus of centralized control over provincial administration by maintaining all appointments and dismissals under the personal control of the emperor.[78]

Haile Selassie reorganized the ministerial system in 1943, building upon the precedent set by Menelik.[79] The 1943 order provided for a Council of Ministers and for a prime minister second in executive authority to the emperor himself. The emperor presided for a time over these cabinet meetings, later relinquishing this task to his prime minister. The formalization of the ministerial system encouraged a vast expansion in the number of central government employees from, according to one estimate, 75 in 1937 to nearly 20,000 in 1977, together with a 17-fold increase in the public budget.[80] But expansion and bureaucratization of the imperial government did not appear to diminish the importance of the emperor's rule even as he reached an advanced age and his government grew vastly in scope and responsibilities. The emperor reviewed the most minute expenditures of his burgeoning bureaucracy and did not actively discourage the practice of his ministers, nominally empowered to act on their own, from waiting upon him for his instructions in the conduct of their business—even when they had no business to transact—in order to reaffirm their loyalty and to curry favor with the emperor.[81]

The emperor's extension of the ministerial system in 1966 to provide for collective decisions by the Council of Ministers and participation by the prime minister in ministerial appointments further stretched the gap between the appearance of an embryonic Westminster system and the continued reality of personal rule.[82] True, Wolde-Ghiorgis Wolde-Johannes exercised enormous power as minister of the pen while responsible solely and directly to the emperor, and Aklilu Habte Wold as prime minister acquired a degree of independence in directing the government while serving at the pleasure of the emperor. Aklilu gained a degree of authority by merging the offices of Minister of the pen and prime minister, attending to the appointment of his friends and associates within ministries, and chairing the Council of Ministers.[83]

In reality, all policy decisions by the council continued to require the emperor's imprimatur. The prime minister and his ministerial colleagues remained responsible only to the emperor and not to Parliament, while the prime minister's initiative in naming ministers was never visible. More generally, the power of ministers to initiate policies within their jurisdictions appeared to be a function of the individual minister's political proximity to the throne, notwithstanding an often quoted speech by the emperor in which he deplored the unwillingness of ministers to exercise power formally bestowed upon them.[84]

The emperor's practice of continuing personal rule within a framework of symbolic political modernization had a two-dimensional impact on the political contours of the postwar empire. On the one hand, the Emperor utilized the reorganization of his government to strengthen further his position vis-à-vis at least the greater nobility. On the other hand, he failed to convince those closest to him that he meant the new structures to enjoy more than symbolic legitimacy. The first dimension of this policy continued the efforts of each of his predecessors in the modern era, while the second dimension was uniquely Haile Selassie's own creation. Clapham's account of the emperor's continued personal rule shows clearly that not even the ruler's closest lieutenants were inclined or convinced to take the new forms seriously. But the degree and nature of their reliance upon the emperor make clear that these same ministers did not find a basis within the traditional power structure for acting independently within the new framework. Markakis argues persuasively that the emperor skillfully blended traditional and more Western-educated officials in his postwar regime and continued to be skillful in playing off his officials against each other.[85] The hypothesis nonetheless emerges that by their own actions these officials demonstrated that only the emperor was able to increase his real political authority through such policies of symbolic modernization.

The emperor's revision of land taxation policies and procedures demonstrated the limits of the emperor's intentions or capacity to weaken the power of more local elites as distinct from the larger nobility. In 1942, taking into account "hardships that our country and our people have undergone during the past five years," the Emperor set the maximum rate of land taxation at 50 percent of prewar levels and reduced the tithe if paid in cash.[86] The Ministry of Finance assumed responsibility for collection of land taxes at differential rates based on fertility. However, assessment of land quality was left in strictly local hands, to be performed by committees composed of the local governor, the local village chief, a local priest, and two elders chosen by unspecified processes.[87]

Mounting opposition in the northern provinces of the traditional empire and in the landlord-dominated parliament obligated the government to limit further the impact of the revised system in these areas. A committee reporting to the emperor on the land tax system concluded with respect to Gojjam that "the Land Tax Proclamation . . . cannot be enforced," primarily in this case because a presumption of individual proprietorship of land in the proclamation struck at the heart of a usufructuary land tenure system that remained central to the political culture of the region.[88] More than twenty years later a similar initiative met with the same result.[89] A revised 1944 proclamation levied the land tax on the province as a whole, not only for Gojjam but for Begemdir and Tigre as well, to be assessed and collected by provincial officials. Subsequently, these provinces paid less than the minimum figure established for poor lands.[90] Moreover, members of the royal family, important provincial nobility and local elites, and some church lands were exempted from land tax.

In short, the emperor's postwar measures to restructure his government strengthened his personal rule more than it centralized the power of the imperial government itself. Officials of the central government derived little increased legitimacy for independent action from the symbolic modernization of governmental structures. Thus they lacked bases for independent action in either traditional or modern terms. Moreover, such "centralization" appears to have had relatively less impact on the traditional provinces of the empire than it did upon the newer ones added by Menelik's conquests. It is possible, therefore, that the emperor's "modernization" of his administration was only a symbolic gloss for strengthened personal rule within the central government itself. Such "modernization" may have carried greater consequences for the empire as a whole in emphasizing a dichotomy in his Shoa-based government's capacity to govern the newer and older realms of the empire.

Compartmentalized Development: Agriculture

Postwar processes of agricultural development resulted in islands of agricultural progress. While strengthening the country's national accounts, they benefited the few while even in appearance improving the lot of only a small number of the emperor's subjects. Outside these islands of economic growth, the traditional economy was affected, if at all, only indirectly and often adversely. Such change as did occur was largely limited, unplanned, and unassisted.

One of the most visible islands of agricultural modernization was the Chilalo Agricultural Development Unit (CADU). Historically converted to tenant-based agriculture by the conquests of Menelik II, Chilalo has had one of the highest population densities in the country, and tenant households may have accounted for as much as 50 percent of the total on the eve of the 1975 land reform. The Swedish International Development Authority (SIDA) found Chilalo attractive for the establishment of a pilot project for intensive rural development in part because of the area's anticipated agricultural potential and in part because of a perception that its inhabitants would respond to such initiatives.[91]

The goals of CADU were to (1) stimulate general regional social and economic development, (2) mobilize popular participation in development processes, (3) generate favorable employment effects, (4) develop appropriate technology, (5) emphasize helping low-income producers, and (6) generate an improved district tax base. The project was comprehensive, including livestock as well as crop production, forestry, research, veterinary programs, training, public health improvements, marketing, credit provision, and infrastructural development. The basic implementation strategy was to build momentum for change among smaller producers by offering first marketing facilities and later increasingly intensive agricultural production assistance. One "model farmer" was selected for every 100 producers, and these were to be the initial beneficiaries of other agricultural inputs.

CADU achieved improved production and yields, and it provided the basis for agricultural research and for less-intensive agricultural development programs elsewhere in the country. But participation in these benefits was uneven and limited. Participating farmers' incomes in one district of the CADU project increased from U.S.$162 per capita to U.S.$441 between 1968 and 1971, but these increases were experienced primarily by owner-occupiers rather than tenants despite efforts in the early 1970s to increase the numbers of participating smaller farmers and tenants.[92] New inputs and farming techniques were introduced, but dissemination was uneven and showed declining participation after the early years. CADU undertook to stabilize market prices and provide a better distribution system than that enjoyed by farmers outside the project. Even with the assistance of outside donors, however, CADU proved unable to compete with the existing market apparatus operated by agents of large buyers in urban areas who retained a capacity to control market information, collude in offering lower prices, capitalize on small farmers' lack of storage facilities and information, and cheat on weights and measures.[93] When it tried to reduce losses by forecasting average prices for the year, CADU still lost money because of large scale imports by the Ethiopian Grain Corporation.

The project operated on what proved to be the erroneous and, in retrospect, naive assumption that larger landholders and local elites would remain neutral to broadened participation in agricultural development by smaller farmers and tenants. During the first seven years of the project, as many as 5,000 tenants were evicted by landholders eager to appropriate the gains for themselves and to introduce mechanization at the expense of tenant farmers. Those not evicted by their landlords found themselves expropriated by higher rents in cash and kind.[94] The emperor's government ignored SIDA's appeal to halt these practices, and SIDA backed down on its threat to withdraw from the project. Meanwhile, the courts did not restore evicted tenants to their lands, and local governments increased tax burdens on CADU participants. Moreover, some self-help projects produced negative benefits, such as a water development effort to which participants contributed both labor and cash, only to be charged for water that was previously free to them.[95] Probably the most durable benefits of CADU were the agricultural research and training programs that provided the basis for less intensive assistance to smaller farmers throughout the country, though these projects were to encounter some of the same obstacles as did CADU.

The imperial government undertook compartmentalized agrarian development in other regions of the country as well. After World War II it began to encourage plantation development in the Awash River Valley to establish its presence in a region only marginally incorporated into the empire prior to the war, develop import-substituting agro-industries consistent with economic orthodoxy of the day, and to some limited degree provide outlets for inexpensive, underemployed labor from the overcrowded highland areas.[96] During the 1950s and 1960s over thirty plantations established irrigated agriculture along the Awash River, displacing large numbers of Afar pastoralists from their traditional and best grazing lands. These plantations varied in size and held varying relationships with the imperial government. The government awarded some estates to politically prominent individuals, while other grantees represented a new breed of professional agriculturalists. The largest and most important estates were joint ventures between the imperial government and foreign firms. All such estates shared one important characteristic: the virtual exclusion of all displaced pastoralists from participation in any but the most peripheral employment. Permanent and seasonal laborers were drawn from almost entirely highland regions, while training programs were similarly restricted. Only medical services on the larger estates were made available to the pastoralists to the degree that the facilities were not taken up by estate personnel.

The estates served a complicated set of political and economic purposes with mixed results. The largest of the estates contributed substantially or completely to the country's requirements for sugar, bananas, and cotton, yet at least the sugar was only competitive within a protected domestic market. They were capital-intensive estates whose technology was inaccessible to largely illiterate and impoverished producers outside the schemes. Though they employed up to 50,000 laborers, the schemes yielded a net export of capital.[97] They established the presence of the Ethiopian government in a peripheral but strategically important region, yet they deeply antagonized the Afar whose loss of grazing lands went uncompensated until the very eve of the regime's demise. However, much of the pastoralists' animosity was directed to the plantations themselves rather than to the sponsoring Ethiopian government.[98]

In larger political terms, the emperor legitimized but also helped corrupt the authority of the traditional Afar sultan among his own people without establishing a basis for alternative leadership. The sultan acquired huge tracts of land in the lower Awash Valley in such a way as to check any further expansion of the Tendaho cotton plantation in his own sphere of influence, while participating as a major shareholder in this joint venture between the government and a British firm. He cooperated with Tendaho in clearing his subjects' herds from unauthorized and destructive grazing, but appeared unable or unwilling to prevent them encroaching in the first place. He represented the interests of lower-valley Afar who sought the restoration of their lands while participating in the affairs of a major plantation that caused their displacement in the first place.

The marginalization of pastoralists in their own lands by the estates did not prevent important social and economic change in their societies.

Small urban centers in the Awash Valley became commercial outposts for business ventures by highland "expatriates." Pastoralists thus became peripheral participants in these settings as consumers, but lacked opportunities and resources to engage in the commercial activities themselves or in the limited educational and health facilities that were established in these towns. The Afar were spectators to urban and commercial development as well as displaced by the commercial estates established within their midst. They were thus especially vulnerable to the drought and famine of the early 1970s.

In the early 1960s the Ethiopian government created the Awash Valley Authority to coordinate overall development in the region. Significantly, it gained only partial jurisdiction over the estates already present, whose obligations were directly to the Ethiopian government or the emperor.[99] For example, one of the most fertile plains in the middle Awash was retained largely undeveloped by a princess of the royal family. Moreover, the entire thrust of the AVA was development of the lands and natural resources of the valley rather than mobilization of resident peoples for economic and social change. To prepare the way for the AVA and for the estates the civil code, in the name of legal reform, had in effect extinguished any rights the pastoralists might have possessed to press their case for recovery of lost lands or compensation.[100] The AVA itself lacked the financial authority to act independently of the landlord-dominated Ethiopian parliament, the power to coordinate the work of various ministries in the valley, or the authority to ameliorate the problems the estates had caused the pastoralists.

The Chilalo and Awash development projects exemplified the strategy and results of the imperial government's postwar agrarian development. The regime established what Hess termed a "veneer of modernization."[101] The processes established did increase the country's productive capacity to a limited extent. However, they masked the monopolization of the benefits by the regime's political establishment that reduced all but a tiny minority of ordinary rural citizens to marginal participants, spectators, and/or losers. Participation in these processes appeared to be shared by newer and more traditional elites alike, giving them a common stake in the sponsoring regime.

The same symbolic and superficial modernization may have carried other larger and more problematic implications for political and economic development within the empire. The majority of these schemes were undertaken within the newer regions of the empire and appeared to be an economic expression of the military and political incorporation of these regions by the emperor's predecessors. At the grass roots level the predominance of temporary and permanent employees from older regions of the country also lent this appearance to the schemes, while those who were rendered tenants of the crown by Menelik's conquests were among those marginalized by the new projects, notwithstanding the project designs and intentions of foreign donors. The projects may also have strengthened, in at least formal terms, a greater direct presence for the central government in some local areas than it had previously enjoyed, implying to some degree a shift in power and political responsibility from locales to the capital.

Imperial Reform

In common with each of his predecessors in the modern era, Haile Selassie I articulated commitments to improve the lot of the realm's ordinary subjects. Emperors from Tewodros through Haile Selassie I inveighed against slavery with varying degrees of intensity, and Haile Selassie's predecessors also sought to limit the depredations of the army upon civilians. Each publicly endorsed the dignity and importance of labor, the disapproval of the Church notwithstanding. Particularly with respect to slavery, imperial calls for improvement in the lot of ordinary subjects were directed to international as well as domestic audiences. It is very difficult, however, to ascertain to what extent the reform initiatives of the earlier emperors were received, as were Haile Selassie's, as symbolic gestures with little real substance.

Haile Selassie's measures to reform the empire in the interests of his humble and impoverished subjects, like those of Menelik II in particular, reflected the end of Ethiopia's isolation from international political and economic currents. Menelik responded to European ideological currents, technological development, and realpolitik. He nurtured the the germ of cabinet-style government initiated by Menelik, lent special status and encouragement to expatriates with technological skills to offer his government, and engaged in his own imperial expansion partly in competition with Europeans. Haile Selassie's domestic reform policies appeared also to have been motivated at least in part by a concern to define and establish Ethiopia's identity in world affairs. Haile Selassie, too, appeared to respond to the realities as well as to the technological potential and ideological currents of a changing international order. He undertook to clothe his regime in the dress of an embryonic Westminster-like constitutional monarchy, he applied the changing economic wisdom of the 1950s and 1960s to the task of promoting such development as would strengthen his regime, and he appeared to fashion his foreign policy to the twin postwar international realities of the Cold War and the retreat of European empires in the face of growing African nationalism.

International realities enabled the imperial regime to bolster Ethiopian national political identity and acquire heroic stature among colonized

African peoples in Menelik's time. In external affairs after World War II, Haile Selassie was increasingly obliged to rely upon parlaying his country's heroism of the earlier era into contemporary diplomatic stature and influence. To his credit, he did so quite successfully for as long as he reigned. Domestically, however, international realities caused Haile Selassie's regime to appear increasingly anachronistic to younger generations of Ethiopians. He attempted to preserve an empire while those of European powers were receding in the world beyond Ethiopia's borders. The lengthy debate over the postwar future of Eritrea resulting in United Nations endorsement of federation with Ethiopia was not only a new chapter in an historic struggle for power in that region but a reminder of the potential domestic meaning of the African continent's transition from empire to nationhood. The independence of Somalia in 1960 and its claims upon Somalis in the Ogaden region of southeastern Ethiopia carried a similar implication. The Organization of African Unity's (OAU) defense of established colonial boundaries benefited the emperor's regime but also highlighted its imperial character. Moreover, while regimes in newly independent countries elsewhere in Africa attacked economic neocolonialism at least in ideological terms, Haile Selassie did not make even a symbolic postwar effort to distinguish and distance imperial economic reform from such influences.

The emperor's skill in coopting modernity-oriented as well as more tradition-bound elites at the national level throughout his rule helped to prolong and entrench his regime. But in thereby undermining the legitimacy of both sets of elites with respect to their potential bases of power, he ultimately weakened not only his regime but the foundations of the Ethiopian polity itself, a reality starkly demonstrated by the tumultuous course of events after his departure. The story of imperial political and economic reform is therefore one of limited, largely symbolic modernization bolstering the emperor's regime in the short to medium term but, in the long term, undermining the bases of Ethiopian statehood and its socioeconomic foundations.

Some of the imperial reforms were clearly prompted by the abortive coup of 1960. This was a direct challenge to the emperor in the name of modernization and for that reason without historical precedent in Ethiopia, but it was an insurgency that failed because the military perpetrators had not organized a broad base of support for their movement consistent with the professed objective.[102] The coup attempt was a warning to the emperor that pressures for economic and social change were beginning to outrun measures introduced by his regime in the name of progressive change. In the failure of the coup he might have derived both some comfort and a disturbing omen: the inadequacy of existing political processes to express aspirations for social and economic change but the sufficiency for a time of those same processes still to frustrate change.

One of the emperor's most important reform initiatives was the promulgation in 1955 of the revised constitution.[103] Its most important provision established a lower house of Parliament to be elected by nearly universal adult suffrage every four years. One complicating factor in its promulgation may have been the difficulty of incorporating an Eritrea with its own embryonic parliamentary institutions into a still-traditional autocracy. On its face, however, the new constitution sought to enlist the participation of both local elites and ordinary Ethiopian citizens in a regime in which the authority of the greater nobility had at least in theory been diminished by the immediate postwar decrees. Like its predecessor, however, the apparent democratizing features of the new constitution were all subject to law of which the emperor remained the unchallenged dispenser, e.g., voting qualifications and eligibility for electoral office. In fact, Parliament set $500 of immovable property or $1000 of movable property as a requirement for candidates in a country where per capita income was well below $100. The Chamber of Deputies gained legislative initiative, but the emperor retained a veto. Promised laws establishing judicial independence did not appear until two decades later on the very eve of the regime's demise, while no modification was contemplated of traditional judicial appeals.

The emperor may have bespoken some of his purposes in decreeing the revised constitution when he stated to the first elected parliament that "You are the bridge that connects us to our people."[104] But popular response to the imperial constitutional overture was considerably less than enthusiastic. Voter turnout was never high and decreased during the four general elections prior to the end of the regime in 1974. Furthermore, the turnover in elected representatives to the Chamber of Deputies was very high, indicating some combination of dissatisfaction with the performance of the institution, indifference, or treatment of electoral office as a prize to be shared rather than a means to the achievement of social ends. The absence of roads and communications for the majority of citizens in rural Ethiopia limited the effectiveness of campaigns and the extent of voting itself. Finally, the elected members of the chamber were, characteristically and predictably, members of the imperial establishment: landed, slightly educated, Orthodox Christian, and civil servants.

The abortive coup of 1960 spurred the emperor's government to further reforms in the decade and a half that was to be left to it. One such initiative was recognition of the right of trade unions to organize, while another was the order in council of 1966, discussed earlier, which furthered the appearance of a Westminster-style constitutional democracy by enlarging the role of the prime minister. Of potentially greater but unrealized significance was the Local Self-Administration Order of 1966.[105] The order granted considerable opportunity to local administrators to deliberate upon and provide for education, public health, public works, water supplies, agricultural and community development, and governance of local trade and commerce. Perhaps most significant, the order provided for the election of *awraja* (or district) councils, and property restrictions for council candidates were omitted. However, the order did not identify the specific functions the councils were to exercise, concentrating instead on elaborate specification of the procedures by which they were to perform their duties. By contrast, the careful specification of the role of district, provincial, and central government administrators indicated clearly the advisory roles these councils were to fill. Despite the circumscribed roles of these councils, the Parliament never passed the enabling legislation to effect the provisions of the order, nor did it determine what sources of local finance would be available to them. The emperor, moreover, did not put public pressure upon the Parliament to enact such legislation.

In an extraconstitutional maneuver, senior officials of the Ministry of Interior on the eve of the regime's fall sought to implement a pilot scheme of local self-administration in seventeen *awrajas* following the model of the unlegislated order. The ministry cautiously sought support from foreign donors, in this way tacitly recognizing the regime's need for strengthened grass roots support at a time when drought, inflation, unemployment, and famine increasingly challenged the ability of the regime to govern.

In other ways, the regime attempted with partial success to coopt potential political opponents in the name of development. One example was the Ethiopian University Service (EUS) program providing that all University students were to spend the third of their four years in direct development efforts benefiting the country. Never popular with the students because it appeared to them a measure to coopt their support for a regime they had increasingly come to despise, the program greatly benefited the Ministry of Education in particular. University students were not only a source of inexpensive classroom staffing but made possible relieving potentially politically vocal regular teachers of unpopular rural assignments. While EUS blunted the image of the university students in their own minds as urban parasites on an oligarchic regime, it also appeared to draw students to a sober appreciation of the realities of poverty and underdevelopment in their country.[106] Perhaps partly for that reason seniors—returned from EUS and within a year of graduation and hoped-for public sector employment—were less in evidence as student body political leaders. EUS, however, served only to dampen, not quell, student hostility to the regime which was intensified by violent reaction to student protests during Haile Selassie's last years in power.

The experience with comprehensive, intensive smallholder agricultural development in CADU, coupled with growing recognition in the Ethiopian ministries and in international financial circles that Third World development processes were not reaching effectively the rural majority, led to further reform measures in the late 1960s and early 1970s. With the assistance of SIDA, the World Bank, and the U.S. Agency for International Development, the Ethiopian government initiated a Minimum Package Program (MPP). The purpose of MPP was to distribute to a large number of farmers a carefully selected assortment of critical agricultural inputs. These inputs—fertilizer, seeds, credit, and marketing facilities—were to stimulate production at a cost that small farmers including tenants could afford. New farming methods and technologies evolved by CADU were to be adapted to the circumstances and requirements of these small producers.

The MPP effectively challenged the inherited imperial strategy of focusing agrarian development within confined spheres and instead broke down barriers to broadened participation in processes of rural development. The program was so successful in generating farmer interest, stimulating higher productivity, and reaching new strata of producers that it was one of the few adopted and expanded by the post-imperial regime. However, under the emperor's government, MPP was also frustrated because it operated upon the same unrealistic premise as CADU—the benign neutrality of landed elites toward progress by their tenants and other impoverished farmers. The objective was to persuade landlords to stabilize the obligations of tenants so that tenants would gain the land tenure security to merit their investment in the agricultural package. The extent of MPP's success before 1974, while real and important, was nonetheless limited by the unreality of this premise. SIDA officials in their reports stated directly that the sustainable success of MPP depended upon land reform measures that the empire's political and economic establishment did not consider in its interests.[107]

Similarly, under pressure from the United Nations Development Program which supported the work of the Awash Valley Authority through the Food and Agriculture Organization, the emperor's government in the early 1970s initiated pilot schemes to resettle Afar pastoralists displaced by the Awash Valley estates. Justified both as compensation of lost grazing lands and as a means of introducing the Afar to enhanced socioeconomic opportunity through settled agriculture, the pilot schemes achieved neither purpose. The Afar were motivated by severe losses during the 1972–73 drought-famine to participate in the schemes. But they were in reality shareholders on schemes in which imported highland surplus agricultural labor did almost all the agricultural work. The project included only scant provision for educational, health, and other social services to assist the Afar in converting to lifestyles of settled agriculturalists, nor were they permitted to keep livestock on the scheme to ease the transition. The Afar settlers did not, therefore, make an unambiguous commitment to the project, nor did their leaders accept it as adequate compensation for lost lands. Under World Bank auspices, however, the scheme was nevertheless to be greatly expanded in the post-Haile Selassie era as the Amibara Irrigation Project. It was more than ten years later before serious consideration was given to a substantial livestock component that would allow the Afar to seek economic development on the basis of their traditional pastoral economies.[108]

Meanwhile, the problems experienced by CADU and MPP in seeking to reach tenant farmers and other small producers victimized by inherited land tenure systems surfaced nationally in the tenancy reform legislation drafted for submission to Parliament in 1968 after years of preparation.[109] The object of the legislation was to make realistic the major premise of the regime's agrarian reform initiatives: stabilization of the relationship between landlords and tenants. Through such legislation tenants might have gained a degree of land tenure security necessary to encourage their participation in agrarian development programs that required investment of their own labor and resources. But even this modest legislative proposal never reached the floor of Parliament. The emperor's government and the houses of Parliament collectively frustrated the efforts of progressives within the administration who had been encouraged by foreign donors to introduce even this modest reform.

While the emperor's regime demonstrated its incapacity or unwillingness to undertake the structural reforms indicated by the declared purposes of programs it endorsed, the political integrity of the empire itself had come under increasing strain. The independence of Somalia encouraged irredentism in the Somali-inhabited Ogaden region. At the same time, following the agreement on Eritrea's federation with Ethiopia, the emperor's government set out to achieve the territory's full incorporation into the empire, a historic milestone achieved formally in 1961 that had eluded Haile Selassie's predecessors. Yet Eritrea's apparent voluntary acceptance of incorporation was in fact the product of intrigue, cooptation, pressure, and outright corruption on the part of the Ethiopian government.[110] The imperial government's Eritrean presence was further established by the Kagnew military communications base in the capital, Asmara, a key element in the country's military assistance agreement with the United States.

The incorporation of Eritrea in 1961 spurred the birth of the Eritrean liberation movement whose two principal expressions have been the

Eritrean Liberation Front and the Eritrean People's Liberation Front, the latter in recent years the more powerful of the two. While the Eritrean economy, notably the industrial base in Asmara, became an integral part of the imperial economy and many Eritreans served in high places in the imperial government, the actions of the liberation movement forced the imperial government into increasing commitments of military forces to the region. Though struggles among the liberation movements themselves have been recurrent, and often bitter and violent, they collectively denied the imperial government full control of the province. Despite support from constellations of Middle Eastern countries, the liberation movements were not able during the remaining years of the empire to force the imperial government to negotiate publicly. While it is generally believed that the liberation movements were initially prepared to accept a resumption of pre-1961 autonomy rather than full independence, the costs of war embittered all sides to such a degree that the options for a negotiated settlement were more remote under the successor military regime than they were during the last years of Haile Selassie's government.

Despite its limited capacity to modernize, the imperial government's fragile legitimacy in the regions of the traditional empire was demonstrated with the same force in 1967 in Gojjam as it had been twenty years earlier. The agricultural income tax proclamation of 1967 slightly modified existing land taxes in ways that again suggested more individual proprietorship over land. Rebellion ensued in Gojjam against what people perceived to be a threat to the complicated double descent system of land tenure in which individuals inherited the right to compete for the use of land from both parents' lines.[111] The ability to compete for the use of land throughout the region went to the heart of Gojjami society and was a principal institution linking them as a people. The government again withdrew the provisions the Gojjami found most objectionable, as it had twenty years earlier, but not before having to resort to military force to suppress the rebellion.

Conclusion

The foregoing analysis suggests that Haile Selassie's measures to modernize and develop the empire did not foster but, rather, inhibited the development of Ethiopian statehood within the empire he inherited. This occurred, first, because his measures not only exacerbated inequalities but, through elite cooptation, blurred formation and articulation of class identifications expressing the realities of the Ethiopian political economy. These realities included capitalist formations incompatible with long-term vestiges of historic feudalism, economic exploitation and impoverishment incompatible with sustained long term development, and inequalities and human misery defying any claims of concern for social justice. The contradictions in the country's political economy were seemingly beyond the capability of a traditional feudal regime to rectify and thus pointed to reformation of the Ethiopian state itself.

Second, Haile Selassie's centralization of power occurred in form, while in substance the emperor aggrandized his personal rule at the expense of more traditional as well as more modernizing elites. More modernizing elites were denied the institutionalized authority their formally modern roles seemed to imply, while their cooptation appears to have cost them credibility as advocates of socioeconomic as well as political change. At the same time, Haile Selassie was suspect to traditional elites from the beginning of his reign. He followed the pattern of his predecessor in denying to all pretenders investiture as *negus,* or king, of regions within the empire. He did not appear to permit those more traditional elites to whom he did grant symbolically important modern roles within his government to thereby enhance their power in traditional terms. If Haile Selassie "decapitated" the traditional feudal hierarchy in this fashion, he did little to limit elites' access to wealth or status or the perpetuation of the system itself below its apex. However, by undermining the political legitimacy of both the greater nobility and more modernizing elites as the price of sustaining his personal authority, the emperor undermined the political fabric of the feudal order itself. Thus, he left open the prospect of state transformation as well as regime change when he left office.

Third, he perpetuated a high degree of regionalism within the older areas of the empire, some of the evidence for which was careful accommodation of the Tigrean line after suppression of the 1943 revolt and forced retreat from two attempts to impose modest tax revision on Gojjam. But his attack on Eritrean federation was inconsistent with any attempt the imperial government might have made to to reconstitute the empire upon more federal lines by marrying contemporary concepts of federalism with historical political patterns within the empire.

Fourth, Haile's Selassie's symbolic and carefully circumscribed economic development initiatives carried real, broadly based, and predominantly negative consequences. Compartmentalized rural development efforts contributed to national income without releasing the productive energies of most of the country's rural producers suppressed by traditional and inegalitarian land tenure arrangements. Meanwhile, elites of all persuasions took full advantage of the opportunity to enhance their own wealth and privilege through these initiatives vis-à-vis the excluded majority. Their economic aggrandizement contrasted with the weakening of the fabric of the state itself that sustained their wealth and status. Such initiatives could be construed as economic complements to the imperial political and military conquests of Menelik and, as such, did little to increase this excluded majority's commitment to the regime or to the Ethiopian state it purposed to embody.

In short, Haile Selassie employed symbolic political and economic change to strengthen and prolong his regime. The realities, however, undermined not only the old regime's tenure in the long run but bases of Ethiopian political identity and statehood that may have emerged and survived during a long history of empire. These larger dimensions of political crisis in Ethiopia were to become apparent in the attempt to transform and build upon underlying foundations of an Ethiopian state after the demise of Haile Selassie's government.

Notes

1. The term "modern" is employed only to distinguish the reigns of Ethiopia's last four emperors from the long line of those who preceded them in chronological terms only.

2. Among the most important sources on empire is S. N. Eisenstadt, *The Decline of Empires*. New York: Prentice-Hall, 1969.

3. While European colonial empires in the Third World have been dismantled, other contemporary states not normally thought of as empires could be considered such, e.g., the Soviet Union and over the long historical term possibly China as well. The interesting historical question is, thus, how and why does an empire evolve into a multinational state outliving the imperial structures within which it was born?

4. Nelson Kasfir, "Class, Political Domination and the African State," in Zaki Ergas (ed.), *The African State in Transition*. New York and London: Macmillan, forthcoming.

5. Sven Rubenson, *The Survival of Ethiopian Independence*. London: Heinemann, 1976. See also M. Abir, *Ethiopia: The Era of Princes*. London: Longman, Green, 1968.

6. *Ibid.*

7. *Ibid.*, pp. 408-9.

8. Among the principal sources on earlier Ethiopian history are J. Spencer Trimmingham, *Islam in Ethiopia*. London: Oxford University Press, 1952; Taddesse Tamrat, *Church and State in Ethiopia 1270-1727*. Oxford: Clarendon Press, 1972; A. Jones and E. Monroe, *A History of Ethiopia*. Oxford: Clarendon Press, 1955; C. F. Beckingham and G. B. Huntingford (eds.), *Some Records of Ethiopia 1593-1646*. London: Hakluyt Society, 1954.

9. Useful sources on the legend are Jones and Monroe, *op. cit.*, and Tamrat, *op. cit.* Robert Hess in *Ethiopia: The Modernization of Autocracy* (Ithaca and London: Cornell University Press, 1970) gives an insightful interpretation of the legend's political significance.

10. John Markakis, *Ethiopia: Anatomy of a Traditional Polity*. London: Oxford University Press, 1974.

11. Among the principal sources on the emperors of the empire's "modern" era are as follows: On Tewodros, S. Rubenson, *op. cit.,* and *Tewodros: King of Kings.* Addis Ababa: Oxford University Press; and Donald Crummey, "Tewodros as Reformer and Modernizer," 10 *Journal of African History,* 3, 1969, pp. 457-69; and "Bandit and Resistance: Noble and Peasant in Nineteenth Century Ethiopia," in S. Rubenson (ed.), *Proceedings of the Seventh International Conference of Ethiopian Studies.* East Lansing: African Studies Center, Michigan State University, 1984. On Menelik, Harold Marcus, *The Life and Times of Menelik II.* London: Clarendon Press, 1975; Kofi Darkwah, *Shewa, Menelik and the Ethiopian Empire 1813-1889.* London: Heinemann, 1975; Rubenson, *Survival, op. cit.* On Johannes, one of the more important studies is by one of his descendants, Zewde Gebre Selassie, *Johannes IV of Ethiopia: A Political Biography.* London: Clarendon Press, 1975; also consult Rubenson, *Survival, op. cit.*

12. Richard A. Caulk, "The Pre-Modern Army and Ethiopian Society 1850-1895," paper presented to the African Studies Association meetings, Boston, November 1986. See also Richard Pankhurst, *Economic History of Ethiopia.* Addis Ababa: Haile Selassie I University Press, 1968, Ch. 12; and "The Ethiopian Army of Former Times," 7 *Ethiopia Observer,* 2, 1964, pp.118-142.

13. A very insightful analysis is to be found in Crummey, "Bandit and Resistance," *op. cit.*

14. Abir, *op. cit.,* and Rubenson, *Survival, op. cit.*

15. Markakis, *op. cit.*

16. There has been quite some debate on the appropriateness of describing traditional Ethiopian society as feudal. See Chapter 1, note 7.

17. Major sources on feudalism in general are Marc Bloch, *Feudal Society.* Chicago: University of Chicago Press, 1961; and E. L. Ganshoff, *Feudalism.* New York: Columbia University Press, 1961.

18. Taddesse Tamrat, "Feudalism in Heaven and on Earth: Ideology and Political Structure in Medieval Ethiopia," in S. Rubenson (ed.), *Proceedings, op. cit.,* pp. 201-13.

19. D. Levine, "Individualism in Feudal Ethiopia," *op. cit.*

20. Pankhurst, *Economic History, op. cit.,* and "The Ethiopian Army," *op. cit.*

21. An avalanche of literature has appeared on the depressed condition of the Ethiopian peasants past and present. One concise summary of the problem is to be found in Richard Pankhurst, "Some Factors Depressing the Standard of Living of Peasants in Traditional Ethiopia," 4 *Journal of Ethiopian Studies,* 2, 1966, pp. 45-98.

22. Pankhurst, *Economic History, op. cit.* Mesfin Wolde Mariam has recently completed a historical analysis of Ethiopian droughts and famines that is soon to be published.

23. Rubenson, *Survival, op. cit.,* and *King of Kings, op. cit.* Also Margaret Morgan, "Continuities and Traditions in Ethiopian History: An Investigation of the Reign of Tewodros," 12 *Ethiopia Observer,* 4, 1969, pp. 245-72.

24. Pankhurst, *Economic History, op. cit.*

25. Jones and Monroe, *op. cit.,* argue that the reaction to Portuguese missionaries' evangelism was indeed a popular uprising.

26. Donald Levine, *Wax and Gold: Tradition and Innovation in Ethiopian Culture*. Chicago: University of Chicago Press, 1965. Gedamu Abraha's review was published in 11 *Ethiopia Observer*, 3, 1967, pp. 229-44.

27. Morgan, *op. cit.*

28. *Ibid.* See also John Markakis, "An Interpretation of Ethiopian Political Tradition," 66 *Presence Africaine*, 1968, pp. 79-97.

29. Jones and Monroe, *op. cit.*

30. Richard Pankhurst and Andreas Eshete, "Self-Help in Ethiopia," 2 *Ethiopia Observer*, 11, 1958, pp. 354-64; Alemayehu Seifu, "Edir in Addis Ababa," 12 *Ethiopia Observer*, 1, 1968, pp. 8-19; Eftychia and Peter Koehn,"Edir as a Vehicle for Urban Development in Addis Ababa," in H. G. Marcus (ed.), *Proceedings of the First United States Conference on Ethiopian Studies*. East Lansing, Michigan: African Studies Center, Michigan State University, 1975, pp. 399-427.

31. Frederick Gamst, "Peasantries and Elites Without Urbanism: The Civilization of Ethiopia," 12 *Comparative Studies in Society and History*, 4, 1970, pp. 373-92.

32. Teshome Wagaw, *Child Rearing Practices in Rural Ethiopia: A Pilot Field Study*. Addis Ababa: Faculty of Education, Haile Selassie I University, 1974.

33. Pankhurst, "The Ethiopian Army," *op. cit.*

34. Rubenson, *Survival, op. cit.*

35. Allan Hoben, *Land Tenure Among the Amhara of Ethiopia*. Chicago: University of Chicago Press, 1973.

36. Jones and Monroe, *op. cit.*

37. Donald Levine, *Greater Ethiopia: The Evolution of a Multicultural Society*. Chicago: University of Chicago Press, 1974.

38. Rubenson, *King of Kings, op. cit.*; Crummey, "Tewodros as Reformer," *op.cit.*; Morgan, *op. cit.*; and Tsegaye Gebre Medhin, "Tewodros," 9 *Ethiopia Observer*, 3, 1965, pp. 209-27 (published version of a play).

39. Crummey, *Proceedings, op. cit.*

40. Tsegaye Gebre Medhin's play dramatized this point.

41. Hess, *op. cit.*

42. Crummey, "Tewodros," *op. cit.*

43. Richard Greenfield, *Ethiopia: A New Political History*. New York: Praeger, 1965; Rubenson, *King of Kings, op. cit.*; and Crummey, "Tewodros," *op. cit.* differ somewhat on the relative importance of Tewodros's attack on the practices of the church in bringing about his downfall.

44. Crummey, *Ibid.*

45. Zewde Gebre Selassie, *op. cit.*

46. Pankhurst, *Economic History, op. cit.*, Ch. 1.

47. Zewde Gebre Selassie, *op. cit.*

48. Greenfield, *op. cit.*

49. Marcus, *op. cit.*; Darkwah, *op. cit.*

50. Among a number of sources about these land tenure practices: John Cohen and Dov Weintraub, *Land and Peasants in Imperial Ethiopia: The Social Background to a Revolution*. Assen, The Netherlands: Van Gorcum and Co., 1975. Also, John M. Cohen, "Ethiopia After Haile Selassie: The Government Land

Factor," 72 *African Affairs*, 289, 1973, pp. 365–82; H. C. Dunning, "Land Reform in Ethiopia: A Case Study in Non-Development," 18 *U.C.L.A. Law Review*, 2, 1970, pp. 271–307; Patrick Gilkes, *The Dying Lion: Feudalism and Modernization in Ethiopia*. New York: St. Martin's Press, 1975; Hoben, *op. cit.*; Ethiopian Government, Ministry of Land Reform and Administration, *Reports* (1967–70); Michael Stahl, *Ethiopia: Political Contradictions in Agricultural Development*. Stockholm: Liber Tryck, 1975.

51. Cohen and Weintraub, *op. cit.*, give this coherent summary of the rationale. Markakis, *op. cit.*, p. 24, speculates on the underlying reasons for Menelik's expansionism.

52. Sven Rubenson, *Wichale XVII: The Attempt to Establish a Protectorate over Ethiopia*. Addis Ababa: Haile Selassie I University, Historical Studies No. 1, 1964. This work is the definitive work on controversy over the interpretation of the treaty.

53. Markakis, *op. cit.*, is one of the few who has speculated on this question.

54. Richard Pankhurst, "Menelik and the Utilization of Foreign Skills," 5 *Journal of Ethiopian Studies*, 1, 1965, pp. 60–83.

55. *Ibid.*, and M. Abir, "Salt, Trade and Politics in Ethiopia in the Zamena Masafint," 4 *Ethiopia Observer* 2, 1960, pp. 1–11.

56. Pankhurst, *Economic History*, *op. cit.*

57. Pankhurst, "Menelik and the Utilization," *op. cit.*

58. Caulk, *op. cit.*; Pankhurst, "Ethiopian Army," *op. cit.*

59. See note 60.

60. Pankhurst, *Economic History*, *op. cit.*

61. Hess, *op. cit.*; Greenfield, *op. cit.*, p. 97.

62. Marcus, *Menelik*, *op. cit.*; and Harold Marcus, "The End of the Reign of Menelik II," 11 *Journal of African History*, #4, 1970, pp. 570–590.

63. Pankhurst, *Economic History*, *op. cit.*

64. Greenfield, *op.cit.*, offers a perceptive picture of the personalities and struggles surrounding the succession.

65. A point that appears not well sorted out in the research is the relative importance of the several aspects of Iyasu's association with the Turkish consul. A probably accurate assumption is that flirtation with Islam was fundamental, but how important were the accompanying geopolitical overtones, among them Ethiopia's posture in the war and the significance of an association with Turkey in terms of regional balances of power?

66. Greenfield, *op. cit.*

67. Among the good sources on the emperor's prewar reign are Margery Perham, *The Government of Ethiopia*. 2nd ed. London: Faber and Faber, 1969; Greenfield, *op. cit.*; and L. Mosley, *Haile Selassie: The Conquering Lion*. Englewood Cliffs, N.J.: Prentice-Hall, 1964.

68. Perham, *op. cit.*

69. An account of the constitution of 1931 along with the text is included in Perham, *op. cit.*

70. John Spencer, "Haile Selassie: Triumph and Tragedy," 18 *Orbis*, 4, 1975, pp. 1129–53.

71. Among the accounts of this period are Laurence Lafore and James Dugan, *Days of Emperor and Clown: The Italo-Ethiopian War of 1935-1936*. Garden City, New York: Doubleday, 1973; and Jones and Monroe, *op. cit.*

72. Richard Pankhurst, "The Ethiopian Patriots: The Lone Struggle 1936-1941," 13 *Ethiopia Observer*, 1, 1970, pp. 40-57.

73. An insightful analysis of the international politics of Haile Selassie's restoration is Harold Marcus, *Ethiopia, Great Britain, and the United States: The Politics of Empire*. Berkeley: University of California Press, 1983. See also Alberto Sbacchi, "Haile Selassie and the Italians 1941-1943," 22 *African Studies Review*, 1, 1979, pp. 25-42.

74. Greenfield, *op. cit.* An analysis of earlier pamphleteers' calls for change is Richard Caulk, History Department, Rutgers University-Camden, "Pamphleteers and Polemicists in Print in Ethiopia 1900-1935," unpublished, n.d.

75. Levine, *Greater Ethiopia, op. cit.*

76. Marcus, *Ethiopia, op. cit.*

77. John M. Cohen, *Local Government Reform in Ethiopia*. Washington, D.C.: Agency for International Development, 1974; John M. Cohen and Peter Koehn, *Ethiopian Provincial and Municipal Government: Imperial Patterns and Post-Revolutionary Changes*. East Lansing, Michigan: Michigan State University, 1979.

78. Decree No. 1 of 1942.

79. Decree No. 1 of 1943.

80. John Spencer, address to the twentieth annual meetings of the African Studies Association, Houston, November, 1977.

81. Christopher Clapham, *Haile Selassie's Government*. New York: Praeger, 1969.

82. Order No. 44 of 1966.

83. Clapham, *op. cit.*

84. *Ibid.*

85. Markakis, *op. cit.*

86. June 8, 1942.

87. Gilkes, *op. cit.* Also Peter Schwab, *Decision-Making in Ethiopia: A Study of the Political Process*. Rutherford, N.J.: Fairleigh Dickinson University, 1972.

88. Quoted in Gebre-Wold Ingida-Worq, "Ethiopia's Traditional System of Land Tenure and Taxation," 5 *Ethiopia Observer*, 4, 1962, pp. 307-339.

89. Examined in Hoben, *op. cit.*

90. Schwab, *op. cit.*

91. In addition to CADU a similar project was established in Wolamo and Ada districts, known as WADU and ADA respectively. However, CADU's was very much the most comprehensive of the three and had the largest impact nationally. All three projects are discussed in Tesfaye Tecle, *The Evolution of Alternative Rural Development Strategies in Ethiopia: Implications for Employment and Income Distribution*. East Lansing, Michigan: Department of Agricultural Economics, and Addis Ababa: Institute for Development Research, Addis Ababa University, 1975. In addition, John M. Cohen has written a number of insightful articles on the CADU experience. Among these are "Effects of Green Revolution Strategies on Tenants and Smallholders in the Chilalo Region of Ethiopia," 9

Journal of Developing Areas, April 1975, pp. 335-58; and "Rural Change in Ethiopia: The Chilalo Agricultural Development Unit," 22 *Economic Development and Cultural Change,* 4, July 1974, pp. 580-614.

92. Tesfaye Tecle, *op. cit.*
93. Cohen, "Effects," *op. cit.*
94. *Ibid.*
95. *Ibid.*
96. Lars Bondestam, "People and Capitalism in the North-Eastern Lowlands of Ethiopia," 12 *Journal of Modern African Studies,* 2, 1974, pp. 423-39; John W. Harbeson, "Afar Pastoralists and Ethiopian Rural Development," 28 *Rural Africana,* 1975, pp. 71-87; John W. Harbeson, "Territorial and Development Politics Among the Afar of Ethiopia," *African Affairs,* 1979, pp. 479-98; and John W. Harbeson and Tefarra-worq Besshah, "Afar Pastoralists in Transition and the Ethiopian Revolution," 9 *Journal of African Studies,* 3, Fall 1978, pp. 249-68.
97. Bondestam, *op. cit.*
98. Harbeson and Tefarra-worq, *op. cit.*
99. Abere Jembere, "The Prerogatives of the Emperor to Determine Powers of Administrative Agencies," 5 *Journal of Ethiopian Law,* 1968, pp. 321ff.
100. Imperial Ethiopian Government, *Second Five Year Plan 1963-1967.* Addis Ababa, October, 1962. On the legal status of the pastoralists' claims see John Bruce, "Legal Considerations-Nomadic Lands," Memorandum, Ministry of Land Reform and Administration, May 20, 1962.
101. Hess, *op. cit.*
102. Christopher Clapham, "The December 1960 Ethiopian Coup d'Etat," 6 *Journal of Modern African Studies,* 4, 1968 pp. 495-507.
103. See Asmelash Beyene (comp.) *Studies in Ethiopian Government and Administration.* Addis Ababa: Faculty of Arts, Haile Selassie I University, March, 1974; Asmelash Beyene and John Markakis, "Representative Institutions in Ethiopia," 11 *Journal of Modern African Studies,* 2, 1967, pp. 193-220.
104. Speech from the throne by Emperor Haile Selassie I, October 1955.
105. No. 43 of 1966.
106. Personal interviews.
107. Based on interviews with officials and review of reports prepared by the Extension Projects Implementation Division of the Ministry of Agriculture, which was responsible for implementation of the MPP. EPID reports made clear the negative impact of land tenure constraints on the progress of the project. The EPID-Phase II Proposals for Expansion (Addis Ababa: EPID, Ministry of Agriculture, 1974) observed, "At the outset it should be emphasized that the current land tenure systems serve as serious disincentives for tenants to buy agricultural inputs and make other improvements on their farms." at p. 66.
108. Harbeson and Tefara-worq Besshah, *op. cit.*; and Harbeson, "Territorial," *op. cit.*
109. Agricultural Tenancy Proclamation of 1971. The proclamation appeared in various draft forms beginning in 1968, but was never officially promulgated.
110. Among the sources on the Eritrean problem: J. Bell, "Endemic Insurgency and International Order: The Eritrean Experience," 18 *Orbis,* 2, 1974, pp. 427-

50; Berekhet Habte Selassie, "The Evolution of the Principle of Self-Determination," 1 *Horn of Africa*, 4, 1978, pp. 3-9; John Campbell, "Background to the Eritrean Conflict," 16 *Africa Report*, 5, May 1971, pp. 19-25; John Campbell, "Rumblings Along the Red Sea: The Eritrean Question," 48 *Foreign Affairs*, 3, 1970, pp. 537-548; L. Ellingson, "The Emergence of Political Parties in Eritrea, 1941-1950," 18 *Journal of African History*, 2, 1977, pp. 261-81; Lloyd Ellingson, "The Origin and Development of the Eritrean Liberation Movement," in Robert L. Hess (ed.), *Proceedings, op. cit.*, Session B, 1979. Chicago: University of Illinois Press, 1979, pp. 613-628; Richard Sherman, *Eritrea: The Unfinished Revolution*. New York: Praeger, 1980; and G. K. N. Trevaskis, *Eritrea: A Colony in Transition*. London: Oxford University Press, 1960.

111. Hoben, *op. cit.*

3

Ethiopia on the Eve of the Transformation

Over the long sweep of the country's history, the evolving character of Ethiopia's political economy left a deep imprint on the peoples within its borders and the geographical, social, and cultural milieu within which they played out their lives. At the same time, these factors were independent as well as dependent variables, significantly shaping the character of the country's political and economic evolution. They influenced the agenda of those who sought to revolutionize Ethiopia and defined constraints on the realization of those agendas. And the nature and extent of change of Ethiopia's physical environment, its societies and cultures, and its economy over the course of the Ethiopian transformation constitute important testimony on the basis of which to assess what has transpired. The purpose of this chapter is to survey Ethiopia's geographical, social, cultural, and economic circumstances on the eve of the transformation.

Geography

Geographical characteristics have played an important role in the formation of the contemporary Ethiopian state.[1] The predominant effects of these features have been simultaneously to (1) inhibit the task of forming a centralized, integrated state realizing a common political identity; (2) inhibit the conquest of Ethiopia by foreign powers; and (3) facilitate the incursion into, as distinct from conquest of, the country by foreign powers.

The mountains in the northwestern portion of Ethiopia were the home of the ancient empire. Much of the area lies 6,000 feet above sea level, with mountain peaks ranging up to 12,000 feet. Extremely rugged terrain, chiseled by generations of erosion, has rendered difficult the daily task of deriving a bare subsistence livelihood from the land. Communications between villages even in close proximity to one another were and remain difficult, facilitating a sense of local autonomy and fostering entrenched diversity in social structure, particularly with respect to land tenure. Ethiopian kings could exile relatives on remote *ambas* (mountains), where their inaccessibility prevented them from continuing competition for political power. Such a cultural and political mosaic in this and other regions presented an immediate challenge to any regime unwilling to adapt universalistic reform initiatives to particularities at the grass roots as Haile Selassie had occasions to discover.

Overcultivation and deforestation of these rugged landscapes to meet home fuel needs have over time produced very high levels of erosion, which in turn have complicated efforts to help the peoples of this region rise out of abject poverty. These same highland areas have also been intensively occupied and cultivated for generations. By one estimate, all the highland regions of the country lose more than 200 tons of soil per square kilometer every year.[2] While the population per square kilometer is only about 33 for the country as a whole, it is much higher in many highland districts. Moreover, population per square kilometer of *cultivated* land may range from 300 to 700 in the highland districts. The acute famine conditions that precipitated the downfall of Haile Selassie's regime in 1973 and plagued the country again in 1984–85 have been most severe in some of these northern highland precincts. The inaccesibility by road of many of these areas has greatly impeded efforts to deliver relief aid. From such areas locked in poverty has come a steady stream of emigrants seeking employment on agricultural estates in more-favored regions of the country.

In 1974 only two all-weather roads linked the major cities of this region: Bahr Dar, Gondar, Mekele, Dessie, and Asmara. Few rural roads had been built to connect agricultural peoples to centers of marketing and communication. The building of a countrywide political community has been discouraged by such sparse infrastructure even as the terrain has permitted dissident local groups a measure of de facto latitude in the conduct of their affairs. Particularly in the early years of the Mengistu regime, local notables enjoyed such geographical advantages in sustaining local resistance to the new order. For example, one of the more prominent of these local rebels, Dejazmach Berhane Meskel, managed to block the military government's writ over part of this region for more than three years. Haile Selassie's government created an airline network serving more than a dozen provincial cities, but these and the two arterial highways still left many of the communities of the region effectively isolated.

Menelik's expansion of the empire's perimeters also magnified the number and complexity of the country's distinct physiographic regions, giving tangible expression to the constitutional problem of state building within the empire. Now included were pastoralists among the Kenya border; the great Awash Valley region to the east, with its irrigable lands of high potential, possible sources of geothermal energy, tourism possibilities, and enormous archaeological interest as the likely birthplace of the human species; and the Arusi and Harar highlands ringing the Somali semidesert plateau, important battlegrounds in the expansion of the empire by Menelik and its defense and preservation by his successors.

To the north are the coastal plains along the Red Sea that were a gateway for Ethiopian highlanders in ancient times in their passage from the Arabian penisula, for Gran's invasions in the sixteenth century, and for Turkish, Egyptian, and Italian invasions in more recent times.[3] The U.S. communications base in Asmara for monitoring developments in the Middle East and the Soviet Union made the region an outpost of the Cold War in Haile Selassie's time. Finally, along Ethiopia's long 1,500-mile border with Sudan lies a lowland region, site of contention between an expanding Egyptian and a reviving Ethiopian empire in the nineteenth century. During Haile Selassie's reign and after, it has been a porous border region facilitating two-way passage of exiles and refugees, whose activities have been a focus for allegations of insurgency support by each country against have been a focus for allegations of insurgency support by each country against the other.

If geographical features illustrate an historical tension between alien and indigenous cultural influences, three rivers have also described potential bridges between them. The Awash, flowing from west of Addis Ababa to near the Djibouti border, is a major source of hydroelectric power as well as irrigated agriculture for communities along its banks. The Wabe Shebelle flows from highland Ethiopia through the Ogaden to Somalia, and its irrigation potential creates a topographical mandate for cooperation between the two countries. Finally, the Blue Nile flows through Sudan, joining the White Nile on its way to Egypt and the Mediterranean Sea. Historically, Egypt and Sudan have feared Ethiopian diversion, overshadowing the river's potential for promoting shared, mutually beneficial economic development.

Societies and Cultures

The diversity of cultures represented in contemporary Ethiopia is dramatized in the first instance by the profusion of primary languages spoken within its borders. A corollary to the marginal European colonization of Ethiopia has been the absence of an imposed lingua franca with which to paper over these differences, as occurred in other African lands. However, most government publications are published in English as well as Amharic, though there was persistent speculation in late 1987

The Eve of Transformation

that English would be increasingly deemphasized at least in official business, including the schools.

Amharic remains the language of power in a national government in which northern Ethiopians still appear to predominate. However, the political preeminence of Amharic has not been sufficient to eclipse the local prevalence of other tongues and language families, even in northern Ethiopia. While Amharic is the predominant language of Shoa, Welo, Gondar, and Gojjam, Tigrinya is spoken in Eritrea and Tigrai in the adjacent northern region of Tigre. Indeed, hostility to the dominance of the Amharic language was a source of great bitterness, at least to educated elites during the empire. University students from non-Amharic speaking areas, for example, greatly resented having to learn Amharic after grade six only to enter the university where English was the official language.[4] The military regime has responded to such pressures by gradually legitimizing the official use of several Ethiopian languages in addition to Amharic.

A second great language family is Orominya (or Gallinya), which is spoken over much of the southern portion of the country and along a strip separating highland Amharic speakers in the north from the eastern lowland dwellers.[5] Sidaminya, spoken in a significant area of southern Ethiopa, reflects the incomplete dominance of Orominya culture over peoples who resisted Oromo intrusion long before the conquests of an Amharic-speaking emperor.[6] Nilotic tongues are heard along the southwestern border of the country. Afarinya prevails in wide, lightly populated areas dominated by Afar seminomadic pastoralists, while in the Ogaden region the Somali tongue dominates, reminding irredentist forces in Somalia of their claims on Ethiopian territory.

In a land of such great linguistic and cultural diversity, religion has played an important integrating as well as divisive role. In the growth of the Ethiopian state from its ancient origins, the Ethiopian Orthodox Church lent an invaluable sense of political identity to otherwise loosely integrated highland peoples, strengthened the legitimacy and authority of the emperors, and served as a basis for mobilizing people against their non-Christian adversaries. In the expansion of the Ethiopian state, conversion to the Orthodox Church was seldom compelled, but was at the same time an important indication of assimilation to the culture of the conquering Amhara and a qualification for sharing local power with them. Today the Ethiopian Church may claim the adherence of approximately one-third of the population, with concentrations of communicants in the northern and southern highland regions of the country. Although it has politicized the upper ranks of the church hierarchy, the military regime has tolerated the Ethiopian Church, perhaps because it has had little choice but to do so. There is visible evidence that the Church continues to enjoy widespread support. Indeed, some new churches were under construction in mid-1987, and church attendance at least in Addis Ababa was high despite bans on Sunday driving and scheduling of obligatory political meetings on Sunday mornings.

The prevalence of Islam in the lowland perimeters of the country and among predominantly pastoral communities reflects the political and military incursions that tested the durability of the ancient highland kingdom in earlier centuries. Today, adherents of Islam may approximate, equal, or even exceed those of Orthodox Christianity. Though Western missionaries worked in Ethiopia during the years of empire, Roman Catholic and Protestant communicants are relatively few in number. Finally, an ancient brand of Judaism has persisted among the Bete Israel (commonly known by the somewhat pejorative term "Falasha," meaning "stranger"), who are concentrated in the northern region of Gondar.[7] They suffered persecution during the imperial era, and their recent airlift to Israel offers prima facie albeit officially disputed evidence suggesting that they have fared little better under the Mengistu regime.

The development of modern Ethiopia has been affected by important internal population movements, a subject upon which extremely little research has been done. In general terms, two great population movements have dominated the history of Ethiopia during the last four centuries: (1) the westward and northern movement of Oromo peoples and their at least partial absorption within the domain of the older empire; and (2) the emigration, and more recently occasionally alleged forced migration, of Amharic-and Tigrinya-speaking peoples from their traditional domains to the south. To these a third movement should be added: the emigration of Ethiopians overseas and to neighboring Sudan and Somalia, which together account for the largest number of refugees and displaced persons of any country in Africa, the result of more than a decade of civil war in Ethiopia.

The long-term consequences of these population movements have been matters of debate. Donald Levine has projected the evolution of a multiethnic greater-Ethiopian society based upon hypothesized complementarities at the most general level between Amharic and Oromo cultures.[8] On the one hand, as a result of the first two population movements, it is true that there has been some blurring of territorial, linguistic, and religious differences between the two groups, especially at the elite level. Many Oromo have converted to the Ethiopian Orthodox Church, Amharicized their names, intermingled with the Amhara geographically, and learned to speak the the Amharic language of their conquerors. On the other hand, Amharic adaptation to Oromo culture has been less visible than the reverse. More fundamentally, each of these population movements has been profoundly destructive of the political and economic fabric of the country. Oromo penetration of Amhara areas contributed to political disintegration and the virtual absence of central authority within the traditional empire from the last quarter of the eighteenth century to the middle of the nineteenth century. The movement of northern peoples southward left a sense of conquest and subjugation of a depth difficult to gauge, for the Oromo liberation movement has not engaged the regime militarily to the same extent as have the Eritrean and more recently the Tigrean movements. Moreover, the swelling of Ethiopian emigres in the last decade has contributed to war and the disruption of at least three national economies in the Horn of Africa. Over and above the human misery that provoked and attended this diaspora, the enormous loss of critical human resources undermined the task of building a new Ethiopia upon the ruins of the empire. In a great many cases these emigres have been individuals of considerable ability and experience, whose presence abroad represents a real loss to a regime that needs all the resources it can muster to achieve its professed objectives. A great many of the Ethiopian emigres have not been devotees of the old regime but rather advocates of different courses and methods of post-imperial transformation, often within the framework of the very socialism the regime has espoused in undertaking its socioeconomic reforms.

Political Economy

Ethiopia was perhaps the poorest country in Africa and one of the half dozen poorest in the world at the end of Haile Selassie's reign in 1974 (Table 3.1). Haile Selassie's policies flirted with political and economic change and development while in fact deploying such new resources as were available for this purpose to broaden and entrench rather than moderate historical poverty and inequality. Evolving patterns of political and socioeconomic stratification were thus rooted not only in tradition itself but in the *use* of such tradition to corrupt the processes of mobility and development the emperor's Western-style policies appeared to set in motion. Patterns of rural political economy exemplified the perpetuation of traditional exploitation upon which imperial institutions had historically rested. The corrupting influence of these traditions upon the legitimacy of superficially modernity is apparent from a review of urban class structure late in the life of old regime. It is also evident in the circumstances of particular groups within that class structure.

Rural Political Economy

The great variability in traditional land tenure systems during the empire is well known even though the full extent of such diversity has

Table 3.1

Ethiopia's Economy in Comparative Perspective

	Ethiopia	Ethiopia World Rank	Africa Average	Developing Countries Average*
Per Capita Income	US$110	119/119	US$400	US$270
Ave. Annual Per Capita Income Growth 1965-1985	0.2%	82/104	1.0%	0.4%
Ave. Annual GDP Growth 1965-1980	2.8%	83/107	5.3%	3.2%
Ave. Annual GDP Growth 1980-1985	0.3%	81/109	-0.7%	2.8%
Ave. Annual GDP Growth in Agriculture 1965-1980	1.2%	68/104	1.9%	2.0%
Ave. Annual GDP Growth in Agriculture 1980-1985	-3.4%	91/96	-0.4%	1.9%
Life Expectancy (Years)	45	117/125	50	52
Population Growth 1965-1980	2.7%	33/128	2.7%	2.7%
Population Growth 1980-1985	2.5%	76/128	3.3%	2.7%
Population/Physician 1965	70,190	121/121	36,570	26,110
Population/Physician 1981	88,120	103/103	26,760	17,350
Population/Nurse 1965	5,970	101/118	5,340	7,350
Population/Nurse 1981	5,000	77/84	2,570	7,620
Calorie Supply 1965	1,832	124/128	2,094	1,997
Calorie Supply 1985	1,681	123/124	2.024	2,073
Primary School Enrollment Ratio 1965	11%	118/122	41%	44%
Primary School Enrollment Ratio 1984	32%	115/120	77%	70%

*excludes India and China

Source: World Bank, World Development Report 1987.
New York: Oxford University Press, 1987.

not been fully documented by anthropological research.[9] In one of the more useful taxonomies, Cohen and Weintraub have identified five groups of traditional land tenure systems that existed under the empire: kinship, village, private, government, and church.[10]

Traditionally, kinship tenure systems were found in the predominantly Amhara regions of northern Ethiopia. In such areas *rist* tenure was based on an individual's ability to claim descent through either parent to a founding ancestor several generations removed.[11] Possession of such claims established one's political identity or citizenship, but the complexity of possible claims under such a system ensured that the actual allocation of holdings was a function not only of the strength of one's genealogical claims but also of such political resources as persuasive skill, status, and income. While *rist* in principle could not be sold, only leased, some evidence of sale has been reported. Under such systems an individual's holdings were frequently fragmented. *Gult* rights lay in the government's authority to tax these lands and in the power of individuals recognized by the crown, who might or might not be resident landlords, to exact tribute from these same lands. In these areas one's landholdings were therefore always vulnerable to rival *rist* claims while the income generated was vulnerable to excessive appropriation by powerful *gult* holders.

In village tenure systems found farther north in parts of Eritrea and Tigre, access to land was based more upon residence than upon kinship.[12] Lands were reallocated periodically to take account of movements in and out of the village. Such holdings could not be sold by the holders. The realistic expectation of periodic reallocation served to discourage substantial or long-term investment in the development of one's holding, although in any given term the degree of insecurity may have been less than under kinship systems where land claims were always in order.

Menelik II imposed land tenure systems for the purpose of consolidating and maintaining the regime's political and military control of preexisting systems in the conquered regions that were to comprise the southern half of the empire. The emperor divided the conquered lands among collaborating traditional elites (who implemented government decrees in return for *gult* and private land tenure in particular districts), royal kinsmen and elites of the realm, local administrators, soldiers from his armies, the Ethiopian Church, and imperial subjects migrating south from overpopulated areas of the north. The size of the grant reflected one's status and power within the realm. The position of the church differed only in that it did not pass on any of the tribute received to the emperor's government. A potentially important 1966 proclamation requiring payment of all tax and tribute to government officials instead of *gult* holders, with compensation to the *gultegna,* appears at most to have been only partially implemented.

Thus, the peoples conquered by Menelik became the tenants and tributaries of the conquerors and their agents. The old regime's own studies suggested that half or more of the population in these areas were reduced to tenancy.[13] Their tributes varied in nature and amount but were believed generally to average 50 percent of produce, but ranging as high as 75 percent, over and above taxes due to local and national authorities. Tenants were subject to eviction by landlords, perhaps a fourth of whom controlled a third or more of the total land area and who were frequently absentees.

Finally, the the empire retained as government land more than 40 percent of the country's total area, 95 percent of which was concentrated in the southern areas incorporated by Menelik's conquests. Government land represented perhaps 15 percent of the country's total arable land. The government superimposed its claims on those historically assumed by resident seminomadic pastoralists. These had been displaced by the thousands from prime riverine grazing zones in favor of semipublic and private agricultural estates that employed surplus labor from overcrowded highland areas in the production of sugar, cotton, and bananas. Pastoralists' sometimes violent protests against such displacement were of no avail, though the government allowed them de facto possession of the remaining lands.

Urban Political Economy

Such inequalities grew and took on new forms as the country experienced superficial modernization in the twentieth century, forms that were most apparent in the country's pattern of urbanization. Ownership of land in urban areas, particularly in Addis Ababa, was concentrated in a very few hands. Urban employees, weakly unionized if at all, struggled to survive on wages of little more than U.S.$1.00 per day, while high officials of the government, members of the royal family, and elites of the old order monopolized urban-based wealth and social services. The capital city, Addis Ababa, in particular exemplified this pattern claiming perhaps two-thirds of all doctors in the country and a disproportionate share of educational resources.

The interrelationships between social class and the urban social environment appeared to be reinforcing for those at the upper and lower ends of the hierarchies of privilege and opportunity. However, they appeared to be conflicting for those in the critical middle range, where movements for reform and revolution have characteristically found their leadership.

On the one hand, prosperous merchants, senior civil servants, senior officers of the armed forces, the clergy, and the judiciary blended easily with the substantial foreign diplomatic community in Addis Ababa. Together, they created a cosmopolitan urban culture quite divorced in many ways from the countryside—from which many nonetheless continued to draw income as absentee landlords—and from the lifestyles of the great majority of urban residents who were poor and who were strictly marginal to the civilization created by these higher status groups.

For these upper echelon groups, wealth, status, and an overlay of urbane cosmopolitan culture were commensurate with political roles as at least de facto upholders of the old regime. These cadres exercised some degree of authority together with the increasingly urban-dwelling traditional landed elites. Haile Selassie never really appeared to have challenged the power base of these elites in the postwar administrative and fiscal reorganization he enacted as long as they accepted his reinforced personal rule.[14] At the same time, through tax credits, exemptions, other forms of official favoritism, or simply the absence of comparable routes to employment and opportunity, these cadres became beholden to the imperial order whether or not they liked being in such a position.

At the other end of the scale were those whose stake in the realm of urban privilege was so modest that they were far less coopted by imperially dominated urban development: street hawkers, minor clerical and office assistants, the most unskilled labor, beggars, prostitutes, petty merchants in the informal sector, and household servants. Incomes, employment security, social status, and opportunity appeared to vary significantly among these groups. However, they held in common, vis-à-vis the much smaller middle and upper classes, marginal participation in the development of the urban economy because of the insecure, temporary, desperate, and/or servile bases of their livelihood.

Prostitution in Addis Ababa was a particularly dramatic illustration of the plight of these lower-class constituencies. Several thousand women, perhaps as much as 5 percent of the city's population, characteristically sought such "employment" as an escape from arguably more desperate rural conditions.[15] Avoiding beggars or the attentions of street hawkers in the city was a daunting experience even for those most hardened to circumstances of poverty in the world's poorest countries. Some household servants, particularly those attached to foreign residents, had relatively secure positions, acceptable living conditions, and manageable survival-level incomes. However, most of those attached to many Ethiopian households were not only paid less but worked hours that differentiated them but little from de facto serfs. The oppressiveness of their working and living conditions was matched only by their lack of opportunity for mobility or self-improvement. Beneath even these were indeterminate and probably variable numbers of unemployed and underemployed who survived, if at all, with the help of the more settled poor.

In common with other African cities, the vast majority of such urban residents lived in huts of dried dung with metal roofs that appeared to differ relatively little from their rural counterparts. The only differences appeared with respect to density and in the degree of concentrated overburdening of sparse, primitive, and unhealthy water and sewage facilities. One rough measure of the proportions of people living in such circumstances was the size of the Addis Ababa telephone book, which was about the size of that for an American city of 50,000 or 60,000 but covering a city of 1,000,000 or more. One factor differentiating urban inequalities in Addis Ababa from those of other major African cities was the extent to which the poor and the affluent lived in proximity to one other. Sharp class and income-based residential segregation was much less evident in Addis Ababa than in many other cities.

On the other hand, the critical "middle-class" cadres, who by virtue of income and employment circumstances might deserve such a label, appear to have suffered from an ambivalence between their quite modest standards of living by Western measures and their relative affluence by national standards. Such middle-level cadres struggled to achieve comfortable living circumstances in an urban environment dominated economically by expatriates and Ethiopians attuned to expensive imported consumer goods. The emperor's import-substitution strategy, in vogue in international circles until quite late in his reign, enabled the emperor to create this politically useful artificial enclave of privilege. The deployment of tax and investment privileges, consistent with the import-substitution strategy, encouraged entrepreneurial dependence upon the government for protection from international competition that such cadres might otherwise not have survived. The fiscal conservatism of Haile Selassie limited the availability of these privileges, heightened their value, and enhanced the emperor's ability to control and manipulate the beneficiaries: principally salaried teachers, students on stipend, industrial labor, and commercial and industrial employers. Three constituencies deserve special attention in terms of these hypotheses: labor, students and teachers, and the military.

Labor

The growth of industry in both the cities and in agricultural plantations led to the emergence of a labor movement that the imperial government recognized in 1962.[16] In absolute terms the wages paid the union members on the eve of the empire's demise, around U.S.$0.75 per day, were somewhat high by national standards. But they were very modest in terms of the city's cost of living, artificially inflated by the protective tariffs on the importation of many consumer goods. But from its inception the labor movement was racked with organizational impediments to effective organization on behalf of members' economic interests. The participation of the government in many industries and agro-industries caused the employees to be beholden to the government for their employment, with correspondingly constricted rights to strike. Like the country as a whole, the central leadership of the Confederation of Ethiopian Labor Unions (CELU) exercised limited leadership at the grass roots. Many locals operated in effect as company unions without a great deal of assistance from the central organization in dealing with company management. This state of affairs was not lost on the rank and file of such unions and appears to have caused them also to view their leaders as creatures of the imperial order, even as they themselves could be construed in the same manner by those who lacked such access to cash wages.[17]

The leadership of CELU never demonstrated effective independence of the imperial government through large-scale strikes, articulation of independent ideological positions, or tough-minded bargaining with management. Small plants were not eligible to unionize, precluding the growth not only of a larger labor movement but of a union presence in firms less beholden to the imperial government for their bases of operation in the country. Nonetheless, CELU did grow fourfold between 1962 and 1974.[18]

The effectiveness and significance of labor's ambivalent position as between the interests of their members and their cooptation by the imperial government was underscored by the absence of increased militancy as membership increased. Not until the emperor was deposed did CELU become more militant, and as a consequence the successor military regime moved successfully to reorganize the labor movement. Foreign assistance from the International Confederation of Free Trade Unions (ICFTU) appeared to have been largely without effect in stimulating the growth of a politically independent and economically resolute labor movement.

Teachers and Students

The emperor gave the grounds of the former imperial palace of Menelik II for the creation of the national university that was to bear his name for the duration of his regime. Students from the university came from diverse social and economic backgrounds, though disproportionately from the capital city itself, Eritrea, and Shoa province. University students were fully funded for their four-year programs of study. Until the time of the attempted coup in 1960, Haile Selassie evinced a markedly paternal interest and devotion to the students, symbolized by his annual Christmas visit to the campus to bestow gifts. Moreover, the civil service remained by far the dominant employer of university graduates until the very eve of the empire's demise.[19] Only on the eve of the revolution did it become clear that governmental employment would be available to a decreasing percentage of the graduates. In each of these ways university graduates were a very privileged elite relative to the populace as a whole. So also were their instructors, whose annual incomes were well above the national average, though for many their obligations increased correspondingly in a familiar pattern. To some extent the university community may have derived a social status reflective of the traditional high esteem in which scholarly pursuits by priests and others were held. In numerical terms, less than 1 percent of students entering elementary school reached the university, and little more than 8 percent reached secondary school.[20] While the relationship between secondary education and subsequent public employment was less pronounced than for university education, secondary graduates were still heavily employed in the public sector.

Students and teachers at the secondary and university level found themselves in ambivalent class positions because of gaps between their positions of privilege and the lives of most of their fellow citizens. At the same time, students were frustrated by what they considered very spartan living conditions even though, relatively speaking, they were included within institutions for the privileged academic elite. They also appeared to find themselves torn between pride and alienation with respect to Ethiopia. They were fiercely nationalistic, but their feelings of national identity were divided between country and region, the latter to a significant degree based on language. Many were incensed at being obliged to learn Amharic at the expense of their own native tongues only to be required then to learn English in preparation for the university where it was the official language. They were torn between solidarity with their country and shame at its anachronistic role within the continent as an island of inegalitarianism and autocracy. In short, many of the students appear to have been aware of and frustrated at being trapped in the contradictory positions in which they found themselves. They were less beguiled than trapped by educational patterns geared to their political cooptation by the emperor's government.[21]

The Military

The position of the military in Haile Selassie's Ethiopia is very important to the subsequent struggles for the post-imperial state. The country's military rulers have presented themselves from the beginning as guardians of the country's integrity and architects of its revitalization. Attacks on the *derg*, on the other hand, have centered not only upon its postponement and/or rejection of civilian democratic rule and its methods of rule but upon its legitimacy as a self-appointed tribune of Ethiopia's poor. Such challenges have implied that the military's initiatives were rooted in officers' aggrandizement of their own political and, possibly, material interests and that its reform measures have been but window dressing to cover this alleged underlying reality. From this perspective the *derg's* succession was a coup signifying only change in forms of inegalitarian autocracies.

A key historical issue is, therefore, whether the junior officers who organized to dismantle the emperor's government and organize a successor regime were or were not among those who were coopted by the dispensations of the *ancien regime*. Four circumstances, all special to Ethiopia, may have a particular bearing on this issue. First, the armed forces were called upon frequently to defend the integrity of the empire against internal challenges, notably in Eritrea, the Ogaden, Bale, Tigre, and Gojjam. Second, the armed forces were particularly visible and effective instruments of the emperor's foreign policy, having been restructured and trained along Western lines with U.S. assistance since World War II. They served with valor and distinction in United Nations efforts both in the Congo and Korea, gaining some possibly significant exposure to international trends and events outside Ethiopia in the process.

Third, the content of training programs for the armed forces after World War II may have socialized them to an ethic quite contradictory to the essential parameters of the imperial regime as well as to the prewar organization of the armed forces. Previous Ethiopian armies had been highly individual rather than corporate in organization, loosely organized rather than regimented in deployment, untrained rather than skilled and professional, contingent upon inspired leadership rather than loyal to institutions or causes in their devotion to duty, spontaneous rather than disciplined and strategic in combat, and ad hoc rather than institutionalized in their service to the state.[22] Such changes in training and organization may have encouraged a sense of loyalty to the state above more parochial allegiances and appear to have been accompanied by closer affiliation with an increasingly radical and militant university student body. To an extent difficult to gauge, such changes in the culture and organization may have set the military officers apart from and caused them to resent the emperor's efforts to exercise personal rule, with the help of spies and informers, more than was the case elsewhere in the public sector.

Fourth, the armed forces appear to have been more decentralized in fact than in their formal structure. Battalions commanded by middle ranking officers lived and worked at some distance from senior officers. Such units appear to have been less tarnished by imperial cooptation than were field-grade officers, and they also appear to have retained substantially decentralized control over weaponry.

Conclusion

Aspects of Ethiopia's physical, social, and cultural, environment reveal distinctive, identifiable, potential foundations for strengthening political cooperation and identity, notwithstanding the many divisive factors. The symbols of political and economic development, had they been tangible and real for more than a few Ethiopians, might have propelled Ethiopia on a very different (though difficult-to-predict) course after the end of Haile Selassie's regime. Standing alone, however, such symbols of change had real and adverse consequences both for the majority of those excluded, i.e., ordinary folk in rural areas, and for those whose cooptation by the regime was the price of their lending credence to those symbols. Such cooptation undermined the leadership claims of those constituencies who sought to make such change real after the demise of the old regime and weakened the integrity of the processes of change they themselves symbolically represented. The apparent melding of forces of change and tradition did little to sustain the imperial order beyond the personal authority of the emperor. As the next chapters will portray, such processes did little to sustain foundations of Ethiopian political identity and statehood that the regime's political legatees sought to transform and build upon in the service of a better Ethiopia for all its peoples.

Notes

1. A good introduction to Ethiopian geography is provided in Mesfin Wolde Mariam, *An Atlas of Ethiopia*. Asmara, Ethiopia: Poligrafico, Priv. Ltd. Co., 1969.

2. Mesfin Wolde Mariam, *op. cit.*

3. Historical analyses of Ethiopian rulers' involvement in the Red Sea region are found in Jones and Monroe, *op. cit.*; Richard Pankhurst, "Ethiopia and the Red Sea and the Gulf of Aden Ports in the Nineteenth and Twentieth Centuries," 8 *Ethiopia Observer*, 1964, pp. 36–104; and Sylvia Pankhurst, "A Short History of Ethiopia's Ancient Seaports and Eritrea—Lost and Regained," 3 *Ethiopia Observer*, 5, 1959 pp. 138–71.

4. Personal interviews with Ethiopian university students, 1973–1975.

5. The degree of cultural and linguistic affinity of peoples today considered to be Oromo remains a matter of political if not scholarly controversy. One example of a perception of Oromo unity is Cornelius Jaenen, "The Galla or Oromo of East Africa," 12 *Journal of Anthropology*, 2 1956, pp. 171–90. For other perspectives, see Herbert S. Lewis, *A Galla Monarchy*. Madison, Wisconsin: University of Wisconsin Press, 1965; and also J. S. Trimmingham, *Islam in Ethiopia*. London: Oxford University Press, 1952.

6. Contrasting views on the origins of the Oromo invasions are expressed by I. M. Lewis, "The Somali Conquest of the Horn of Africa," 1 *Journal of*

African History, 2, 1960, pp. 212–29; and Herbert S. Lewis, "Origins of the Galla and Somali," 7 *Journal of African History,* 1, 1966, pp. 27–46.

7. For a pathbreaking study of Falasha religion and history that questions the authenticity of their Jewish heritage and suggests the importance of hitherto unrecognized Ethiopian Orthodox Church influences on Falasha customs, see Kay Kaufman Shelemay, *Music, Ritual, and Falasha History.* East Lansing: Michigan State University Press, 1986.

8. Levine, *Greater Ethiopia, op. cit.*

9. A useful short summary is Balambaras Mahteme Selassie Wolde Maskal, "The Land System of Ethiopia," 1 *Ethiopia Observer,* 9, 1957, pp. 283–301

10. Cohen and Weintraub, *op. cit.*; Dunning, *op. cit.*; Hoben, *op. cit.*

11. Hoben, *op. cit.*

12. Cohen and Weintraub, *op. cit.*; S. F. Nadel, "Land Tenure on the Eritrean Plateau," 16 *Africa,* 1,2, 1946, pp. 1–22 and 99–109; George Sevard, *The Peoples of Ethiopia.* 3 volumes. Addis Ababa: Haile Selassie I University, 1970, pp. 435–39; Dan Franz Bauer, "Land, Leadership and Legitimacy Among the Inderta Tigray of Ethiopia" (unpublished Ph.D. dissertation), University of Rochester, 1972.

13. Ministry of Land Reform, *Reports, op. cit.*

14. Clapham, *op. cit.,* Ch. 2.

15. Lekatch Deressa, presentation to the International African Studies Conference, Addis Ababa, December 1973.

16. See a study by Seleshi Sisaye, "Urban Migration and the Labor Movement in Ethiopia," in Robert Hess (ed.), *Proceedings, op. cit.*

17. Interviews by author with unionized employees of Awash Valley estates, 1974–75.

18. Seleshi, *op. cit.*

19. Markakis, *op. cit.*

20. Imperial Ethiopian Government, Ministry of Education, *Education Sector Review.* Addis Ababa, 1973.

21. Personal interviews by author with university students, 1973–75.

22. Donald Levine, "The Military in Ethiopian Politics: Capabilities and Constraints," in Henry Bienen (ed.), *The Military Intervenes: Case Studies in Political Development.* New York: Russell Sage, 1968; John W. Harbeson, "Radical Military Rule and Ethiopian Political Development," paper presented to African Studies Association meetings, Boston, 1978.

4

The Beginnings of Change

The Ethiopian cabinet resigned on the evening of February 27, 1974, the first such action in Ethiopian political history. More than the beginning of the end of Haile Selassie's regime barely seven months later, the cabinet's resignation signaled the beginning of a still unresolved crisis of the Ethiopian state. The underlying issues in that crisis have been (1) whether and on what basis a multiethnic Ethiopian state emerged within the framework of the empire and survived its demise, and (2) how and by what processes it should be preserved while also being transformed.

The working out of that crisis has occurred in three identifiable phases. The first phase, the subject of this chapter, began with the old cabinet's departure and extended to the execution by the military of arrested notables of the old order in November 1974, two months after it deposed the emperor. The second and third phases will be considered in Chapters 5 and 6.

Causes

The fundamental causes of the end of the empire were three. First, the emperor through personal rule both deinstitutionalized the traditional order he inherited and denied legitimacy to the modernizing institutions and roles he formulated. The political vitality of the empire thus declined with the advancing age of the emperor himself. Second, deinstitutionalization of the Ethiopian state appeared to encourage the apostles of both tradition and transformation to seek to preempt the future by hastening the downfall of the emperor's regime in order to secure the mantle for themselves. Third, the legitimacy of the emperor's regime depended in part on preserving the largely symbolic content of his modernization policies by limiting their "implementation" to well-compartmentalized circumstances wherein the political consequences of the gap between pretense and practice could be at least partially contained. But events and the emperor's own actions increasingly prevented such containment, exposing not only the policies' hollow mockery of reality but the resulting weakness and incapacity of the regime to address critical economic and social problems, thus hastening the collapse of the empire and the struggle to define a new political future for the country. Events in the early 1970s, especially the drought and famine of 1972 and 1973, exposed the superficiality of the emperor's carefully circumscribed and controlled programs of economic development and the breadth and depth of suffering they ignored or intensified.

Drought and Famine

Drought and famine conditions were nothing new to Ethiopia.[1] Along with plagues and epidemics of various descriptions, drought and famine had afflicted Ethiopian peoples throughout the country's long history, but no previous imperial regime appears to have been threatened through indifference to the resulting suffering. Why then should the government's handling of the famine of 1972 and 1973 have been an important precipitant of its downfall? Several explanations are possible. To some extent rulers and ruled alike appear to have viewed such disasters, along with marauding armies and plagues, as the natural lot of humankind. However, there is another perhaps more plausible explanation.

The devastations of drought and famine in the past appear to have been used by emperors to reinforce the quasi-feudal order over which they ruled by leading the many who suffered to greater dependence upon the nobility, both lay and clerical, who possessed the only grain surpluses. Provinces recently conquered were obliged to provide grain to the leaders of afflicted peoples who had conquered them. The emperor reinforced his authority over his nobility by distributing sequestered grains to them, and those in the political hierarchy did likewise in distributing symbolic amounts of grain to Ethiopians of low estate who looked to them for the means of survival. Competing with such use of natural disasters for traditional political ends was an inclination on the part of Menelik to deal more systematically with drought conditions by, on at least one occasion, rationing water use for the populace as a whole. There were thus symbolic dimensions to earlier drought amelioration initiatives by Haile Selassie's predecessors, but these actions were consistent with, and served in fact to reinforce, the status quo.

In 1972 and 1973, forced by external publicity to confront pervasive drought and famine, the government could no longer respond only in symbolic terms but was obliged to deal with evolving underlying socioeconomic realities and thereby to expose further the hypocrisy of its postwar "modernization" policies. The government's paralysis reflected the fact that Haile Selassie had used political symbols to legitimize and strengthen neither traditional nor modern institutions nor some amalgam of them. The resulting official paralysis, exposed by international publicity, both revealed the decline of Haile Selassie's government and prompted challenges to its authority.

The crisis of 1972 and 1973 did not spring without warning upon an unsuspecting Ethiopia. However imperfect, the Ethiopian government had rainfall records dating back some years, which reflected an observable pattern of declining rainfall in the latter 1960s and early 1970s. Moreover, the Ministry of Agriculture knew by late 1972 that the rains had failed in the northern parts of the country. By the time of the spring 1973 Organization of African Unity meetings in Addis Ababa, the government knew that the spring 1973 rains had been completely insufficient.[2]

The Ministry of Agriculture produced evidence in March 1973 indicating that many crop-producing districts were about to harvest much below normal and wholly inadequate crops that would threaten the livelihood of a quarter of a million people in Welo region alone. Moreover, its evidence showed that the worst-affected areas were lowland districts, where viable cultivation was marginal to begin with, inhabited by peoples escaping overpopulated highland precincts. Strikingly, however, the same statistics revealed that many districts elsewhere in the country would produce not only normal but above-normal harvests.[3] But the institutionalization of grain markets and distribution systems in the country was too inadequate and/or was considered an inappropriate mechanism for responding to the northern crisis. Meanwhile, the draft Fourth Five-Year Plan in preparation at the time contained a general call for economic growth with equity but without reference to the critical case at hand.[4]

The sheer magnitude of the crisis and unprecedented international and diplomatic attention to the country's plight combined to force the emperor and his ministers to recognize the scope of human suffering involved. Estimates were that more than a quarter of a million people starved to death, and the Relief and Rehabilitation Commission produced data suggesting that by November 1973 nearly 1.6 million people were afflicted by the drought and famine. The same estimates pointed out clearly that improved rains in 1974 and 1975 only diminished the rate of increase in the numbers of those who were affected.

By spring 1973, reports of the suffering had been generated by lower-level officials of the Ethiopian government itself as well as in foreign embassies and donor agencies. Foreign governments did not refuse aid or directly attempt to force the Ethiopian government to recognize the crisis, but neither did they deliver goods in the required quantities until the government publicly acknowledged the problem.[5] The government resuscitated a ministerial level National Emergency Relief Committee (NERC) that refused to accede to the wishes of potential donors for a public, coordinated effort to meet the human suffering. However, one of the reports of a UNICEF official found its way to London, which led television producer Jonathan Dimbleby to seek and somehow gain access to the affected areas. His film exposé, shown in the fall of 1973, produced a flood of international journalistic interest and contributions for a relief effort.

In the spring of 1973, the migration of 1500 Welo-region famine victims to Addis Ababa to petition the emperor was turned away by the police. Students and others in the city were outraged by government efforts to prevent physical evidence of the problem from marring the OAU conference, but they were unable to mobilize public opinion. The students mobilized only themselves, raising a remarkable $40,000 for drought relief by forgoing their breakfasts. Crowds of peasants lined the arterial highway between Addis Ababa and the Eritrean capital of Asmara to plead for handouts from drivers of passing vehicles. But they succeeded only in mobilizing the truckers, who brought bread to cast to the petitioners in order to speed their passage.

The international publicity and mobilization of assistance that Dimbleby's BBC documentary aroused did appear to bring greater pressure upon the highest levels of the Ethiopian government than had local protests and demonstrations. But the initial response was largely negative. Ethiopian representatives at the United Nations reportedly reacted angrily to inquiries about the drought and famine, viewing them as interferences in the country's internal affairs.[6] However, in November 1973 Haile Selassie personally visited the drought-affected areas and appeared to be moved and surprised by what he saw. He issued a proclamation promising measures not only to relieve the suffering but to undo the injustices wrought by poor peasants being obliged to sell their land to the rich at low prices in order to buy food at inflated prices. The emperor thus bestowed his personal blessing on efforts that had quietly been initiated by private agencies and coordinated by a junior minister from the Ministry of National Community Development. The emperor's belated endorsement of the relief effort allowed it to expand and gain strength, but it did not allow his regime to mend the political damage already done to it. More fundamentally, the emperor's visit demonstrated the continued reality of his personal rule, which was thereby correspondingly undermined.

Belated official Ethiopian notice of the famine crisis in northern parts of the country was matched, according to Shepherd, by equal delay on the part of the potential assisting nations in publicizing the situation and calling for assistance efforts.[7] The foreign governments and private agencies did face a dilemma, however. They had the choice of remaining silent, respecting the sovereignty of the Ethiopian government and accepting some of the responsibility for the delayed response. Alternatively, they could have spoken out and endangered their credibility with the regime and the opportunity to be of assistance. They might also have endangered the regime's own credibility, the likely impact of which could only be guessed.

The size of the relief effort in quantitative terms (once fully mobilized) magnified the qualitative shortcomings of the imperial political system. Some grain delivered for the relief effort before the emperor's visit to Welo never reached its destination, nor did at least some of the money collected by the university students. The price of grain rose precipitously, since some foreign governments were reluctant to provide greater assistance until the government utilized its own grain reserves. Even after the Aklilu cabinet resigned, published reports appeared stating that both domestic grain and grain imported for relief purposes were being exported.[8] In ways such as these, longer-term patterns of Ethiopian politics prevailed, largely unmodified by crisis circumstances accompanied by the glare of international publicity.

Education Policy

While trouble brewed over the government's handling of famine conditions in northern Ethiopia, the government released a new education policy that had been months in preparation.[9] The release of the policy indicated how badly the government had misjudged the ferment arising from the famine, while the policy itself proved to be another instance of the long-term counterproductivity of the regime's symbolic modernization policies to the development of the Ethiopian state.

The *Education Sector Review,* published in January 1974, proposed to restructure educational priorities in order to broaden participation by the majority of citizens in the priorities in order to broaden participation by the majority of citizens in the country's educational resources. It proposed to reduce the rate of increase in investment in formal higher education in favor of greatly increased support for primary education and nonformal instruction. Given the great returns to those benefiting from a university education, the Review proposed to increase the loan component of university students' financial-aid packages. The Review recognized that traditional employment opportunities for university graduates in the public sector were not likely to keep pace with the output of degree recipients. The possibility of unemployed university graduates who could not be politically coopted by governmental employment might well have worried the emperor's government in political terms, even as government economists pointed to the potential waste involved.

In these proposals the emperor's government faced a serious dilemma. On the one hand, while the report in effect revalued upward the "currency" of the government's patronage by diminishing the growth of access to it, it also threatened the interests of a constituency that already enjoyed it. It was not immediately apparent that by revolting against the policy, educators could recover the political damage to themselves inflicted by the newly dramatized extent of their previous cooptation. On the other hand, apart from the potential wastefulness of expanding governmental employment to meet the supply of available employees, such expansion of employment opportunity might have devalued the "currency" represented by the government's patronage and, therefore, its effectiveness as a means of cooptation. In short, even the limited economic development that the regime's policies permitted undermined the strategy implicit in the government's sponsorship of it.

The most controversial conclusion of the *Education Sector Review* was the proposal to place relatively greater emphasis on primary and nonformal education. From one perspective, the Review addressed directly the problem of Ethiopian underdevelopment during the preceding two decades: only superficial and limited attention to the requirements of the vast majority of citizens at the grass roots level. Ironically, the government's halfway measures of the past discredited what was arguably a genuinely reformist proposal in the eyes of those most critical of the regime's inadequacies. The teachers and students did not oppose basic education for adult citizens at the grass roots on a comprehensive basis, nor did they object to making at least primary education more universally available to the school-aged population. Rather, the teachers complained (particularly because they were at the time engaged in salary negotiations with the government) that the net effect of the proposals would be to force teachers to accept employment in lower grades at correspondingly lower rates of pay. From their vantage point the government was simultaneously considering raising rates of pay for each grade while contemplating forcing more teachers to teach at lower rates of pay commensurate with primary-school instruction levels. To them it appeared the regime was supporting education while damaging the interests of those responsible for it.

The students, for their part, viewed the policy as another attempt by the government to coopt them. University education such as theirs had been the primary channel out of a life of predominantly rural poverty and domination by landed elites. The *Review's* proposal, in their estimation, amounted to an attempt to provide rural citizens at the grass roots just enough instruction to enable them to function more effectively and yet also be quiescent with respect to rural inequalities and absence of opportunities for mobility. The students saw the cooptational dimension from the perspective of peoples at the grass roots without perhaps realizing the impact of the policy in betraying the extent of their own previous cooptation.

An alternative view expressed by some ministry officials was that such mass-oriented nonformal education would contribute to more effective articulation of demands for change at the grass roots, demands that would have focued on existing land tenure arrangements and the inequalities they perpetuated. From this unofficial ministry point of view, students and teachers opposing the policy resisted genuine reform measures in a way that drew attention to their own supposed interests in preserving an elite educational process leading to university education and comfortable subsequent civil service careers for the fortunate few.

Both students and teachers maintained that the real political intent and the effect of the proposed educational policy were revealed by the government's harsh response to the suffering of famine victims and to their demands for land reform on their behalf. In January 1974, the teachers and students went on strike in opposition to the new policy. By one account, their strike contributed substantially to mobilizing unrest in the provincial towns and the countryside.[10] While the true relationship of that unrest to the teachers and students' strike is unclear, it is possible that at least at that point the degree of teachers' and students' cooptation by the old regime appeared less pronounced at the local level than nationally.

Thus the policy, liberal and progressive in itself, provoked hostility from the regime's seemingly liberal and progressive-minded teachers and students. However, their material interests had become aligned with the hierarchical order of the *ancien regime,* even though by virtue of their official roles they only symbolized the regime's *apparent* progressive intentions. In issuing the policy, the regime undermined its own credibility by betraying the material interests of teachers and students whose cooptation had helped the regime to appear progressive. In their response teachers and students betrayed the extent to which their tangible interests had become identified with the traditional order notwithstanding their apparent oppositional roles, proclaimed objectives, and often genuine intentions. But by demonstrating the extent of their cooptation, the policy undermined not only the regime but the bases of an Ethiopian state itself. This it did by damaging the credibility of a constituency from which leadership for a future regime might have been expected to emerge.

Inflation

Inflation was an immediate precipitant of the Aklilu government's resignation and the initial phases of the Ethiopian transformation. The price of oil rose exponentially as a result of the Arab oil embargo, raising prices of a whole range of imported goods as well as oil. Prices overall

Table 4.1

Index of Retail Prices, Addis Ababa, 1964-1971

(1963 = 100)

	1964	1967	1969	1971
Household items	106	130	130	133
Clothing	107	124	129	141
Transportation	100	100	100	100
Medical care	100	110	124	137
Personal care	113	147	156	160
Food	121	133	135	159

Adapted from International Bank for Reconstruction and Development, Ethiopia: Agricultural Sector Survey, Vol. 1, May 30, 1972.

rose by 16.5 percent in 1973, and by 80 percent for food in the first quarter of 1974. While substantial, the 1973 increases were not dramatic by international standards and those of 1974 occurred after the beginning of the struggle. The effects on particular communities may therefore have been as important in political terms as the overall rates of increase on the country at large.

The imperial government badly misjudged its public standing when, in late January, it announced that the price of automobile gasoline would rise from approximately U.S.$1.00 per gallon to U.S.$1.50, a precipitous increase to a level that was still not especially high by international standards. The price hike occurred in the wake of the Arab oil embargo, leaving the impression that the government was simply responding as were other governments throughout the world. The trouble was that the government did not permit the bus and taxi drivers in the capital city to raise their rates accordingly. The transportation workers, however, were among those hardest hit by patterns of inflation over the preceding decade.

The Chamber of Deputies' response to the problem demonstrated the continuity of traditional institutions and the counterproductivity of imperial symbolic modernization to the further development of an Ethiopian state itself as well as to the regime. Though elite-dominated, the chamber had maintained a steady stream of criticism of the government on its handling of the drought, criticism that had by and large not found its way into the press. When the fuel price hike was announced, the chamber called Minister for Commerce, Industry, and Tourism Kitema

Yefru on the carpet. Where, the chamber demanded to know, was the government's authority under the 1955 constitution to decree such a price hike unilaterally? Since it amounted to a tax levy requiring the chamber's prior authorization, parliamentarians argued that the government had acted unconstitutionally. In the course of the debate, the minister found himself obliged to admit that the reason for the price rise lay not directly with the Arab states, a popular target with the regime given their level of support for Eritrean liberation forces, but with inefficient management of the government's principal oil refinery at Assab. Four days of general unrest and rioting attended the announcement of the price hike as students and other urban constituencies joined with taxi drivers and, after considerable pressure, the bus drivers. The unrest per se as well as the issues involved shocked the country, perhaps especially the cities, into realizing the regime's vulnerability and the magnitude of political damage done it by the protests.

Parliament's objections to the price hike rang rather hollow in some circles, since a few months earlier both ministers and parliamentarians had helped themselves to substantial salary increases. The parliamentarians voted themselves a 25 percent salary increase even as they were beginning to criticize the government's indifference to the plight of the famine victims. Later that spring the government mandated a 10 percent salary contribution from all civil servants and moved to reduce the oil price hike a few weeks after its promulgation, but these compensatory economic measures did not undo the more fundamental political damage. The oil price hike had betrayed the government's merely symbolic commitment to the new constitution, introduced with much fanfare nearly two decades earlier. In acting out their constitutionally prescribed role, the parliamentarians demonstrated the government's hypocrisy but also the degree to which they had compromised themselves.

Transport workers and teachers and, later, other organized groups within the urban sector were strengthened in their determination to strike and demonstrate against the government both because political elites' self-determined raises manifested indifference to the drought and inflation affecting others and because these elites had resisted the similar wage demands of other constituencies. Haile Selassie's government tried to attribute the urban groups' protest to concern for their own material self-interest. In so doing, the government in effect used against these urban cadres the ambivalence of their relationship to the old regime that had been fostered by its own policies.

At the time of these protests, the Ethiopian Grain Corporation announced that there would be no grain shortage for the forthcoming year because production increases and better rains had come about in the fall. It pledged $U.S.2.5 million for the construction of new grain storage facilities. The deaf ear turned by the strikers to such blandishments proved that at the time the proximate economic causes for their unrest reflected a political hostility to the regime far deeper than the economic grievances themselves.

That spring Kifle Hagas, a vice minister of interior, introduced the awraja self-administration proposal, ostensibly demonstrating the government's renewed interest in extending the scope of popular political participation. But by then the scale and intensity of the demonstrations were beyond the government's reach, even with proposals that might have augered real and important major reorientation of the imperial government.

The Emperor and His Dynasty

Beneath the surface, though rarely articulated directly, Emperor Haile Selassie I's advancing age appears to have been itself a cause of unrest, as diverse constituencies began to prepare for a change of regime. These preparations began with those close to the emperor as early as 1961. In that year a ministerial committee suggested that the emperor set in motion a transition to a constitutional monarchy by yielding most governmental powers to his ministers in fact and not just in appearance. Indeed, the emperor's own son, Asfa Wossen, was reported to have been in favor of such constitutional change.[11] One striking point about these initiatives was that they betrayed the unreality of the 1955 constitution, which on its face accomplished much of that objective several years earlier. But they also indicated that even those most closely identified with and dependent on the emperor had begun to look beyond his regime more than a decade before it in fact ended. However, as events were to reveal, lengthy covert and informal preparations for regime change were not sufficient to prevent civil war over the imperial succession.

The political uncertainty introduced by the simple fact of the emperor's advancing age was complicated by the illness of Asfa Wossen. The emperor had proclaimed that his dynasty would rule in perpetuity. Yet Asfa Wossen's residence in London, and his apparent disability throughout most of the regime's last years, caused heightened political maneuvering since it was not apparent even in traditional dynastic terms what the political future held in store. Rumors circulated, though apparently without foundation, that the emperor was becoming senile. Even to conservative elites not greatly moved by the famine in Welo, Haile Selassie's government's mishandling of the crisis must have been unsettling. At a minimum the crisis suggested that he was out of touch with events and that his much-heralded encyclopedic and detailed knowledge of the workings of his government had failed him. The emperor himself lent credence to this view by announcing in March 1974, when the momentum of change was considerable, that Prince Zara Yacob would be second in line to Asfa Wossen—as if such information would calm the masses or, at that point, even the more conservative elites.

As the subsequent account of the transformation's first phase will suggest, conservative forces appear to have mobilized for a change of regime out of concern for the uncertain dynastic prospect, suggestions of the emperor's declining capacity, and an inclination to restore the powers of the traditional nobility that Haile Selassie had followed his predecessors in seeking to curtail.[12] Aklilu Habte, the emperor's longtime prime minister, was a commoner, and he had inserted his followers in a great number of key positions in the government, lending credence to the prospect that the exclusion of the traditional nobility would thus be institutionalized and outlast Haile Selassie's personal rule. This prompted at least one effort at a preemptive conservative coup for which U.S. assistance had been sought, apparently unsuccessfully.[13] However, as the subsequent section will suggest, such forces also tried to gain control of events in the early months of 1974 as it became apparent that Haile Selassie's own reign was nearing an end.

Though the conservative initiative proved unsuccessful and subsequently played but a small role in the competition for leadership after Haile Selassie's departure, it did suggest that Haile Selassie had restrained but had not extinguished such forces in his quest for strengthened personal rule. It also suggested that the emperor's skillful practice of *shum shir* (appoint, dismiss—and, therefore, divide and rule) had been only partly effective. On the one hand, it had successfully played off more and less conservative elites against each other during his postwar rule, but on the other hand, it may have been less successfully employed to reconcile the more traditional elites to the more progressive ones than vice versa.

Military Insurgency

Insurgency within units of the armed forces played a critical role in bringing down the *ancien regime*. On January 12, noncommissioned officers of the fourth brigade of the fourth division, stationed in the drought-afflicted southern district of Neghelli, mutinied and arrested their commanding officers. The NCOs had been personally affected by the drought because their water pump had broken down, and they were not permitted to use the officers' water supply. They demanded redress of grievances by the emperor personally and an on-site investigation of their grievances by the prime minister, the minister of defense, and the commander of the ground forces. The last, General Deresse, was then

The Beginnings of Change

detained when he visited the camp and was forced to live as the men rather than the officers did. Exactly one month later unrest occurred at the airforce base in Debra Zeit, a short distance east of Addis Ababa, as enlisted men on the base demanded improved working conditions and higher pay as a compensation for refraining from striking.

In addressing the soldiers' demands, the cabinet was augmented by two of the emperor's closest associates, Abiy Abebe, the president of the Senate, and Ras Asrata Kassa, president of the Crown Council and himself a potential claimant to the throne. This enlarged council recommended a pay increase for the privates in the army from $36 per month to $45. At the same time, it granted some of the teachers' demands for salary increases, reduced the fuel price increase, and postponed implementation of the *Education Sector Review* recommendations in the wake of the near mutinies and the urban disorders. The emperor himself announced these responses to the unrest, preceding them by a stroll through the traditional and often turbulent market sector of the capital with a minimum of security precautions. In this manner he sought to demonstrate his continued personal command of the situation and the country. However, he also seemed to emphasize in so doing that he and not his cabinet ministers was in charge, the cabinet system notwithstanding.

Armed forces unrest spread when, on February 25, the second division located in Asmara mutinied. Noncommissioned officers arrested their commanders and took control of the airport, banks, and other public installations in both Asmara and the Red Sea port city of Massawa. While avowing their continued loyalty to the emperor, the troops demanded further pay increases, improved food and clothing, and a freer political climate in which the demands their commanding officers had tried to suppress could be heard and addressed. The second division had also been the most heavily employed unit domestically, bearing primary responsibility for containing the persistent Eritrean insurgency. The NCOs expressed distress not only with their working conditions but with the frustrating and inconclusive course of the war against people they supposed to be their countrymen. This unit in particular had had direct, immediate, and sustained evidence of the imperial regime's vulnerability and difficulty in uniting the country. But the emperor refused their further demands, claiming the country could not afford to meet them. The fourth division and the airforce expressed sympathy with the demands of the second division, which promptly termed the emperor's response unsatisfactory.

Two days later the airforce seized Debra Zeit and the third division took over public facilities in the eastern towns of Dire Dawa and Harar not far from the Somali border. The taxicab and bus drivers had returned to work, but the students and teachers continued to strike and demonstrate against a government preoccupied with mutiny. Their demands escalated to include the end of the monarchy, land reform, disestablishment of the Orthodox Church, and freedom of speech and expression. At this point the students were essentially alone on the most fundamental of their publicly expressed demands: an end to the monarchy. The navy, commanded by the emperor's nephew, Rear Admiral Eskinder Desta, responded as it would to a severe storm and put out to sea from its base in Massawa. A delegation of high-ranking officers sent to negotiate with the troops in Asmara was seized and imprisoned except for one of their number sent back to reiterate and enlarge upon their demands which now included improved pensions. Then the engineering corps and transport workers mutinied in Addis Ababa.

Somewhat similar negotiations between the emperor and his armed forces occurred in 1960 *after* they had proved their loyalty to the emperor by helping to abort the coup attempt inspired by officers of the imperial bodyguard. However, it was not clear that the negotiations in 1960 extended much beyond negotiations over salary and working conditions per se. In 1974 the armed forces had not provided any such up-front evidence of their loyalty. Their insurgency appeared to augur more profound changes than had resulted fourteen years earlier, though the military units did not publicly challenge the legitimacy of the regime at this stage. Conversely, the emperor's dependence upon the armed forces had become more apparent with the development of the Eritrean civil war and, to a lesser extent, revolts in Gojjam and elsewhere.

A key issue was whether the armed forces were simply seeking to advance their material interests in striking for improved wages, working conditions, and pensions or whether their insurgency had broader ramifications. For his part, the emperor had declined to use the military against the other strikers. The armed forces units did not publicly criticize the strikers, and there were some unconfirmed reports that the military had expressed sympathy for them. Moreover, the military's demands came to include far broader demands. The emperor's allegations that strikers, military and civilian, were concentrating exclusively on advancing their own self-interest failed to elicit much support, nor did it set constituency against constituency. However, in part because none of the striking units other than the students had publicly withdrawn loyalty to the emperor, it was not clear who or what group could unite the protesters or even that such a leadership role needed to be established.

Reform, Revolution, or Creeping Coup?[14]

A remarkable diary of the events of January and February of this period, alleged to be that of Ras Asrata Kassa, recounted what transpired within the emperor's Jubilee Palace in the days surrounding the resignation of the Aklilu cabinet.[15] The diary reported that the prime minister and his brother, Minister for Justice Akala-worq Habte Wold, urged the cabinet's resignation on hearing that the armed forces mutiny had become general and included units in the capital city itself. Endalkachew Makonnen, soon to become prime minister in a new cabinet, was not present, but ministers who were did not object. General Abiy and Ras Asrata, the emperor's close associates brought in for the discussions, objected that ministers of the emperor simply did not resign, that there was no precedent for such action, that the Amharic language included no word equivalent to "resignation," and that their actions would not be popularly understood or approved. The emperor asked the cabinet to reconsider its request to resign in the absence of specific evidence that such was demanded. But the cabinet resigned anyhow, the announcement being reported on the radio stations the same evening.

The following day, some within the Council of Ministers were reported to have argued against the Emperor's designation of General Abiy as the next prime minister on the grounds that basic changes were understandably being demanded and the emperor should therefore become his own prime minister for a time with Abiy as his minister for defense. The emperor was reported to have declined, changing his mind about Abiy only when he was given what later seems to have been a false report that the army preferred Endalkachew Makonnen, the son of a former high minister in the emperor's government and closely linked to the Shoan nobility. He was also related by marriage to Asrata Kassa. Later that day the Emperor announced that Endalkachew would be the new prime minister and, seeming to contradict at least the spirit of his 1966 reforms, named additional ministers: General Abiy as minister of defense and a little-known but respected general, Wolde Selassie Bereket, as the new commander of the ground forces. At the same time, the emperor acceded to the army's full demands for wage increases, bringing the new basic pay rate to $75 per month, more than twice their previous rate of compensation.

Several aspects of the transition between governments deserve attention. First, the nature of the transition demonstrated once again the political bankruptcy of the constitutional structures supposedly legitimized by the emperor himself. The emperor further confirmed the heightened role of his personal rule with adverse consequences for other political institutions whether traditional or modern in form. But most important, the course of this transition revealed the emperor's own diminished grasp of political power. For example, the emperor and his ministers appear to have acted largely on the basis of rumor. They also appeared not to have known whether the cabinet's resignation was specifically demanded or whom the armed forces would accept as the new prime minister. The cabinet's resignation appeared to be an expression of the cabinet's own lack of self-confidence, a generalized sense that they had lost control of events and political forces in the country. They chose to defer to an emperor whose own political authority appeared to be ebbing.

The first days of the transition were less disorderly than eerie. The city was incredibly quiet, with buses and cabs again not functioning. Only the marching of students and the sound of occasional helicopters disturbed the uneasy quiet. The police made no effort, as they always had before, to interfere when students took to marching or singing revolutionary songs. There was an almost palpable atmosphere of suspended political animation, at least in Addis Ababa—the passage of political time in a historic empire arrested, the marching and demonstrating of students given a surreal quality by the tacit abeyance of the political structures against which they inveighed.

Second, the emperor's appointment of Endalkachew Makonnen could have been read as encouraging or reflecting resurgence by the Shoan nobility the emperor and his predecessors had long been at pains to try to limit.[16] The long tenure of Aklilu, a commoner, his successful efforts to place supporters in key positions within the government, and the possibility that he might thereby be strong enough to influence the succession in the event of Haile Selassie's departure were an obvious challenge to any of the nobility who might have looked to the end of the emperor's reign as an opportunity to enact a restoration of a still-remembered political tradition. To such potential conspirators the appointment of Endalkachew was an encouraging development, for he was related to Asrata Kassa, son of Ras Kassa whose claim to the throne had rivaled that of the emperor a generation earlier.[17] However, the emperor, and perhaps these conservative forces as well, apparently failed to anticipate damaging attacks on the appointment by the striking constituencies based on Endelkachew's prominent membership in the cabinet from which he had just resigned. For the conservative forces around the emperor, who may have been influential in the naming of Endalkachew, the symbolism of cabinet-style government also carried real and adverse consequences. One of their number, and by extension the company of traditional elites generally, was politically damaged by his membership in a cabinet whose resignation came to symbolize the bankruptcy both of the institution itself and of the traditions defied by the Aklilu cabinet when it resigned.

In naming both the minister for defense and the chief of the ground forces, the emperor seemed intent upon reestablishing conservative leadership over the armed forces by omitting any reference to General Assefa Ayene. The chief of staff was known to hold relatively liberal views and to be popular within military circles. He had also been the subject of considerable speculation concerning his political future and ambitions after the emperor's departure. The appointments seemed to suggest that the emperor wanted to box in General Assefa by appointing both his superior and his most immediate subordinate.

If Endalkachew's appointment by itself seemed to be a bid for influence by the Shoan nobility and also to cashier even the image of legitimacy for cabinet government, the appointments of the remainder of the cabinet suggested the opposite: the rejuvenation of the cabinet as an institution and a renewed commitment to progress. The new cabinet was noteworthy for the greater education, professional qualifications, and apparent greater liberalism of its members. Widely noted at the time was the resemblance of the new cabinet to the one appointed after the abortive coup of 1960, whose more liberal members, however, gradually departed to positions more peripheral in domestic political terms. Michael Imru, given the ministry of commerce and industry and then transferred to the prime minister's office, had been a minister in the 1961 reform cabinet and was a son of Ras Imru Haile-Selassie. The ras was the emperor's cousin and was much admired even by radical students for his heroism during World War II and for voluntarily turning over much of his land to his tenants (which earned him the nickname "red ras"). Another prominent member of the 1961 reform cabinet, Dejazmach Zewde Gebre Selassie, became minister of interior. A descendant of the ruling house of Tigre and related through his mother to the crown prince, he had been fired as minister of justice in 1961 because the emperor found his reform plans unacceptable. He subsequently served abroad in diplomatic posts and is a well-regarded biographer of his ancestor, Johannes IV. A professor in the Haile Selassie I University medical school became the first medical doctor to hold the health portfolio. Similarly, the new minister for public works was a professionally trained engineer, and World Bank economists became ministers for education and for agriculture. Endalkachew himself held a master's degree from Oriel College, Oxford.

Collectively, the new cabinet was younger and better educated than its predecessors. Two-thirds held postgraduate degrees compared with one-third of the old group, and 75 percent held baccalaureate degrees as against 50 percent for the old cabinet. The average age of the new cabinet was 47 compared with 55 for its predecessor. On the other hand, while the members had far greater professional experience, they lacked political experience by comparison with the Aklilu cabinet. At the same time, both cabinets were at once cosmopolitan and parochial. A majority of both cabinets had been educated overseas and many claimed fluency in international languages other than English. Yet most also claimed only fluency in Amharic among Ethiopian languages; both were drawn disproportionately from Addis Ababa and from Shoa province. The new cabinet, like the old one, had close links to the crown despite the liberal reputations of many of its members.

The fate of the Endalkachew cabinet as well as its appointment, and the preceding resignation of the Aklilu cabinet, established dramatically the significance and the fundamentally injurious consequences of Haile Selassie's postwar policies of symbolic modernization. What Haile Selassie had accomplished was the cooptation of traditional as well as "modernizing" elites in part through membership in institutions such as the cabinet in which he apparently, but in reality only symbolically, vested the authority to govern. Elites at all points along this spectrum invested their own political resources as well as those of the constituencies they represented. As previous sections have shown, the emperor gained enhanced personal authority through these measures, leaving other elites only the legitimacy afforded by the symbolically authoritative institutions he purported to create.

The resignation of the cabinet signified more than the failure of a particular administration; it confirmed the insignificance of the institution itself under the emperor's regime. Asrata Kassa's objections to the cabinet's resignation revealed the political price paid by traditionalist elites for their membership. The inability of the cabinet to deal with the distress of the strikers or the famine victims established the cost of membership for more progressive elites who allowed themselves to be coopted. But as a consequence of the emperor's continued and even enhanced personal rule since World War II as well his policies of elite cooptation, neither more conservative nor more progressive forces had visible leaders to help them regroup and prepare for the major political transition that was upon the country. The emperor thus undermined not only his own regime but, in compromising both leaders and the ideological foundations of their leadership, the possibility for agreement on a successor government.

The Endalkachew cabinet presided over the demise of Haile Selassie's regime and of the monarchy itself. His regime never achieved any degree of political legitimacy in the first instance because the break with the discredited Aklilu administration was not complete. Not only Endalkachew himself, but two other members of his cabinet, Foreign Minister Minasse Haile and Planning Minister Tekalign Gedamu, remained from the old cabinet. Moreover, the subsequent divisions within the military ranks verified that there had been no consensus on Endalkachew's appointment from this quarter. During the course of his five-month tenure, long-simmering issues of corruption, gross malfeasance, and personal self-aggrandizement among officials of the old regime surfaced not only among the demonstrators but within Parliament, and these fueled pressures for more radical political change. Endalkachew himself was widely accused of not only unseemly political ambition but of having used his long tenure as minister for commerce and industry to amass an enlarged personal fortune. However, events were to overtake the pursuit of investigations against individual ministers, even ones as important as that involving the prime minister.

From March onward, virtually every organized group in Ethiopian society participated in repeated work stoppages and other demonstrations in support of demands ranging from wages and working conditions to fundamental reorganization of Ethiopian society. In provincial cities and towns throughout the country, groups of citizens formed revolutionary committees of varying descriptions and followed the earlier example of some military units in seizing control of public offices and arresting officials in support of their demands.[18] Meanwhile, units of the armed forces themselves were initially very divided and confused by events, and with their commanding officers themselves compromised, they did not immediately move to restore order.

The Endalkachew administration, for its part, made very little effort to restrain the contagious spread of political demonstrations out of an apparent mixture of motives: genuine desire to establish greater freedom of speech and expression as had been demanded and at the same time a sense that it lacked sufficient political control over the means of coercion to enforce a restoration of order. The restraint shown by the government was, however, widely interpreted as a sign of weakness more than commitment to principles. The government pleaded for people to return to work while it pledged to organize itself to pursue the very reforms being demanded. The people responded with more strikes and demonstrations. The thrust of the demonstrations did not center on the replacement of the Endalkachew administration with another, nor did they appeal to the emperor's authority to dismiss it. Rather they simply denied the legitimacy and credibility of the emperor's government itself. These demonstrations were anarchist in neither substance nor spirit; rather, they stripped away the ebbing legitimacy of the feudal empire to focus on the basis of Ethiopian statehood itself, posing the fundamental questions of the future: How would the state be reestablished and transformed in the wake of the empire's demise?

The Day of the Leaflet

The first weeks of March were the days of political leafleting. Students, labor groups, military units, teachers, and other constituencies of all descriptions undertook to create and mobilize public opinion within the capital city through the distribution of leaflets and pamphlets reproduced by underground presses. They were distributed by hand, from the backs of trucks, from military helicopters, and by people roaming on foot.

During this period the streets of Addis Ababa, especially in the vicinity of the university, were frequently dotted by clusters of people gathered about one individual with a fresh leaflet in football huddle-like formation intently listening to the latest contributions to an unprecedented public political debate. The press amplified the leafleting campaign by becoming far more outspoken.

A dominant theme of almost all the leaflets was a demand for comprehensive reforms although the political framework framework within which such reforms should occur was not specified. Their rhetoric, while angry and uncompromising, did not generally suggest doctrinaire ideological commitments by their authors. References to Marx, Lenin, Mao, or to communism generally were rare. On the other hand, the means of expression itself, its persistence in the face of the Endalkachew government's attempt to formulate reform programs, and the substance of the demands were revolutionary against the background of preexisting conditions. In one sense the leaflets were the antithesis of the politics of the empire in emphasizing substantive rights and demands as against the forms established for their realization that did not produce results. Their expressions of opinion stood outside of and unmodified by institutional frameworks wherein the emperor had previously undertaken to coopt participants. They expressed genuine demands of ordinary citizens without reference to the concerns of imperial authority, where all initiatives had previously been undertaken with the approval of the emperor.

Endalkachew himself was the topic of many of the leaflets. They drew attention to his relationship to the old regime, and the teachers remembered him as a corrupt albeit short-term minister for education. A leaflet from the University Teachers' Association inquired: "How can he [Endalkachew] be the man to revise the constitution when we are trying to put him on trial with his companions—the deposed ministers?" A large number of leaflets decried the excesses of the old cabinet and demanded that the individuals be tried on charges similar to those directed at Endalkachew. Notably, however, almost all the leaflets demanded legal process against these and other former officials rather than that they be shot peremptorily or afforded anything less than a fair trial. Few of the leaflets at this time were directed at the emperor personally, and, except for the two prime ministers, they did not they single out particular personalities with any degree of frequency. One of the few moves by the police to interfere with the demonstrations and strikes occurred when students, while burning Endalkachew in effigy in one of the city's public squares, began to prepare an effigy of the emperor for similar treatment.

Beyond attacks on political figures and demands for recognition of the very freedom of expression they were asserting, the leafleteers articulated a range of demands for political and socioeconomic reform. While those more urban-based groups did center on their immediate concerns with prices, wages, and taxes, they also issued calls for reforms of more countrywide significance: more and better schools, freedom of association, democratic rule, an end to corruption generally and in specific institutions in particular like the judiciary, and an end to economic mismanagement. Among the most common themes of the leaflets was the call for land reform, which seemed to center almost entirely on the rural areas. Quite remarkable for their infrequency, on the other hand, were attacks on the government's handling of the famine.

The leaflets emanating from the military contained a mixture of concerns, both specific to the situations of rank and file soldiers and of more general importance to the country as a whole. Most of the military leaflets drew particular attention to the fact that rank and file soldiers would no longer be the slaves, errand boys, or personal servants of their officers. "We no longer serve as domestic servants to our bosses," one stated. But most of the leaflets for which armed forces authorship was claimed articulated a wide variety of demands of interest to the country as a whole. One, circulated the day after Endalkachew was appointed prime minister, called for "freedom of writing," freedom to hold meetings and demonstrations, establishment of political parties and a "democratic way of election of officials," land to the tenant, improvement of labor relations, release of political prisoners, stern price controls, trials for the former ministers, and periodic salary increments for civil servants and armed forces personnel. The same memorandum threatened a "disturbance" if these demands were not met and called for a civilian-military committee to oversee realization of the demands.

The military leaflets revealed particular sensitivity on two points: the importance of bringing about change with a minimum of bloodshed and the army's determination to see that gains it had wrested from the departed administration be the basis for similar gains by other constituencies. One emphasized that "we have surmounted the abortive coup without any bloodshed" and that "appointment of officials should not be made by one person only, it should be the choice of the majority." Another stated "it is of no good to our country if we fight each other" and "we do not want to damage public property or cause casualties [and] we do not want to mutiny against the emperor or the country." The reference to bloodshed and property loss came against the background of considerable damage to property and of some personal injuries as well. Another leaflet made the army's own wage gains the entering wedge for working-class wage increases.

> The monthly income of the working people is going down, down, every day. . . We, Armed Forces, are not happy at all by the increase of salary

we get while the public is suffering from the high cost of living. We will not retreat from supporting the workers in their struggle for higher wages and better working conditions.[19]

A distinctive feature of the military's leaflets was the implicit bid for leadership, attested by its clear sensitivity to the soldiers having received increased wages while other categories of employees were not similarly favored—notably the famine victims and the rural poor generally. In this the military units responded to the emperor's attack on the armed forces as self-serving in seeking yet further wage increases, a complaint that appeared only rarely in other leaflets. While evidencing a degree of internal debate over the military's proper course in that period of great uncertainty, the military leaflets' somewhat defensive posture did foreshadow a future problem: the military's difficulty in casting itself as the tribune and advocate of the millions in whose name it would enact far-reaching reforms.

Plans for Reform

From March to May, the emperor and his new cabinet articulated plans for reform, while virtually every organized group in the city and in many of the provincial towns demonstrated their unwillingness to accept as legitimate the administration that planned them. The emperor, confirming the new cabinet appointments in a speech to the nation on March 6, announced that a commission was to be created to draft a new revised constitution expanding on the one promulgated in 1955. He attempted to place the events of the preceding month in an evolutionary perspective. He saw the disturbances as manifestations of the need to take a further step in constitutional development, implying but not stating that the goal was some form of constitutional monarchy. Among the promised major features of the new constitution was to be a provision making the prime minister responsible to Parliament. The same day, in a speech to a meeting of journalists, Endalkachew professed agreement in principle to the idea of enshrining free speech in the constitution. A week later the new government announced formation of a task force to draw up an austerity budget to compensate for the costs of famine and political upheaval: diminished tax revenue combined with newly granted wage increases to the armed forces and other striking groups. The budget was prepared and signed into law by the emperor two weeks later. The new cabinet also gave well-publicized attention to planning for drought-famine assistance not only in northern Ethiopia but in southern regions where similar problems had appeared and among pastoralists whose needs had previously been ignored.

The emperor announced on March 26 that a special commission of inquiry would be appointed to investigate charges of corruption and maladministration against present and former officials. At the same time, he stated that wage increases would also be granted to some of the country's poorest employees, thereby emphasizing the idea that only the relatively well-to-do had gained wage increments during the preceding weeks of turmoil. A commission was also to be established to consider broader problems of working conditions about which workers had complained. There were suggestions in Parliament that a land reform program might be legislated, perhaps even the draft landlord-tenant legislation of 1968 that had been stalled for almost six years.

On April 9, the new cabinet then issued a comprehensive policy statement detailing its designs for reform, confirming at the same time that land reform measures as well as a new constitutional draft would be prepared before the end of the summer.[20] The policy attempted to confront, as official policy statements of the past had not, the gravity of the problems facing the country, referring to the "national crisis" and the country's "manifold problems." It pledged the government to attack these problems "without regard to personal consequences," including full voluntary disclosure by cabinet members of their property holdings and how they came to acquire them. It promised full support to the newly announced commission of inquiry in its deliberations.

The cabinet's policy statement articulated a broad panoply of reforms placed in the context of the circumstances producing the current crisis, the views of the pamphleteers, and concern for national unity. The statement cited the need for resolution of the government's fiscal crisis caused by wage increases, famine relief demands, and tax shortfalls. It observed the importance of maintaining national unity while at the same time strengthening the country's many honored traditions, both "pillars of national culture." In the statement the cabinet pledged full support to rights already enshrined in the existing constitution, "particularly the rights of conscience, speech, and peaceful assembly." It reaffirmed the *Education Sector Review's* call for a "reorientation" of educational resources.

The cabinet's policy paper outlined five fundamental objectives: accelerating the pace of development, narrowing income inequalities, generating popular participation in development, strengthening self-reliance in relationship to foreign assistance, and enacting land reform measures. In pursuit of these objectives, the cabinet undertook to enact tax reform "to improve equitability by broadening the tax base to reach those who have the capacity to pay more" as well as by improving collection, providing credit to broaden the base of capital formation, and instituting price controls. It centered its economic reforms on the need to give "due regard" to the interests of producers so as to enable them to receive equitable return for their efforts. To this end it took account of the requirement for improved public health in order to eradicate diseases deeply rooted in ignorance and poverty, and it recognized the need to reorient development programs "from urban to rural areas where the vast majority of the population resides and where the benefits of development have not yet reached."

Finally, the government's policy document anticipated enactment of land reform. The premise of such land reform proposals was to be the need to improve agricultural productivity, diminished by fragmentation of holdings, overcultivation, and deforestation. The cabinet recognized the special problems affecting the livelihood of pastoralists. The anticipated land reform program was to include limitation on the size of holdings, allocation of land only to those prepared to work it, legal clarification of landlord-tenant relations that had already been proposed six years earlier, encouragement of pastoralists to take up agriculture, settlement programs to relieve overpopulation, and forest and soil protection measures.

From Reform to Revolution?

In their evident spontaneity and in their scope and depth, the strikes and demonstrations were revolutionary. Some of the demands articulated were also revolutionary in their implications, partly because of their substance and partly because they held Haile Selassie's government to account for results commensurate with the promises implicit in its symbolic commitments to progressive change. The revolutionary dimensions of the strikes and demonstrations were confirmed by the emperor's commitment to constitutional reform, a policy responsive in substance to most of the insurgents' demands, and an inquiry into official misdeeds to rebuild legitimacy for his regime. Perhaps never before had such comprehensive reform at the national level come about in response to such direct public pressure.

The emperor was unable to rely upon the resources of cooptation and containment to mask the true limits of his commitment to reform. The day after Endalkachew's appointment and the plan to revise the Constitution were announced, thousands of students demonstrated through the principal market areas of Addis Ababa, chanting "death to Aklilu, death to Endalkachew" as well as the by then familiar demands for democracy, free speech, and "land to the tiller." Effigies of the former prime minister in a noose were paraded by the students. The armed forces had still not returned to their barracks. Elements of the fourth division had arrested many of the former ministers. There were reports of shooting, demonstrations, and strikes in many provincial towns, especially in Bale and Keffa provinces south of the capital. Teachers in both the secondary schools and at the university remained sharply divided over whether to support the new regime, while vitriolic leaflets from their students decried their indecision.

The demonstrations, strikes, and military unrest continued with few interruptions throughout the next several weeks and were almost completely uninfluenced in tone or substance by the cabinet's comprehensive policy statement. The armed forces units decided briefly to give the new cabinet a chance, returning captured ministers to the emperor and renewing their loyalty in meetings in the Jubilee Palace. Then came Adwa Day which commemorated the country's famous military victory over Italian armies in 1896. Incredibly, former prime minister Aklilu appeared publicly in the company of the emperor at the day's religious celebrations in Ghiorgis Cathedral. While the nation paused to observe the historic national military triumph, senior officers continued to negotiate with the units of the second division and the airforce while attempting to calm a small demonstration by units of the imperial bodyguard.

The Confederation of Ethiopian Labor Unions followed with the announcement of a general strike in support of a seventeen-point list of demands, the most critical of which were the demands for a minimum wage of U.S.$.75 per day for each worker and firmly administered price controls. The strike lasted three days and may have been supported by as many as 100,000 workers. CELU won its demanded wage hikes but not the price controls. The comfortable relationship between the negotiators for the minister and the leadership of CELU was suggested by the leisurely breakfast the two groups' leaders were seen enjoying together in the fashionable Hilton Hotel across from Jubilee Palace in the midst of the strike. But CELU did not itself always speak for all labor groups, and the general strike became simply a signal to locals within CELU to strike independently and more than once.

The civil aviation workers struck almost immediately after the general strike was concluded, followed by the telecommunications, ministry of finance, and municipality workers. The bus drivers struck a second time, and the nurses association demanded improved wages and working conditions. People's revolutionary committees seized control of provincial cities. Afar pastoralists from the Awash Valley of northeastern Ethiopia came to town to demand the return of grazing lands taken from them for the officially sponsored agricultural plantations. The government's drafting of an austerity budget in these circumstances, pointing out the cost of the wage agreements already reached, was received by the striking groups as a provocation, a gauntlet thrown down to discourage further work stoppages, which instead were promptly forthcoming.

In vain did a March 19 front page editorial in the government controlled press, the *Ethiopian Herald,* observe that urban-based strikes were preventing the government from attacking the famine and enacting the reforms being demanded for the benefit of the great rural majority. But the strikes weren't simply urban. In addition to the revolutionary committees, 200,000 priests of the Ethiopian Orthodox Church threatened to join the ranks of the strikers. Landlords and provincial officials were attacked and arrested in many areas throughout rural Ethiopia. Meanwhile, flooding in regions of the Awash threatened to render still more desperate the conditions of Afar pastoralists who were among the worst hit by the earlier drought conditions. Open conflict between landlords and tenants was reported in the southern province of Sidamo, destroying much of the harvest. In the face of all these developments, the government felt obliged to reaffirm that the prime minister, concerned though he was with security conditions, had not resigned and was not about to do so. One small source of encouragement to the government was the provisional decision of the university students to resume classes pending progress on a newly revised constitution. They returned to classes for less than a week. Meanwhile, the emperor retained the custody of his former ministers, expending some of his own ebbing political legitimacy to lend sanctuary to those attacked as corrupt and as the cause of the distress by those demonstrating in the streets.

The Chamber of Deputies joined the chorus of demands for change in April with its demands upon the emperor, further dramatizing both the seriousness of the political crisis and its own lack of institutionalized authority to deal with it. The ties of many members to the collapsing imperial order suggested that they were simply attempting to save themselves by calling for the dismissal of corrupt provincial governors in Arusi, Keffa, and Illubabor regions. They mounted a very specific attack on alleged corruption by the new minister for information, Ahadu Sabure, in connection with his earlier tour as ambassador to Somalia. It inquired into the alleged massive squandering of funds by provincial and district administrators in Illubabor.

The chamber asserted an historic degree of independence in revising the emperor's plan for a commission of inquiry by enlarging its membership, broadening its charge, and providing for the commission's election by the country's various constituencies. Equally dramatically, the chamber refused to permit Endalkachew even to present his administration's new policy statement until he had first answered questions regarding the government's response to spreading drought and famine conditions in rural areas. At about the same time, a demonstration of more than 10,000 persons erupted in the Tigrean town of Adi Ugri over the absence of a water supply as well as electric power. University students, meanwhile, returned to the attack with a hunger strike protesting the government's refusal to release political prisoners, especially those taken into custody during the unrest of the preceding weeks. These included members of the police and armed forces as well as civilians. They also joined, somewhat ironically, with the Chamber of Deputies in demanding more effective measures to deal with the drought and famine conditions.

The imperial government made a vain effort to act as though business was as usual, but in fact it only demonstrated its increasing irrelevance to the political disturbances swirling about it. The emperor went about appointing provincial officials, and he held audiences in the traditional fashion while an estimated 10,000 demonstrators chanted throughout the city, producing among other results the resignation of the city's lord mayor. Other officials sought to resolve a work stoppage that prevented the distribution of milk throughout the capital. While the prime minister met with assembled police to persuade them to support his efforts, the emperor gambled that his announcement of Zara Yacob's place in the line of succession after Asfa Wossen would ease political tension. He also sought to distance himself from the unrest by ordering the ex-ministers out of the palace, or permitting them to be forced out. Meanwhile, the finance ministry workers returned to their posts, but the postal employees decided to strike.

One single event climaxed and summed up the season of strikes and demonstrations, effectively ending weeks of nondialogue between the imperial government with its posture of reform with business as usual, and virtually all organized groups with their continued protests. On April 21, nearly 100,000 persons demonstrated in the streets of Addis Ababa in behalf of religious freedom. Mobilized by Moslems for the cause of Islam in Ethiopia, the demonstration was joined by many other groups of all religious persuasions, ethnic affiliations and occupations. The demonstration was remarkable for its extremely tight, almost regimental, organization. Each wave of marchers had its own captains, who maintained the orderly procession their charges. By its organization and discipline, the demonstration contrasted sharply with the confusion of previous weeks and dramatized clearly that the power to bring order out of chaos lay elsewhere than with the imperial government. Little else happened in the city that day. Many stores were closed, other groups went on strike, and embassies suggested that people not venture far from home. Thus there was little to distract attention from this well-organized demonstration of people power. Moreover, the demonstration struck at a fundamental weakness of the *ancien regime*—its residual dependence upon and close relationship with the Orthodox Church for legitimacy when that church represented less than a majority of the population. Efforts by the Church to organize a counterdemonstration a few days later flopped miserably; the handful of demonstrators were consoled only by an audience with the emperor.

The Origins of Military Rule

While these developments occupied center stage, at least in the capital city, the units of the armed forces never quite returned to their barracks to stay. While returning arrested ministers to the emperor and formally submitting to his authority, these units insisted nonetheless that land reform and attention to the issues raised by the *Education Sector Review* be given high priority on the new government's agenda. In effect, theirs was a conditional submission to the authority of the emperor. But fragmented leadership undermined the military's effectiveness in attempting to direct the processes of change. There were divisions within and between military units themselves, exacerbated by the efforts of Endalkachew in particular to mobilize them behind his regime.[21]

Following a period of military participation in generating the political crisis that prompted and dogged the creation of the Endalkachew government, the military gradually asserted an increasing leadership role vaguely anticipated in some of the leaflets. From shortly after Endalkachew's appointment until approximately June, a committee of military officers headed by Colonel Alam-Zawd Tessema took some initiatives in cooperation with the government to seek to restore some degree of order while the Endalkachew administration prepared its promised policy reforms. The government's failure to achieve such reform and the colonel's relationship to the government provoked further divisions and unrest within the military. In its wake emerged an armed forces coordination committee that conducted the formal dismantling of the old regime. With this process not only the imperial order but, more generally, civilian government disappeared, yielding to a military rule that was to continue formally until September 1984.

This transition to military rule is of great moment in assessing the controversy over the formation of a post-imperial Ethiopian state. Those who have opposed the *derg's* rule have claimed that the military staged a preemptive coup, upstaging and eventually submerging a legitimate Ethiopian revolutionary movement exemplified by the strikes and demonstrations of Spring 1974.[22] By contrast, the *derg* has defended its rule as bringing to fruition the aspirations voiced in that period of protest and providing the only available organizational base for pursuing the revolution at that point.[23] The critical question then is how the military came to assume power during this period. Did it act with the consent and support of the demonstrating civilian cadres? Was the military the enemy or the friend of the Endalkachew administration? Alternatively,

The Beginnings of Change

did it fashion an independent course between the government and the protesters? Subsequently, has it kept or broken faith with the fundamental changes demanded by military and civilian strikers during this period? The next chapter will center on this last issue.

Insurgents in the second division at Asmara and in the airforce at Debra Zeit struck again on March 25 and 26. Prompted by the administration's reliance on the military to quell the continuing civilian unrest, they sought the removal and arrest of their commanding officers and demanded evidence that the government was serious about a commission of inquiry, constitutional reform, and the promised wage increases. Most serious of all was a reported threat by the airforce insurgents to march on Addis Ababa and rearrest the old ministers themselves, hold a summary trial, and carry out the sentences in the middle of the palace grounds. In response, the Endalkachew government attempted with some success to reassure the second division concerning the promised reforms, and it was at this point that the emperor appears to have dismissed the former ministers from the palace, leaving them more open to arrest and trial. Steps were taken to prevent the ex-officials from departing the country, and Aklilu was himself foiled in one such attempt.

Simultaneously, acting on orders from the prime minister, an Addis Ababa paratrooper unit under Colonel Alam-Zawd Tessema's command encircled the Debra Zeit base in response to the airmen's threats. They also seized control of key installations in Addis Ababa since a substantial number of the Debra Zeit personnel were believed already to have entered the city to follow through on the rumored threat. Sixty or more insurgent officers were arrested, many of whom had been in leadership roles in the earlier mutinies.

In April Alam-Zawd surfaced publicly as the chairman of an armed forces coordinating committee, with junior aircraftman Girma Fisseha as his deputy. Their proclaimed purpose was to relieve political tensions by arresting in the first instance the former cabinet ministers excluding Endalkachew and others who continued in the new administration. In addition they published a long list of former cabinet ministers, judges, high civil servants, senior clerics, and senior military officers who were invited to surrender themselves at the Addis Ababa army headquarters. The list included Ras Mesfin Sileshi, governor of Shoa province and one of the largest and most prominent landlords in the country; Kassa Wolde Mariam, former president of Haile Selassie I University and related by marriage to the emperor; Rear Admiral Eskinder Desta, a nephew of the emperor; and virtually all former cabinet ministers and high officials of earlier years, such as former agriculture minister Abebe Retta. All but two members of the powerful Enqu Selassie family surrendered peacefully and voluntarily. They appear to have surrendered peacefully because they presumed legal process of the old order still to exist and to remain in effect under the ultimate protection of the emperor, an impression sustained by Alam-Zawd's apparent cooperation with the Endalkachew administration and the emperor. In surrendering peacefully, these notables of the *ancien regime* contributed greatly to sustaining the impression within the country and the world that reform would in fact take place in Ethiopia by peaceful and evolutionary means and under the emperor's ultimate aegis.

The actions of this first armed forces coordinating committee were a dramatic and fateful illustration of an imperial government creating the image of progress as an apparent means of restoring or shoring up the status quo ante. However, it came to light that Colonel Alam-Zawd was a cousin of Endalkachew, who in turn was related to Asrata Kassa. In itself such consanguinity might not have carried great significance until the committee he chaired announced its support for the Endalkachew government and for its call that strikes and demonstrations come to an end. By these actions Alam-Zawd angered airforce personnel for acting against fellow officers, and he may also have misled his own paratroopers, who reportedly believed he was moving against the emperor and his government rather than on their behalf.[24] Alam-Zawd's position thus cast into doubt the real and perceived purpose of the arrests. Observers and the arrested themselves could not be sure whether the arrests were to be a prelude to further changes (that eventually transpired) or whether they were simply a means of defusing the political unrest by preempting further action against the government.

Other issues led members of the armed forces to conclude that the administration sought to coopt them, through divide-and-rule tactics, toward a program of retrenchment rather than to lead progress toward the objectives articulated by the many striking and demonstrating constituencies. Among the most important of these indications was the initiative of members of the Chamber of Deputies to seek the release of the former cabinet ministers. In addition, the arrest of General Assefa Ayene caused further dismay within the armed forces, for he was not only a popular figure within the armed forces but may have been preparing to lead a coup against the emperor and the new government. The third division was also angered by Endalkachew's removal of their commander, Major General Nega Tegegne, to the governorship of Begemdir and Simien (later Gondar) province. Though not apparently radical in his views and later associated with conservative opposition to the *derg*, General Nega appears to have been one of the more popular senior officers, and his removal was interpreted as retaliation for the division's seizure of the public facilities. Finally, Endalkachew created a National Security Commission, composed of junior officers supportive of Endalkachew, for the purpose of restraining military as well as civilian protest and dissent.

Endalkachew's initiatives appear to have exacerbated both unrest and disunity within the armed forces. Insurgents within the airforce issued a public criticism of Alam-Zawd, and by implication Endalkachew, for using force against fellow officers. It has been reported that paratroopers themselves serving under Alam-Zawd thought they were acting in support of a coup against Haile Selassie, when in fact they were acting to shore up his newly appointed government.[25] There was general resentment among the armed forces against the Endalkachew administration's initiatives to restrain military insurgency by reinforcing divisions within their ranks. However, opinions within the armed forces on the direction and process of further political change appear to have diverged widely. Some sought the overthrow of the emperor, others sought a military government with the emperor as figurehead, while still others were prepared to work with Endalkachew. These very divisions, accentuated by Endalkachew through such tactics as his proposal for a National Security Commission and his use of Alam-Zawd's paratrooper units, came to a focus in fighting between the paratrooper units and the airforce in mid-June. The defeat of the paratroopers, who were perhaps also misled in this instance concerning their commander's true purposes, forced Alam-Zawd into exile and hiding.[26]

A new armed forces coordinating committee came into being in late May, the origin of the *derg* that was to rule Ethiopia after the departure of Haile Selassie. The purposes and processes at work in the formation of the *derg* constitute crucial evidence in assessing whether this committee intended to supplant or to advance the revolutionary momentum demonstrated both by civilians and within the military units themselves. The answer to that question in turn bore on the controversy that has surrounded the *derg's* leadership of the country in the ensuing decade.

As Haggai Erlich has observed, the new *derg* was in reality a "*derg* of *dergs*" since those chosen were representatives of political committees already active within the various units.[27] Each unit of the armed forces was asked to send three representatives to the fourth division's headquarters in Addis Ababa at which, apparently on the basis of an impressive speech, Mengistu Haile Mariam was elected chairman. Lieutenant Colonel Atnafu Abate, who was to share power with Mengistu for over two years, appears to have been instrumental in the formation of this assembly. The process of the *derg's* formation was itself revolutionary, for there was no precedent for any such democratically and nationally elected body, albeit within a single profession, without the blessing of the emperor's government. This process lent some credence to the military committee's claim to represent the nation, reinforced by the humble origins of many of the members and the officers' socialization to think in terms of national unity.[28]

A critical issue is the relationship of the *derg's* formation to the civilian organizations and constituencies whose strikes and demonstrations in behalf of political and socioeconomic change defined the country's political crisis. The author and most other students of this period have observed that middle and junior officers had personal linkages to the civilian groups, e.g., their attendance at Haile Selassie I University. Moreover, some of the leaflets attributed to the military expressed strong support for the demands these civilian groups articulated. There were, however, two problems. First, there appears to have been a degree of consensus on the kinds of social and economic reforms that were required—many of which were even included in the new cabinet's policy statement. However, on the crucial issue of the political framework within which these reforms should be accomplished—the fundamental issue that was to divide the country for the next decade—there was no evident agreement. The civilian and military groups that were articulate on this point offered divergent counsel. They were not in agreement on whether the reforms should be accomplished under the emperor or whether he should be overthrown, nor were they clear on how the government should be organized under either constitutional framework.

Second, nothing of what is known about the formation of the *derg* establishes how either civilian or military constituencies envisioned civilian-military relations under a reforming administration, also a vital dimension of the decade's subsequent controversies. The fact that each of the representatives came from an independent military unit required that decisions be taken by consensus if the outcome was not to be further intramilitary conflict. That reality in itself appears to have slowed the articulation of the new group's positions on these and other issues.

Given these circumstances, it is difficult to conclude that the *derg* intended to preempt or to sidetrack the revolutionary momentum developed by civilian and some military units in the preceding months. The clearest motivating factor in the formation of the military committee appears to have been the serious conflict among the military units themselves, to which the actions of Alam-Zawd's units were clearly and widely recognized to contribute. Since the linkage of Colonel Alam-Zawd to Endalkachew's government was established during the period, it followed that the military units at a minimum resented the government for those actions. Therefore, if in its formative days and weeks the *derg* did seek to reshape or alter the direction of the political uprisings of the previous months, it does not appear to have wished to do so by way of shoring up the Endalkachew government. Further clarification of these

The Beginnings of Change

issues therefore appears to require examination of subsequent events rather than the organizationl stage of the military committee.

The hallmark of the first public phase of the *derg's* activity during the summer of 1974 was caution. Intervals passed between the publication of new lists of those who were to surrender, the military committee seeming to wait to gauge the public response before proceeding further. At the same time, it dealt with problems of internal organization at a time when the public had begun to feel the weight of the military's presence on the political scene. Such internal pressures, as well as the inherent weight of their role in the country's rapidly changing political scene, may well have influenced the *derg's* caution as much as any inherent commitment to evolutionary reform and political change. While the military committee was sorting itself out internally and continuing the dismantling of the old regime "externally," it issued its first policy pronouncement in mid-July.

The central theme of the policy statement was national unity, and the phrase "Ethiopia Tikdem" (Ethiopia First) that it employed was to become the regime's motto for the first several months of the post-Haile Selassie era.[29] The same statement articulated a number of social and economic policies that closely resembled those expressed by the Endalkachew cabinet's April policy pronouncement. The single most important difference was the military's commitment to continue to play an important role in the country's immediate political future, an assertion that was not publicly challenged at the time. If the question of the political and constitutional framework of the country remained largely unaddressed in this period, there appeared to be a general consensus on the broad outlines of the socioeconomic changes that were required.

With the publication of its "Ethiopia Tikdem" statement, the *derg* began in earnest to dissolve what was left of the old regime. The arrests had already extended into the ranks of those presently trying to govern the country. Now the pattern of arrests shifted from exclusively members of the Aklilu administration to include also Alam-Zawd and others with roles in supporting the Endalkachew administration. Armed forces chief of staff General Assefa Ayene had been detained previously. Defense Minister Abiy Abebe dropped out of sight for several weeks and was eventually arrested, as was the foreign minister, Dr. Minasse Haile. Toward the end of July, Endalkachew himself was arrested, and Michael Imru was persuaded to succeed him. While the pressure of demonstrations by students and other groups mounted again, in August the *derg* began to arrest individuals within the emperor's own personal entourage. The Crown Council was abolished as was his *chilot,* or private court, which had remained independent of the regular judicial system. For much of

August the emperor came under virtual house arrest within the Jubilee Palace, emerging under escort primarily to attend church. In naming his cabinet, Michael Imru retained most of Endalkachew's remaining ministers in their existing posts, but he replaced Abiy Abebe at the ministry of defense with Lieutenant General Aman Andom, who retained also the portfolio of chief of staff. Aman had been a distinguished general some years earlier in campaigns against Somalia in the Ogaden. While still minister for defense he made a fact-finding investigation in Eritrea, demonstrating not only that he could do so without being harmed but also the possibility of engaging liberation groups in dialogue.

The arrest of Emperor Haile Selassie I on September 12, the day following celebrations of the Ethiopian new year, was actually anticlimactic because it had been so long anticipated by the military's actions of the preceding months. The gentility of the whole process continued to the end, the emperor's cousin, Ras Imru, being invited to participate in the deposition "ceremony." The arresting officers read a speech explaining to the emperor what was about to happen, and he is reported to have accepted his new circumstances with good grace, complaining only when asked to ride away from the palace in a Volkswagen rather than one of his far more pretentious vehicles.

Some have argued that the emperor had by this time actually become senile and had little comprehension of what was actually happening. This hypothesis may be supported or contradicted by reports that within his prison in the basement of Menelik's old palace, he retained quarters more luxurious than those of his compatriots and insisted on being treated imperially even in captivity—to the extent of having guards who also acted as servants. The emperor did in any event leave office with grace, sustaining an aura of peaceful evolutionary change by maintaining his dignity with the cooperation of those who arrested him. This same aura was reinforced by the new government's reference to Asfa Wossen as the future head of state upon his return.[30]

For the country as a whole, the day of the emperor's departure was one of celebration. The 7:30 P.M. curfew proved unnecessary, and it lasted only that day. Businesses and government offices generally extended the holiday begun with the previous day's new year celebrations. Groups of people strolled the streets of Addis Ababa, enjoying the fine weather as though they were tourists seeing the sights. Tanks were stationed in front of the Jubilee Palace as well as other key installations throughout the city, but the soldiers themselves participated in the holiday mood. Passersby brought flowers to the soldiers, which appeared in their caps and in the muzzles of the tanks.

Conclusion

The mood of the country on the day the monarchy ended was less one of anticipating the commencement of further thoroughgoing revolutionary changes or of using the event as an opportunity to mobilize for further struggles than it was of pleasure and even self-congratulation at the culmination of a peaceful process of dismantling the empire. For a moment the country put aside the problems and crises that had produced this remarkable process of political change. People savored newfound political freedom and the sense that a great political burden had been lifted. But a fundamental problem lurked just below the surface during these days: How should the post-imperial Ethiopian polity be reconstituted, and by what processes should decisions on this question be addressed? That these questions had not been publicly addressed in the weeks since the emergence of the *derg* was in retrospect one of the most significant dimensions of the emperor's last days in power.

Notes

1. Mesfin Wolde Mariam has produced a history of drought and famine in Ethiopia that is forthcoming. Also, Richard Pankhurst, *An Economic History of Ethiopia*. Addis Ababa: Haile Selassie I University, 1968.
2. Jack Shepherd, *The Politics of Starvation*. Washington: Carnegie Endowment for International Peace, 1975.
3. *Ibid.*
4. Addis Ababa: Government of Ethiopia, 1973, in draft.
5. Shepherd, *op. cit.*
6. Interviews.
7. Shepherd, *op. cit.*
8. Marilyn Hall, "The Ethiopian Revolution: Group Interaction and Civil-Military Relations" (unpublished Ph.D. dissertation), George Washington University, 1977.
9. Imperial Ethiopian Government, Ministry of Education, *Education Sector Review*. Addis Ababa: 1973.
10. Hall, *op. cit.*
11. *Ibid.*
12. *Ibid.*
13. *Ibid.*
14. The analysis in this section is based on personal observation as well as numerous interviews with Ethiopians and some expatriate observers while the author was resident in Addis Ababa during February-September 1974.
15. "Ethiopia: Crisis Diary," *Africa,* May 1974.
16. Hall, *op. cit.* and interviews.

17. Christopher Clapham, *Haile Selassie's Government*. New York: Praeger, 1969.
18. Hall, *op. cit.*; David and Marina Ottaway, *Ethiopia: Empire in Revolution*. New York: Africana, 1978.
19. Unpublished leaflet circulated in Addis Ababa, March 1975.
20. *Policy State of the New Council of Ministers*. Addis Ababa: Ministry of Information, April 9, 1974.
21. Hall, *op. cit.* and interviews.
22. Interviews.
23. Hall, *op. cit.*
24. *Ibid.*
25. "The Establishment of the Derg: Turning of a Protest Movement into a Revolution," in Robert L. Hess (ed.), *Proceedings of the Fifth International Conference on Ethiopian Studies*. Chicago, April 1978.
26. Hall, *op. cit.*
27. Erlich, *op. cit.*
28. The socialization of the officer corps is discussed in Donald Levine, "Ethiopia: Identity, Authority, and Realism," in Lucian Pye and Sidney Verba (eds.), *Political Culture and Political Development*. Princeton, New Jersey: Princeton University Press, 1965. Also Clapham, *op. cit.*
29. *Ethiopian Mirror*, No. 4, July 1974.
30. Addis Ababa: Government of Ethiopia, Proclamation No. 1, 1974.

5

The Crisis of the Post-Imperial State

The military committee's dethronement of Emperor Haile Selassie I launched the Ethiopian ship of state into waters never before charted in the country's long history. The unity of insurgent forces attending the dismantling of his regime disappeared within hours of his departure. In leading the assault on the *ancien regime,* the military committee gave little or no indication of what course it would take when victory was achieved. When the moment arrived, the military projected real as distinct from merely symbolic constitutional democracy in the country's future, and it claimed the role of architect of the transition. Many constituencies that accepted military leadership in abolishing Haile Selassie's government immediately contested the military's seizure of power to prepare and enact the transformation of the Ethiopian state itself.[1]

The crisis over state transformation critically influenced, and was influenced by, parallel processes of socioeconomic transformation. Though the regime and its adversaries agreed on the necessity and broad outlines of this socioeconomic transformation, they differed and fought with each other over which should be primary and which derivative. The military regime proposed to revolutionize the country's socioeconomic structures as a foundation for the reconstruction of the Ethiopian state, and it claimed for itself the role of midwife and architect of both. The regime's adversaries rejected the military's self-proclaimed roles, demanding that the political transformation occur first and immediately as the basis for subsequent socioeconomic transformation.

The actual processes of conflict over these principles concerning the appropriate course of political and socioeconomic transformation yielded de facto results very different from those the contending parties envisaged. In warring with its adversaries for survival, the military found its de facto role evolving from a transitional one of conducting the transformation of the Ethiopian state to the long-term one of equating realization of the post-imperial state with the consolidation of its own regime. Correspondingly, conflict over whether socioeconomic transformation should be preparation for or derivative from reconstruction of the state reshaped the socioeconomic transformation in actuality as a means of consolidating the regime's changing political role.

The de facto metamorphosis of the military's role in the *processes* of state and socioeconomic transformation produced a corresponding de facto change in the *ends* of those processes themselves. The quest to define and realize principles of a post-imperial state was overtaken by escalated civil wars over the historical tensions in the nature of the Ethiopian state itself that threatened its very existence. On the one hand, the campaigns to undo feudal centralization at the expense of Eritrean autonomy became a war to end the empire in favor of the independence of component nationalities rather than to transform it into a socialist republic. The magnitude of this struggle was enlarged by war with Somalia over the Ogaden and the emergence of Tigrean and Oromo liberation movements. On the other hand, the struggle over who should conduct the transformation of the state and its underlying socioeconomic structure mutated into a struggle over to what extent, if at all, consolidation of the regime brought to fruition the objectives of such transformations. Placed in context, the issue became to what extent, if at all, the military had exceeded the accomplishments of the *ancien regime* by adding substance to the symbols of such transformation.

Thus this chapter examines, in order, (1) the imperial antecedents of the state transformation crisis, (2) key features of the projected social revolution and the impact upon it of the state transformation crisis, and (3) the metamorphosis of the state transformation crisis from the initial struggle over process to include the ends and nature of a post-imperial state itself during the course of the military's struggle with its "domestic" and "international" adversaries.[2]

The Troubled Legacy

The military government's claim to establish and define the nature of the future Ethiopian state was bedeviled by the legacy of the imperial regime it deposed. In the first place, interregna between the reigns of at least the modern emperors were characterized by competition among contenders, and the eventual winners required considerable periods of time to consolidate their authority. The idea that any one individual or institution could or should assume the authority to redetermine the structure of the state itself, not simply anoint the progenitor of a successor regime, carried little if any historical precedent.

In the second place, in promulgating the Ethiopian constitutions of 1931 and 1955, Haile Selassie treated restructuring of the state as a largely symbolic exercise to help perpetuate a traditional regime by lending it new and apparent legitimacy in a global and regional environment of political change. The military's problem in promising to establish a new constitution was to differentiate sufficiently its methods and objectives from superficially similar measures by Haile Selassie's governments, including the Endalkachew government earlier that year, in order to convince many constituencies that history was not simply repeating itself. The military did promise to create a civilian advisory group "on economic, political, social, and economic development projects and other national affairs."[3] But it failed to persuade its critics that such a body would be any more influential than the Parliament, now suspended along with the 1955 Constitution as a whole. In fact, the advisory group never met.

From the moment Haile Selassie was deposed, the military found itself at odds with other primarily civilian constituencies, with whom it had shared the goal of regime change, but which sought to claim or share the process of redefining the Ethiopian state. The *derg* responded both by defending militarily what it claimed would be its transitional rule and by fighting to extinguish secessionist insurgencies. The result was prolonged, multifaceted civil war, continuing and enlarging on ones fought by the deposed emperor and from which the regime has by no means fully escaped.

Provisional Military Rule: Long-Term Consequences

The military committee's "creeping coup" created a widespread expectation that its ultimate objective was the removal of Haile Selassie from the throne and the termination of his government, though its protestations of loyalty to the emperor left its ultimate intentions ambiguous. Did the military intend simply to establish a reform-oriented successor regime, or did it propose to reconstitute the Ethiopian state itself? The gradual, extended process of dismantling the emperor's regime preserved this fundamental ambiguity as well as drew attention away from the questions of what kind of successor regime would be established and how it would be constituted. The committee's "Ethiopia Tikdem" statement sounded themes of national renewal and of reform along the lines demanded by the strikers, demonstrators, and pamphleteers. However, it did not address the questions of whether and how the Ethiopian state itself would be reconstituted or how its basic socioeconomic structures would be transformed.[4] Such was the power of the illusion of change under Haile Selassie's regime that even the manner of its demise preempted public consideration of the basic issues of state formation and socioeconomic transformation that had been submerged for so long during its heyday.

The potentially revolutionary implications of the peaceful demise of Haile Selassie's government may have been slow to dawn upon even the military coordinating committee members themselves. Paradoxically, in demonstrating exaggerated respect for the person of the emperor and his lieutenants out of caution and possibly trepidation, the military committee may have been beguiled by its own actions into failing to realize the deeper issues of state transformation that it would be obliged to confront. Thus the first pronouncement of the Provisional Military Administrative Council (PMAC) was ambiguous on these fundamental issues. The PMAC's inaugural proclamation announced its own formation and promised that Asfa Wossen, the ailing son of the former emperor, would assume the throne.[5] At the same time, while assuming full power to govern, the PMAC indicated that it would relinquish power to a new government once a constitution had been adopted by a popularly constituted assembly. However, the new administration did not announce even an approximate timetable for effecting such a transition.

The PMAC sought to establish its own credentials in part by reference to the imperial regime it had just deposed. The same proclamation mixed criticism of the former emperor's abuse of power with what might have been interpreted as compassionate realization that the ex-emperor after all had become a very old man in a very big job. Rather remarkably the PMAC stated that the emperor's power had "been conferred upon him by the Ethiopian people," while noting that the parliament with which he ruled had in effect served itself rather than the Ethiopian people. While suggesting that democratic institutions had been only a facade under the emperor, the PMAC did not seek to establish in the public mind how the substance or process of establishing what was to be a popularly based post-imperial constitution would be different from and more successful than attempts made under the emperor. Failure to establish this difference appears to have helped undermine the PMAC's credibility with those who were to be its critics and rivals.

Finally, General Aman Andom became head of state following the emperor's departure. A popular general who had distinguished himself in earlier campaigns against Somali insurgencies, Aman conveyed an image of a vigorous national identity with which the old order was accused of having lost touch. What he represented or symbolized in terms of the post-imperial transformation of Ethiopia remained unclear. Meanwhile, the anonymity of the military committee that dismantled Haile Selassie's regime was for a time preserved as Aman served as the regime's visible leader.

Thus the PMAC did not immediately confront the fundamental issues of state and socioeconomic transformation raised by its removal of the emperor and his regime. Rather, these issues were forced upon the *derg* by others. It is very important to note that the vision of a new order held by the military committee's challengers did not at first appear to differ greatly from that suggested in its first proclamation. The *derg's* opponents, however, saw democratic rights and processes as both means and end, whereas the military committee appeared to justify its less democratic means by reference to the democratic ends it claimed to share with its opponents.

The Confederation of Ethiopian Labor Unions (CELU), university students, and even units of the armed forces immediately challenged the PMAC's self-proclaimed role as a transitional regime between the new and old orders that would remain in power until pressing security problems and socioeconomic ills could be eased. CELU, for example, rejected the PMAC's preemption of the power to prescribe the contours of the post-imperial Ethiopian state. The confederation called for broad-based participation in this process by designating representatives of various interest groups to form a provisional people's government. Such representatives were to design a new order that would legitimize the exercise of freedom of speech, press, and assembly and permit the holding of free elections from which a popularly chosen government would emerge. Groups to be represented in such a provisional government included teachers, students, civil servants, the armed forces, businessmen, provincial administrations, and CELU itself.[6]

CELU's statement implicitly conceded the difficulty of achieving a popularly elected government in circumstances wherein voluntary associations of any kind had been alternatively actively discouraged by the emperor's government and coopted by it when they were allowed to form. But CELU and the other groups were not prepared to concede that flawed democracy under the old order disqualified groups that worked within it from participating in the formation of a more democratic post-imperial Ethiopia. In support of these demands, hundreds of university students demonstrated in the streets of Addis Ababa, calling for the end of the PMAC and the institution of a popular government. The engineering and army aviation corps, both resident in Addis Ababa, supported these demands, including CELU's threat of a general strike if they were not met immediately.

The PMAC made clear that it would neither sponsor nor permit popularly based demands for processes for state transformation in the foreseeable future. It arrested the leaders of CELU, killed several members of the aviation and engineering units, and banned all strikes, demonstrations, unauthorized assemblages. It also set up special military tribunals to deal swiftly with offenders. Its only major concession to the demands upon it was to authorize a civilian advisory council of approximately fifty members, distinct from the previously established commission of inquiry, which in fact never came into being. The *derg* thereby seemed to claim implicitly that preexisting interest groups lacked legitimacy as representatives of their constituencies through their association with the old regime despite their participation in events of preceding months that had precipitated its overthrow. In so doing, however, the *derg* dramatized a contradiction underlying its rule: The transitional regime's attacks on its challengers seemed to them to indicate that the regime was more permanent than temporary, thereby undermining its own proclaimed basis of legitimacy.[7] To its opponents, therefore, the *derg* appeared to deny those whose actions helped spark the overthrow of the regime of the opportunity to extend that participation to the reconstitution of the Ethiopian state on more democratic foundations. To these opponents, the military committee appeared to have staged a preemptive coup against an anticipated Ethiopian revolution instead of having acted as its true prophet and midwife.

If the direction and objectives of the PMAC's policies caused immediate apprehension and opposition, the regime also faced difficulty in defining its relationship to the one it had just displaced. First, having arrested over two hundred of the most influential political figures in the old order, the *derg* found itself internally divided over the question of what to do with the prisoners and how to do it. Should they be summarily executed? Should they be court-martialed? Should they be tried as they might have been under the procedures of the old regime or given fair trials by some newer and/or higher standard? Second, how should a transitional military regime address the continuing problem of Eritrean insurgency? Should it seek to quell Eritrean liberation groups by military means as had Haile Selassie, or should it attempt to open a dialogue that might result in partial restoration of Eritrean autonomy, the status quo ante 1961? Finally, how should power be exercised within the regime itself? Was Aman's role that of an interim head of state until the return of the emperor's son, as Proclamation No. I suggested?[8] Should the distinction between head of state and head of government be drawn differently and more sharply than under the old order? Should Aman serve as a mere figurehead or should his powers be more extensive? Two months after the dethronement of the emperor, these differences were to provoke the first and most dramatic internal coup within the military regime, with lasting consequences for the course of the post-imperial transformation.

These constitutional questions began to unfold with the work of a commission of inquiry, established by parliamentary mandate in the spring of 1974, which continued to work over the summer and to function well into the first months of the military's new regime. The question was how the regime should use the evidence the commission gathered against those of the *ancien regime* it had arrested.

Soon after he became head of state, Aman's argument with his fellow officers over the treatment of prisoners of the old regime raised the further question of his own role in the transitional regime. General Aman was reported to have been opposed to the death penalty and to the special criminal code provision promulgated shortly after the military committee assumed power. A distinguished military officer whose zeal in prosecuting the 1964 war with Somalia proved difficult even for the emperor to restrain, Aman reportedly wished to establish for himself a more independent and powerful role than the members of the coordinating committee envisaged. Characterized by high officials who knew him well as flamboyant and strong-willed but of solid competence and deep devotion to the principles in which he believed, Aman appears to have been unwilling to confine himself to a mere figurehead role.

Before and after the overthrow of the emperor, Aman undertook to mediate the on-going civil war in Eritrea. He presented the *derg* and the country with a unqiue opportunity for reaching accommodation with at least some elements of the Eritrean liberation forces. Not only did Aman claim Eritrean heritage; but he was neither Ethiopian Orthodox nor Moslem but rather Lutheran, making him appear neutral as between different religious communities in Eritrea and in the country at large. Partly for these reasons he was able to tour Eritrean villages extensively, listen to grievances, and explore possible solutions to the fifteen-year-old conflict, which he did both just before and shortly after the military assumed power. While no solutions appeared to emerge from his expeditions, the liberation campaigns appeared to be more than normally restrained during this period. However, as one high civilian official of the period has pointed out, many in the Addis Ababa regime lacked the confidence in Aman to undertake these ventures, precisely because he was Eritrean, his previous military service in behalf of Ethiopian unity notwithstanding.[9]

While these issues simmered within the *derg* along with those concerning what kind of land reform to enact, the PMAC did little on its own initiative in the first two months except to publish findings concerning the extent of royal landholdings. Compared to the dramatic process of dismantling the old regime, the first two months of the new order appeared anticlimactic and curiously uneventful.

The military committee's most important initative was to announce the formation of the *zemecha* (Amharic-campaign), a program for sending university and high school students and their teachers to the countryside to raise the political consciousness of rural folk, stimulate a sense of national identity at the grass roots, and teach basic skills needed to improve living standards. The plan was in fact a radical extension of the Ethiopian University Service program. A mark of the military regime's tenuous legitimacy in the eyes of its earlier allies was the vigorous debate among the university students over whether to accept such assignments, notwithstanding the fact that the idea had originated with students themselves earlier that year. In a test vote taken after meetings with the regime's leaders, about 60 percent of the university students were reported to have voted against the plan, though there were many abstentions.

The "Saturday Night Massacre"

Preceded by rumors that Aman was on his way out and by the first surfacing of then Major Mengistu Haile Mariam as a leading figure within the *derg,* the issues dividing it exploded on the night of November 23, 1974. General Aman was shot in his home on the outskirts of Addis Ababa, after reportedly boycotting his own office for several days, while nearly sixty other previously arrested high-ranking figures of the old regime were executed.

This "Saturday night massacre" shattered the reputation of Ethiopia's transition as a bloodless, peaceful process of revolutionary change. Previously, precisely because the overthrow had been accomplished with minimal bloodshed, many Ethiopians appeared to applaud the ouster of Haile Selassie and his regime even if they objected to the military's post-imperial strategies for political and socioeconomic transformation. Conversely, the executions sharply polarized the country between those who were and those who were not prepared to countenance violence against the old regime as a means to the transformation of the Ethiopian state.

The details of what happened that fateful Saturday night, and the reasons for it, have never been fully explained. But its impact on the course of Ethiopia's post-imperial development was nonetheless profound and of long duration. It has never been clear whether or not the *derg* members approved the executions on the basis of indictments returned by the commission of inquiry. Nor is it known whether the executions were approved en masse, voted upon individually, or even formally debated at all. Some in the capital claimed to know the exact votes on several prominent officials who were killed and on some who survived execution. Some also claimed to know who pulled the triggers and what the victims told their executioners before dying.[10] But none of these reports has ever been verified, and it may never be possible to do so. The officially cited reasons for executing Aman were the differences described above, but rumors also circulated that one important reason for the executions of the prisoners was a perceived need to compensate for an anticipated hostile reaction in civilian and military circles to the execution of a popular general.

The "Saturday night massacre" shocked the world as well as the country. A number of African nations expressed concern for the fate of the emperor, who had symbolized African independence for them despite his autocratic rule at home. An emergency session of the United Nations General Assembly voted 120-0 to censure Ethiopia for its brutality, an expression with which Ethiopia's own ambassador to the U.N. publicly sympathized before he resigned. Secretary General Kurt Waldheim made urgent representations to the military regime to avoid repeat performances of the massacre. Finally, the executions severely strained Ethiopia's relations with the United States, its principal international patron, with whom relations had already become frayed in the last years of the emperor's rule over levels of U.S. military support for Ethiopia.

Ethiopia's "Saturday night massacre" shattered the illusion, cultivated both by the military itself and by those who surrendered to it without resistance, that the transformation of the Ethiopian state would be evolutionary and deliberate and be built on elements of continuity with the deposed old regime. That very illusion of continuity may have contributed to the military committee's opponents fearing such continuity would be real, not just symbolic, leading them to demand immediate popular participation in the restructuring of the Ethiopian state. Indeed, fears that Aman's actions bespoke just such political continuity with the old order may well also have been an important factor in the decision of Mengistu and his cohorts to kill Aman and execute the prisoners.

If the "creeping coup" terminated Haile Selassie's government, the "Saturday night massacre" dissolved the constitutional foundations upon which it had rested. It established that constitutional questions, such as those with which the *derg* had been wrestling internally since overthrowing the emperor's government, would be resolved without reference to any precedents evolved during the imperial era. The symbolic restructuring of the Ethiopian state through the constitutions promulgated by Haile Selassie would carry no validity outlasting his regime which they were intended primarily to legitimize. Thus, the military committee assumed an assignment far more profound than legitimizing and consolidating its rule as the government of the country. It assumed responsibility for both preserving and at the same time reconstituting the Ethiopian state.

The manner in which the *derg* assumed these profound constitutional responsibilities established important precedents that seemed to presage the results of its undertaking. This Saturday night putsch by its very nature occurred within the narrow confines of the still-semisecret military committee, leaving the vast majority of Ethiopian people mere spectators to events of fundamental importance to their political and economic future as Ethiopian citizens. The event was received by Eritrean liberation forces as tacit rescinding of the dialogue begun by Aman and may have been read similarly in other regions as well.

In taking this plunge, the military upheld no political objectives, institutions or processes outside its own ranks. The "Saturday night massacre" thus starkly posed the fundamental question long papered over by Haile Selassie's symbolic constitutional reforms: What bases, if any, for an Ethiopian state survived the dramatic demise of the empire, which had been restored, expanded, and ruled by Haile Selassie and his modern predecessors? How could the Ethiopian state be reconstituted? What processes could be legitimized for redefining the bases of the Ethiopian state? If Proclamation No. 1 caused many civilian groups to fear the military regime's essential continuity with the methods of the imperial government, the executions raised the opposite and more serious problem: How would the bases of Ethiopian statehood that appeared to have been maintained and evolved under the regimes of the emperors be sustained and appropriately transformed in post-imperial processes of transforming the Ethiopian state? How would the military legitimize its own role in these processes?

Revolutionary Policies

The reconstituted military regime began immediately to address the fundamental issues the "Saturday night massacre" raised dramatically. It undertook to revolutionize the socioeconomic foundations upon which it proposed eventually to constitute a transformed, post-imperial state. The military government began by asserting its objective to be the establishment of Ethiopian socialism, following this declaration with a statement of broad economic policy. It put its plans into operation first with the nationalization of major industries and commercial firms and subsequently the promulgation of far-reaching and fundamental rural and urban land reform programs. It also began a series of mass literacy campaigns. To accomplish these objectives the military committee set about to accomplish the reorientation of the inherited imperial bureaucracy and to mobilize rural folk for the anticipated socioeconomic revolution through the use of brigades of students and teachers known as the *zemecha*.

The blueprints for Ethiopia's socioeconomic revolution and the actual processes by which they were implemented established very contrasting implications for the foundations of the projected post-imperial state. The latter were forged in hundreds of communities at the grass roots as the product of *zemecha* campaigners' expectations, tenants and peasants responses, holdover social and political elites reactions against threats to their interests, and the *derg's* decisions on whom to support when conflicts arose among these groups. The contrast between the constitutional issues implicit in the design of the socioeconomic revolution and those that emerged in the processes of implementation were particularly apparent in the rural land reform.

On the one hand, the socialism manifesto, the economic policy, and the rural and urban land reforms broadly projected a new Ethiopian state based on political dignity for ordinary Ethiopians and the possibility of their active participation in the implementation of reforms initiated for their benefit. The reforms raised directly, for the first time in Ethiopian history, the question of altering the traditional political relationships between the center and the grass roots. Though noteworthy for their ambiguities on this important question, the reforms contemplated grass roots institutions within which local communities *might* discharge a significant array of responsibilities. These institutions were to be the base for higher-level representative institutions reaching up to the center. Such participatory grass roots political economy apparently was to complement centralized control over inherited large-scale enterprises, both urban and rural. In short, these designs projected a socioeconomic revolution featuring the possibility of a substantial degree of democratic socialism.

On the other hand, implementation of the rural land reform in particular brought the military regime face to face at the grass roots with pressures for broadened participation in the country's projected revolution that it had already resisted at the center. To be sure, peasant and tenant responses to the reform itself varied substantially from circumstance to circumstance and region to region. However, from this confrontation, implementation patterns emerged that departed greatly not only from the implications of the reform as designed by the regime but also from the claimed objectives of its adversaries. The results of this confrontation at the grass roots were in turn to broaden the preexisting conflict at the center between the military government and its opponents. The regime's administration of the reforms alienated the *zemecha* students in particular, the most articulate and ardent supporters of revolutionary change through land reform. Their alienation contributed to renewed and strengthened civilian socialist opposition to the *derg*. In turn, such alienation, in combination with an intensified Eritrean struggle, was to create a serious challenge to the military's rule and leave in doubt the constitutional basis of a post-imperial Ethiopia.

Ethiopian Socialism

The restructured military regime sought ideological legitimacy after the fact of its seizure of power in the "Saturday night massacre." The new blueprint proclaimed that the meaning of Ethiopia Tikdem was to be Ethiopian socialism.[11] In many respects the new manifesto closely resembled in tone and substance other formulations of African socialism, notably that of Tanzania. It called for recognition of the basic principles of human dignity, the dignity of work, freedom from discrimination on religious, ethnic, national, or religious lines, and the importance of full equality. However, the proclamation was distinctive in two ways. First, in calling for the eradication of the "limitless idolatry of private gain which has chained our people to poverty and which has so humiliated our country in the eyes of the world," the *derg* showed a more virulent antagonism to private enterprise than that displayed in many other formulations of African socialism.

Second, in proclaiming the "restoration" of local powers of self-administration with the aid of the central government, the military government sought to link the Ethiopian state-to-be to legitimate foundations for Ethiopian statehood assumed to have survived the regimes of the emperors. The manifesto did not go into detail concerning the nature of these traditions upon which it proposed to build. However, the idea of such local self-administration never appeared even as a vague objective in the constitutions of the emperors' regimes.

The Ethiopian socialism manifesto helped to build for the military government a constituency among the university and high school students, long the most vocal advocates of revolutionary change. In combination with threats of loss of passports, employment opportunities, and further educational opportunity if they failed to participate in the *zemecha*, the new manifesto persuaded the students to accept this assignment where previously at least a plurality of the university students had voted it down.

Next, the military regime issued its first major economic policy proposing a mixed economy in January 1975, again characteristic of African socialism policies in other countries.[12] The policy outlined and distinguished forms of enterprise that were to be nationalized, left in private hands, or pursued jointly by the government and private entrepreneurs. Simultaneously, it announced the nationalization of a large number of commercial and industrial firms. While advocating nationalization of the "commanding heights" of the economy, the policy underscored the desirability and even necessity of relying upon competition and private enterprise in many sectors.

Taken together, the Ethiopian Socialism and Economic Policy pronouncements left ambiguous the nature and degree of the change to be undertaken. First, they betrayed the existence of important differences on economic policy within the military government. Whereas the socialism manifesto inveighed against the "limitless idolatry of private gain" the economic policy specifically encouraged private enterprise in many sectors as healthy and necessary. Second, the economic policy also seemed to imply more fundamental change than it actually delivered. The economic policy spoke of nationalization of major firms, when in fact imperial government participation in many of these same firms had already been substantial under Haile Selassie I. Third, while the nationalizations appeared comprehensive in scope, they had few consequences for most Ethiopians locked away on their small plots in rural areas. The scope of nationalization appeared limited primarily to urban concerns, although the scope of public participation in both the commercial and industrial sectors was in fact to be broadened considerably in subsequent years. Fourth, the document promised compensation for nationalized firms, sharply qualified by excluding those the regime considered to have profiteered unjustly under the old order.[13]

Promulgation of the new policies gained the *derg* political momentum and allowed it to attempt to consolidate its own rule and inaugurate fundamental socioeconomic reforms while suspending the question of how its blueprint for the new Ethiopian state would be implemented. The major exception was in Eritrea, where liberation forces resumed and intensified their war against the Addis Ababa government following the execution of General Aman. Since his execution, possibilities for a negotiated settlement stopping short of full Eritrean independence have appeared to be infrequent and fleeting. Nevertheless, strengthened by these initial policy declarations, the military regime was able to undertake the consolidation of its own authority, launch a major rural mobilization campaign (the *zemecha*), and promulgate rural and urban land reforms that along with literacy campaigns were to be the cornerstones of the military regime's program for social and economic reconstruction.

The regime's administrative capacities for undertaking major social and economic reforms were restricted since it inherited a civil service whose structures and personnel were of Haile Selassie's creation. The military government began the overhaul of its inherited administration through crash seminars in development management for groups of field administrators. These training programs were perhaps unavoidably short, hastily conceived, and for those reasons of questionable initial impact. Moreover, the numbers of participants involved were small in relationship to the size of the civil service as a whole. Not until *after* its major social and economic reforms were launched did the military government find the opportunity to undertake the more fundamental tasks of revamping inherited administrative structures, reeducating administrative cadres, and effecting large-scale replacement of administrative personnel with individuals of its own choosing (including a significant number of military officers). The delay in administrative restructuring cost the regime not only efficiency but legitimacy in part because the it was obliged to rely heavily on a still-fragile support base in the thousands of students recruited for the *zemecha*. Such reliance did not strengthen but rather shattered this working coalition, leaving the military regime an ostensibly socialist regime alienated from the principal advocates of socialism.

The rural mobilization campaign, or *zemecha,* was reportedly originally conceived by university students themselves in the months prior to the fall of Haile Selassie's government. The military government seized upon the idea, identifying the students as the vanguard of its revolutionary initiative. It proposed to send up to 60,000 students and their teachers into the countryside to promote the revolution by achieving demonstrable improvements in the living conditions of rural citizenry. The assignments given the *zemecha* participants ranged from teaching basic health practices and literacy to education of rural people in the cultural heritage of their own country to briefing them on the nature and intentions of the revolutionary government. Like the new civil service cadres, the participants received but minimal training in the tasks they were to perform, which was especially notable given the importance of the venture to the regime's quest for broad-based legitimacy. The military government's limited opportunity and resources for restructuring and restaffing its inherited administration and for training the *zemecha* participants were to bear bitter fruit in the implementation of the rural and urban land reforms, inflicting lasting damage to the regime's crucial quest for legitimacy.

Rural Land Reform

Only the *derg's* deposing of Haile Selassie rivaled the promulgation of the rural land reform in evoking positive outpouring of public support.[14] Heralded by the public, festive launching of the first *zemecha* brigades and followed by massive parades marking the first-ever celebration in Ethiopia of May Day, rural land reform marked the pinnacle of visible public support for the military government. Proclamation No. 31 was indeed the PMAC's direct answer to the central rallying point of the revolutionary prophets, the university and high school students, who had long called for "land to the tiller." At no time before or since the termination of the imperial government did the revolution appear to more people to have come closer to fruition.

The rural land reform proclamation culminated many years of efforts to address one of the most visible failings and inequities of the old order.

An imperial promise of land reform followed quashing of the 1960 abortive coup attempt and prompted the unsuccessful effort to legislate protection of tenants' rights.[15] Similarly, Haile Selassie's regime had attempted to measure landholdings and to classify them in terms of land quality. But larger landlords were virtually unimpeded in their efforts to prevent their holdings from being registered. When they were registered, such landlords were able to have them classified as poor without reference to their real agricultural or pastoral value. Landlords also dominated local courts and administrative posts which they used to protect their holdngs with little or no interference from higher levels of bureaucracy.[16] Extensive, costly, and time-consuming litigation over land rights became less tolerable because of the kickbacks required to persuade judges to expedite cases. Moreover, while agriculture was and has remained the overwhelmingly dominant sector of Ethiopia's economy, neither landlords nor tenants possessed much incentive to develop their lands. Landlords suffered no penalties for not developing their holdings, while tenants risked expropriation or eviction if they sought to develop their holdings.[17] Peasants with small holdings characteristically lacked the knowledge, capital, and holdings of sufficient size to develop them even if they did find the incentive to do so. Small producers' vulnerability to drought and famine appeared to many observers to be directly related to inequities in land distribution.[18]

Proclamation No. 31 was the military government's answer to the inherited land-based socioeconomic inequities of the old regime. It was the product of more than six months of intensive discussion against the background of earlier proposals for land reform in which civil servants as well as military and political figures engaged.[19] The proclamation rejected arguments made during this period for, on the one hand, simple reliance upon limitation of holding size and, on the other hand, full collectivization. Instead, Proclamation No. 31 placed all rural land under public ownership, with localized community control over individual families who were to hold land on a usufructuary basis.[20]

The rural land reform was unambiguous in its commitment to ending rural socioeconomic and political inequality and exploitation that were the hallmarks of the *ancien regime*. Initially, however, the reform left open to conflicting interpretations the constitution of the post-imperial state it prophesied. First, the proclamation was, as John Bruce has observed, unambiguous in making all rural lands the "collective property of the Ethiopian people."[21] At the same time, the proclamation left unclear how that collective ownership was to be institutionalized. The fundamental issue left unresolved was the balance of responsibility for administering the land reform at the grass roots as between the central government and the peasant associations created for this purpose under the reform.

Cohen and Koehn have asserted that the proclamation "turns into fact the historical fiction that the crown owns all the empire's land [but] only the state is the residual title holder rather than the monarch."[22] Could or would the military regime successfully claim to be the embodiment of the new Ethiopian state (just as the emperor embodied the imperial state) even though it had formally proclaimed itself to be only a provisional administration? If, on the other hand, the rural land was to be the property of the people as a whole, i.e., of the state as an association of all Ethiopians independent of any government—especially a transitional one—who would the proclamation entitle to act on behalf of the the collectivity?

Such vagueness on the identity of the post-imperial Ethiopian state was a logical consequence of the regime's strategy of effecting a transformation of inherited socioeconomic structures before establishing the formal constitution of the Ethiopian state. However, a practical corollary of fundamental significance was the regime's difficulty in legitimizing its own role in effecting the socioeconomic transformation.

Second, the proclamation provided for the redistribution of rural land while leaving vague the bases of tenure on the land for those to whom it was redistributed. Bruce argued that while the "rights of allottees in their allotments do not summarize conveniently, [they] may be described as a species of usufruct."[23] That was the apparent implication of the proclamation, and it appears to have been nearly universally so interpreted at the time by recipient tenants and peasants. However, the proclamation guaranteed access to rural land without providing allottees any security of tenure on any particular parcel of land or of lasting boundaries for the parcels they received. This feature of the reform was reflected in the sharp restriction on rights of succession in land and on encumbering the land with debt.[24] Nothing in the proclamation guaranteed that households allotted land would be permitted to maintain private use of these plots. At the same time, while the power and obligation of peasant associations to distribute the land was explicit, their continuing authority to *re*distribute in the light of changing population-land ratios was only implicit. Finally, nothing in the proclamation guaranteed peasant associations any autonomy vis-à-vis the central government in the determination of redistribution decisions. Thus, crucial bases of rural citizenship in post-imperial Ethiopia, i.e., the bases of land tenure in relationship to peasant associations and the central government, remained ambiguously defined.

The *derg's* interpretation of peasants' and tenants' claims under the proclamation, that they held household usufructuary tenure, at least for the present was further confirmed by their resistance to *zemecha* students in some southern areas. The students sought to move rural households into more collective tenure even though the regime-sponsored reform had not excluded that eventual possibility.[25]

Third, the rural land reform promised broadened access and rough equality in the size of holdings in the new Ethiopia, but left largely to conjecture the way in which relations of production would be structured. In whom would the country invest scarce resources to increase agricultural output and productivity? After equal access to land occurred, how would rural economic equality be sustained? Landholdings were to be limited to no more than ten hectares per farm family, but the reform did not anticipate how this equality would be sustained between peasant associations with increasingly unequal land-population ratios. Moreover, within peasant associations the relative size of families and of the quality of land were not taken into account in the proclamation. In addition, the proclamation set priorities for access to land that emphasized local residents at the expense of those from other areas, placing at a disadvantage those regions with the most acute population densities.[26] The rooting of producers in the locales of their present residence was further accentuated by the prohibition against sale or exchange of land.[27] Strikingly, a government committed to socialism sought to abolish by fiat, rather than to mobilize, an agricultural working class by forbidding all but the aged and infirm to hire labor.[28] At the same time, the proclamation discriminated against such labor by giving priority in land allocation ahead of such laborers to those "who reside within the area but do not have work or sufficient means of livelihood." Both former laborers and such underemployed persons were assigned lower priorities in land allocation than tenants, evicted tenants, and even landlords expropriated under the legislation.[29]

The rural land reform by itself did not necessarily vest control of the agricultural economy in the former peasants and tenants who gained access to land under its provisions. With the benefit of hindsight, it is possible to see that the proclamation's provision for large farms held a key to the future of the country's rural economy, one in which household farms would not necessarily be those upon whom the government would rely in generating increased agricultural production. This was because the proclamation did not commit the government necessarily to breaking up large estates and allocating them to small producers, allowing the possibility (which has since become reality) of heavy government reliance upon state farms to sustain the country's agriculture.[30]

Fourth, Proclamation No. 31 provided for extensive grass roots administration of the land reform by beneficiary peasants and tenants themselves, while leaving open the possibility for a degree of government intervention at local levels that had precedents in the country's imperial past. While perhaps commendable in not saddling the country with detailed provisions, the proclamation nevertheless implied but did not guarantee democratic processes within the association.³¹ At the grass roots level, peasant associations were to be formed at the village level with a minimum jurisdiction of 800 hectares. They were to be responsible for land distribution, administration of government land use directions, conservation of natural resources, adjudication of disputes, formation of marketing and credit cooperatives, establishment of schools and clinics, undertaking of villagization projects, and caring for the helpless among the young and old.³² Subsequent proclamations were to add raising of local militias for local defense and to supplementing the ranks of the national army to these already extensive functions. A hierarchy of peasant associations was to be erected on these village foundations at the district, regional, and provincial levels. The proclamation provided an indirect selection process with each level of peasant association providing delegates to the next higher level. While the impression was created that these delegates might be democratically elected, the proclamation did not so state.³³

The proclamation empowered the Ministry of Land Reform and Administration to assist and advise the peasant associations at every level in respect to all their functions, including their formation.³⁴ While *zemecha* participants were to become active in the organization of peasant associations, the proclamation explained that ministry officials would supervise the formation and operation of the associations. In particular, such officers were to participate as chairs of judicial tribunals above the village level. Moreover, while encouraging peasant associations to provide for schools and clinics, the government reserved the power of eminent domain to seize land (with compensation) for such public facilities.³⁵ Finally, the government provided itself the power to correct the collective land redistribution efforts of peasant associations by resettling or creating cottage industries for those who, notwithstanding the proclamation, found themselves with little or no land.³⁶

In short, the proclamation provided the structures for decentralized and democratic administration of land reform at the grass roots, but the regime wrote few if any provisions into the reform that would ensure such a result. Rather, the proclamation implied such democracy and decentralization while including provisions specifically enabling the government to limit or eliminate such principles in practice.

Fifth, the proclamation specifically took into account that distinctive cultures and traditions required exceptions to its general provisions, but it insisted that decisions regarding those exceptions be made at the central level. The proclamation thus recognized fundamental culturally defined differences in local political economies without conceding as a corollary any lessening in the unitary quality of the Ethiopian state. Accordingly, the proclamation took special cognizance of "communal" lands in northern Ethiopia and also those of pastoralists.[37]

On the one hand, the proclamation tacitly conceded the distinctiveness and legitimacy of traditional land distribution processes in northern *rist* tenure areas by indirectly excluding peasant associations formed in such areas from land distribution responsibilities. The proclamation also recognized uniquely complex landholding patterns in these areas. It denied those who held land in their own right possessory rights over other lands they cultivated as tenants, while elsewhere tenants were categorically awarded such claims.[38]

On the other hand, the Proclamation also decreed the end of such traditional land allocation mechanisms by outlawing any further land claims in such areas. Critics of *rist* tenure pointed to the pervasive and on-going litigation and perpetual tenure insecurity it produced.[39] However, as Cohen and Koehn remarked: "By freezing a transitory pattern of landholdings, Article 20 threatens both the complex set of traditional institutions which have formed around this system of land holding and the process of upward mobility through the successful prosecution of land claims."[40] Moreover, the regime's freezing in place a pattern likely to produce renewed or increased fragmentation was open to question on technical agricultural development grounds.[41] This provision made explicit for the *rist* areas a problem implicit in the reform as a whole: the lack of provision for *on-going* redistribution to preserve the competing interests of security and equity in landholdings after the original reallocation occurred.

Similarly, in "nomadic" areas the proclamation decreed that "nomadic people shall have possessory rights over the lands they customarily use for grazing or other purposes related to agriculture."[42] Associations were also tacitly excused from any redistributive function since grazing areas, as the proclamation recognized, are normally held and managed in common at the clan level.[43] At first reading, the proclamation thus appeared to extend to pastoralists a degree of security they had not enjoyed under the emperor's government under which they had been, as Bruce observed, effectively tenants-at-will of the government.[44] Yet "possessory rights" themselves afforded pastoralists little real security against government decisions to further encroach on their grazing lands through creation or enlargement of state farms as had occurred under the government of Haile Selassie I.[45] Left unaddressed in the proclamation was the issue of how far the military government would continue, alter, extend, encourage, or discourage a transition of pastoralists toward more sedentary agricultural pursuits.[46] Provisions elsewhere in the proclamation regarding government authorization to resettle pastoralists and government management of state farms left to speculation how official development policy might continue or alter past practices.

Sixth, the proclamation opened up the fundamental questions of who should determine what taxes should be imposed, how they should be apportioned, to whom they should be paid, and why. Indeed, in the months preceding as well as following the proclamation, tax receipts were reported to have declined sharply, which carried important implications for the functioning of the government. Thus, even as the land reform proclamation left the military government room to counteract the expectation of considerable local democratic self-management that it created, it put at risk much of the financial and political basis of its authority to do so.

In short, the rural land reform proclamation combined commitment to social equity and the possibility of substantially participatory democratic socialism. Ambivalence on several key issues left uncertain, however, whether abolition of the feudal oligarchy was to foretell a historic change in the relationships between the center and the grassroots—a monarch absolute in theory exercising his powers in fact within quite a circumscribed sphere. These fundamental issues were to be sorted out in the implementation of the rural land reform.

Urban Land Reform

Concentration of wealth, services, and opportunities in urban areas, particularly capital cities, has long been one of the defining features of less-developed countries. In Haile Selassie's Ethiopia, a highly inegalitarian pattern of landholding in Addis Ababa reflected and accentuated both such geographically based inequality as well as inequalities within the city itself. Absentee rural landlords speculated in urban real estate with tribute accumulated at least in part from their holdings in rural areas. Thus, they contributed to skyrocketing urban land costs resulting from a lack of investment alternatives.[47] Absence of economic opportunities to invest in agriculture resulted in large part from traditional land tenure patterns that afforded privileges to rural elites and economic insecurity to most rural citizens.

Mesfin Wolde Mariam estimated in 1966 that 5 percent of the residents of the capital city owned 95 percent of privately held land.[48] The imperial government's own official figures showed that nearly 70 percent of all rural dwellings were rented in 1972. In the days and weeks preceding promulgation of the urban land reform, the *derg* published evidence that a few officials of Haile Selassie's government had held much of this land.[49]

The military government proclaimed the nationalization of urban lands and extra houses on July 26, 1975, one of the most far-reaching reforms of its kind in the African continent. It declared that the principles of Ethiopian socialism required that urban and rural land be treated on the same basis, i.e., as the collective property of the Ethiopian people.[50] Proclamation No. 47 nationalized all urban land.

The proclamation avoided the ambiguities of "public" ownership in the rural land reform by making urban real estate "the property of the government."[51] Individuals were to be permitted ownership of a single house and the use of as much as 500 square meters of land for residential purposes. All "extra" houses were to be nationalized, defined as all those not held by individuals as their own residence or by individuals or organizations for business purposes. Individuals were to be compensated for extra houses except where evidence came to light that they had been acquired in a corrupt fashion during the old regime. Individuals owning more than one house were to be permitted to choose which one they would retain for residential purposes. Rents were to be government-controlled and categorically reduced, the greatest reductions to be awarded to tenants of the most inexpensive dwellings. Those who derived an income exclusively from house rental in urban areas were to be given a public dole of $250 per month in lieu of rental income.

Proclamation No. 47 provided for the creation of urban neighborhood cooperatives, or *kebelles,* that would be responsible for collecting rents on the less expensive dwellings and for employing such rents to undertake a wide range of governmental functions within small neighborhood jurisdictions: home rental, defense, street maintenance, dispute adjudication, building of new dwellings, and providing generally for the welfare of their constituents. One of the most important of these functions was to be the operation of stores selling *tef* (a wheat-like grain unique to Ethiopia) at lower than market rates.[52] Spouses and children were permitted to inherit their families' urban landholdings, but could not otherwise transfer or encumber them. Houses could be sold or transferred, but the government retained the right of first refusal. Land remaining unused for business or residential purposes was made subject to eminent domain proceedings, provided the government afforded "compensation in kind."[53]

The urban land reform proclamation, like its rural counterpart, appeared to strengthen local neighborhood-level self-governance. But where the rural land reform left considerable potential for reasserted central government intervention, the urban land reform made such central government powers far more explicit. While the proclamation gave substantial responsibilities to the *kebelles,* it also vested broad and relatively uncircumscribed powers in the Ministry of Public Works which now added housing to its portfolio, e.g., "to issue regulations to give effect to the purposes and provisions" of the proclamation.[54] The government assumed wide powers to gain information from individuals and organizations on financial relationships involving urban land, with criminal penalties to follow refusal to provide such information. The ministry, moreover, became the landlord for all urban property and, at the same time, responsible for effecting any redistribution necessary to house the urban landless. Moreover, the ministry was to oversee the work of all *kebelles,* including their financial dealings in particular.

Similarly, the urban land reform proclamation was more specific about the financial obligations of urban dwellers to government than the rural land reform was with respect to the millions of households. Where the rural land reform abolished existing rental obligations to private landlords without immediately substituting new ones to the central government, the urban land reform made the ministry the recipient of such rents under a new schedule published in the proclamation itself. At the same time, the proclamation left unclear how municipal governments would be compensated for the loss of rental revenues to the central government.

Although the urban land reform vested broad oversight and management powers over the *kebelles* in the ministry, the proclamation left unclear their legal and political status vis-à-vis the ministry. Moreover, the proclamation did not elucidate the legal and political relationship of members to the neighborhood organizations. The urban land reform proclamation, like its rural counterpart, provided for a hierarchy of district and regional *kebelles* to bridge the organizational gap between the central government ministry and the multitude of neighborhood cooperatives at the grass roots. But *how* such broader-based cooperatives would function in relationship to the ministry and the local neighborhood organizations was not immediately clear. Would the higher-level organizations be employed by the ministry in an advisory capacity to assist in formulating regulations and policies? Would the ministry in turn delegate the implementation of its policies to the higher-level organizations, or would the local organizations simply transmit orders issued by the ministry? Such questions were not to be answered explicitly for more than a year.

The urban land reform did not by itself alter production relations as did the rural proclamation. It removed one of the most important remaining sources of accumulation available to those whose businesses or rural lands may have been nationalized, but the military regime placed in its own hands discretion in determining how extensively to liquidate the investments of urban elites in real property. Although no compensation was to be paid for urban lands seized, the extent to which urban elites lose investments in houses was made to depend upon what the government considered fair compensation for such dwellings, how the government judged the ethics of their previous dealings in land, and the extent to which the government in fact chose to exercise its new power to preempt the sale of such houses. The investments of such elites in small businesses were not affected at this stage by this proclamation or by any others.

At the same time, while the proclamation opened an opportunity and some encouragement to build modest housing for the country's urban poor, whether such new and improved housing would be forthcoming depended upon the government's willingness to infuse substantial amounts of capital for that purpose.[55] Meanwhile, however, the proclamation did immediately reduce rents substantially, particularly for the very poorest urban tenants, but without abolishing the tenancy relationship. Where rural households appeared to gain a measure of individual proprietorship over their lands, ambiguities in their relationship to peasant associations notwithstanding, the urban land reform eliminated such ambiguity by perpetuating the tenancy relationship either to local associations or to the government itself. The urban land reform did not include any rights for former tenants to retain particular lands and thus, like the rural land reform, left its principal beneficiaries with an uncertain measure of tenure security.

Land Reform Implementation

The *derg* delayed formally constituting of the post-imperial Ethiopian state for nearly a decade after the overthrow of the emperor. Its real foundations, however, were forged on the anvil of insurgency and armed struggle involving the military regime and its adversaries throughout most of this period. In the course of such conflicts the combatants' actions set enduring precedents and established stable expectations that effectively defined the working powers and limits of government, the rights and duties of citizens, the degrees of vertical and horizontal political integration, and the identity of the Ethiopian state. Because the constitutional parameters evolved in the land reform implementation process represented only "working answers" to the underlying issues, the conflicts over them remained unresolved and subject to further escalation. These conflicts carried lasting consequences for the de facto structure of the post-imperial Ethiopian state for which such reforms were to establish the social and economic foundations.

Long-exploited by the feudal or quasi-feudal structures of the *ancien regime,* peasants and tenants were to be the primary beneficiaries of the reform. Peasant associations were authorized by the land reform proclamation to be the organizations through which they would implement its provisions in their own interests. The prospect of benefiting from land reform, however, did not automatically produce mobilization of peasants and tenants to implement the proclamation as the government intended. First, initial peasant and tenant responses to the proclamation appeared to be broadly favorable but variable in relationship to the degree of exploitation and the sharpness of class differentiation they had previously experienced and suffered. In general terms such stratification was most explicit in southern regions where lands had been seized in Menelik's conquests and assigned to his armies, vassals, and local collaborators. Responses to the proclamation were more ambivalent in the north, where though exploitation clearly existed, traditional land tenure institutions somewhat blurred class distinctions.[56] Here, too, traditions of regional loyalty limited the enforceability of any writ emanating from Addis Ababa.[57] While many peasants and tenants actively supported and even anticipated the land reform, they were not necessarily enamored of the government in Addis Ababa or of its chosen initial emissaries, the students.

Second, the reform was designed to take effect in two phases: expropriation of landed elites, followed by redistribution of lands in accordance with the provisions of the proclamation. Peasants and tenants thus initially gained control of the lands they already cultivated which did not necessarily dispose them to want to engage in subsequent redistribution. Though probably unavoidable, phase one of the reform created conflict between peasants' interests in *immediate* control over land, particularly at the start of the growing season when the proclamation was issued, and what appeared to be the military regime's intentions regarding the *eventual* disposition of the land under the 1975 proclamation. For example, phase one gave temporary legitimacy to holdings of unequal size, to unequal distribution of critical agricultural resources such as oxen, and in most cases to male household leadership despite the proclamation's insistence that any person be allotted land "without differentiation of the sexes."[58] Moreover, the reform itself contemplated giving land to former landlords who had been dispossessed of their holdings, even before those they may have evicted, in fact legitimizing the claims of some northern inheritors of Menelik's conquered patrimony.

Third, the military government faced a critical problem of agency: upon whom to rely to help peasants and tenants create peasant associations to empower themselves to take control of the land from their former exploiters and implement the envisaged social transformation. The regime's lack of previously organized cadres for such purposes, e.g., local party workers such as those upon whom the Mugabe administration has relied in Zimbabwe, was a crucial local expression of the difficulties caused by its asserted autonomy from the very classes it purported to help. Lacking an apparatus of its own, the military government borrowed, or perhaps coopted, one in the *zemecha* students and their instructors. The students had been among the foremost advocates of "land to the tiller" and in general set about the task of mobilizing the peasantry with real enthusiasm; but their loyalties were to their revolutionary ideology and to land reform, which they took as its realization, rather than to the government. Some students indeed considered the interruption of their studies a punishment for demanding immediate civilian government after the emperor's government fell.[59] After a year the students left, and cadres of the newly established Provisional Office of Mass Organizational Affairs (POMOA) to some degree assumed their relationship to the new associations. Marina Ottaway described POMOA's relationship to the military government as similar to that of the students. They were, she argued, "radical intellectuals who disliked the military and had agreed to collaborate with it in the hope of eventually being able to seize power."[60]

Fourth, the initial effect of the proclamation was to enlarge a political power vacuum at local levels by undermining what remained of the administrative structure inherited from the old regime. The government did make serious efforts to replace or retrain officials in the weeks preceding and following promulgation of the land reform. However, local administrative cadres of the government's own choosing were not yet sufficiently established in the critical first weeks and months after announcement of the reform to manage socioeconomic transformations of the magnitude it implied. Consequently, the military regime faced a difficult, dangerous choice of varying magnitudes in different locales in implementing the reform: to risk anarchy in effecting the reform fully or to strengthen existing local cadres temporarily at the potential price of having the reform subverted and its beneficiaries and proponents alienated.

The combination of these factors produced contradictory results during the first critical months of the land reform initiative. On the one hand, the land reform *program* itself gained broad if uneven acceptance among the peasants and tenants it was particularly designed to benefit. Resisting landlords were dispossessed and peasants and former tenants gained the land. Within a year more than 15,000 peasant associations had been formed in all areas of the country with the general exception of Eritrea.

On the other hand, the land reform *process* substantially alienated the military regime's surrogate cadres, the students and POMOA coopted to implement the reform on its behalf. Local people in some cases embraced the students as liberators, in others greeted them skeptically but eventually supported them, and in still other instances rejected the students. In some districts, the *zemecha* students sought to redistribute and/or collectivize landholdings beyond what the government was prepared to countenance or local people were prepared to accept. In those cases where the *zemetcha* students were able to mobilize peasants and tenants to accomplish such revolutionary land reform, local administrators and police seen as identified with the landlord classes became the target of revolutionary fervor. The military regime in general treated such uprisings as threats to public order rather than revolutionary change and responded accordingly. Students were in many cases antagonized, driven off, imprisoned, and frequently killed. In the process the government alienated those most committed to the revolutionary change portended by the land reform. An additional serious consequence was a lost opportunity for the government to establish political linkages to the people it was trying to help. Another counterproductive result was that students and intellectuals, already no friends of military rule, came to view the military regime as the enemy rather than the prophet of the revolution that was to be. For them the military regime's asserted autonomy from the forces of social revolution became an enduring obstacle rather than an asset.[61]

The alienation of the chosen agents of rural land reform exposed the constitutional issues implicit in Proclamation No. 31. First, the regime restrained *zemecha* participants from seeking to mobilize peasants in support of more collectivization than the reform mandated, at least for the immediate future. The process created confusion in local communities over whether the students did or did not represent the government, thereby undermining the government's efforts to achieve a new and unprecedented measure of local administrative control. Second, tension between the regime and the students on the pace of redistribution and collectivization exacerbated problems of tenure insecurity, with serious potential consequences for agricultural development. Third, the government's interventions undermined the credibility of peasant associations as potential instruments of decentralized, participatory peasant decision making.

The military government responded to the incipient grass roots constitutional crisis by reasserting its authority over rural households through administrative subordination of peasant associations while at the same time seeming to invest such peasant associations with new and greater powers to be exercised democratically. On the one hand, Proclamation No. 71 of 1975 appeared to strengthen local rural development decision making by increasing the authority and vastly extending the responsibilities of peasant associations and by clarifying its internal procedures.[62] A directive issued shortly after the land reform was announced sought to clarify the political rights and democratic structure of peasant associations without reference to their responsibilities to the military administration.[63]

Furthermore, Proclamation No. 71 endowed grass roots peasant associations with legal personality, expanded their portfolio of functions, and decreed their increased organizational complexity. In addition to responsibilities granted them under Proclamation No. 31, Proclamation

No. 71 emphasized the responsibility of peasant associations for the "political, economic, and social rights" of peasants, for enabling "the peasantry to administer itself," for mobilizing the peasantry against residual feudalism and imperialism abroad in the countryside, for spearheading the political education of their constituents, and for bearing legal responsibility for their stewardship of lands within their jurisdiction. At the same time, they were to collaborate to form service cooperatives for marketing, production input distribution, credit, milling, organization of cottage industries, and provision of consumer goods. Finally, anticipating further stages of land reform, the *derg* directed the associations to promote formation of producers cooperatives that would gradually assert communalization of household lands and instruments of production.

On the other hand, the same proclamation contemplated greater integration and subordination of peasant associations as grass roots arms of official development efforts. The proclamation directed the creation of revolutionary administrative and development committees. Within such committees, representatives of peasant associations were to participate along with central government field administrators in the exercise of broad powers to enforce all laws and official policies and to coordinate the activities of peasant associations in stimulating development. But nothing in the new proclamation spoke of the responsibilities and roles of peasant associations in articulating the interests of peasants to the government at any level. Provisions for the creation of local defense squads and for local tribunals' expanded civil and criminal jurisdiction appeared to be a direct response to the *derg's* difficulty in establishing its authority at the grass roots. Finally, Proclamation No. 77 of 1976 reestablished the government's claims to land use and income tax remissions, though these considerably lightened for the time being the financial burdens on local producers by contrast to those they were expected to carry under the old order.[64]

This continuing ambivalence between decentralized, local participation and central direction in the furtherance of rural land reform was less apparent in the case of the urban land reform. Proclamation No. 104 of October 1976 amplified the powers of urban *kebelles,* particularly those of higher and central urban dwellers associations. The clear subordination of local authorities to the central government in the urban land reform stood in contrast to the rural land reform proclamation. Proclamation No. 104 lacked the ambivalence of the corresponding rural land reform proclamations. It did not emphasize the autonomy of local *kebelles,* but it did appear to vest considerable authority in the hierarchies of urban dwellers associations without establishing parallel administrative chains of command.

Thus, the implementation of rural land reform at the grass roots prefigured the terms of a constitutional struggle at the national level that would engulf the country in insurgency, armed conflict, civil war, and international conflict within the region. The military regime's asserted autonomy as a putatively transitional government appeared both to threaten and be threatened by the processes of constituting the post-imperial Ethiopian state. In asserting its own authority as a transitional administration the military regime assumed in practice the mantle of defender of a unitary Ethiopian state even though it proposed measures of regional autonomy. Opposition groups, which now included many former *zemecha* students, reacted negatively to the government's manner of military rule, however, rather than to its constitutional design or its prescriptions for socioeconomic transformation over which the only real differences were about the pace of its various stages.

In the resulting strife the positions of the military regime and its challengers became self-fulfilling. Each group viewed the other's military actions as confirmation of its true respective objectives and approaches regarding state formation, ideological formations to the contrary notwithstanding. Thus, military struggle has not been the *prelude* to establishment of a post-imperial state, but has been *itself* a major factor in defining the character of a de facto post-imperial state. In their struggles with each other the regime and its opponents have effectively constituted the post-imperial Ethiopian state on terms far different from, and to many Ethiopians less legitimate than, those envisaged by any of the parties to the struggle. The ultimate result was to be a de facto military dictatorship, something that did not appear to be sought by either the *derg* or its opponents, shades of ideological difference among them notwithstanding.

The Politics of State Transformation

The implementation of the land reform shattered the coalition between the military government and *zemetcha* students and teachers already made fragile by constitutional struggles that became overt the day the emperor was deposed. The resulting alienation of the most vocally socialist constituencies from a regime pledged to implement socialism contributed, in turn, to escalation of the constitutional crisis at the central level, for *zemecha* campaigners broadly aligned themselves with urban opposition groups in the wake of their experiences in the countryside. The opposition's challenges between 1975 and 1978 seriously threatened the regime's survival in power, further endangered by serious revolts within its own ranks. At the same time, emboldened Eritrean movements and a major

Somali military challenge in the Ogaden threatened the country's territorial integrity.

These insurgencies greatly dramatized and magnified the military government's fundamental problem of strengthening the inherited foundations of statehood while preparing the way for their transformation. In domestic policies such as the land reforms its problem was to exercise de facto authority (to a degree never contemplated by the emperors) in the interests of socioeconomic revolution, without seeming to replicate the style and forms of imperial rule. In foreign policy it struggled to defend the country's territorial integrity against insurgencies that attacked the imperial institutions by which it had been preserved previously. The more the regime's rule was militarily challenged, and the more it responded to these challenges in kind, the greater its difficulty in preventing the charges of its opponents from appearing to be self-fulfilling.

Revolutionary Dissent

A central feature of the opposition to military rule in Ethiopia has been its reservoir of strength among constituencies with whom the *derg* appeared to share the objectives of revolutionizing inherited socioeconomic structures and the imperial state in order to achieve socialism in some form. On the first anniversary of the regime's rule, the Confederation of Ethiopian Labor Unions renewed its challenge to the government to broaden participation in processes of state formation. Previously, in May 1975, the military regime had shut down CELU, asserting that foreign intrigue was responsible for the confederation's challenge to its leadership. In CELU's apparent progressive stance in favoring popular participation in post-imperial state building, the military regime saw a cover shielding from public review functionaries still loyal to the emperor's regime by which allegedly they had been coopted. It installed a new CELU leadership, but it, too, presented demands the following September that closely resembled those its predecessors had articulated earlier.

CELU's demands included a new call for civilian, popular participation in a transitional administration to prepare the way for the anticipated socialist order. In advancing these claims, the confederation purported to speak for constituencies outside as well as within its own ranks. It called for an end to "persecution" of *zemetcha* students; dispossession of "bureaucratic capitalists" held over from the old order; working-class leadership of a transitional government; broad provision for rights of free speech, association, and press; and improved access for ordinary Ethiopians to adequate health care and educational resources.

The *derg* charged again that CELU's demands were in fact mere ideological window dressing for advancing the interests of a working class privileged by the standards of the old order. The military regime would not recognize as valid or legitimate CELU's clearly adopted stance as tribune not only for its own membership but for other groups already alienated from the regime. It responded with a military show of force against demonstrations by students and others supporting CELU's platform and then moved to disband CELU. With a new proclamation in December 1975, the government upheld the dignity of labor and promised material recognition of labor's efforts, but at the same time it replaced the leadership of the movement with individuals presumed to be more prepared to accept the rule of the military regime.[65]

Underlying this bitter confrontation was a fundamental theoretical question over which the military regime and its adversaries were to war with one another for the next several years: the relationship of processes of social revolution to those of state transformation. By the standards of industrialized countries, class formation characteristic of advanced capitalist countries was partial in degree and limited in scope by the time the old regime was overthrown. Through the tactics of the emperor such capitalist development as had occurred had generally reinforced and been melded with the traditional feudal order. From this perspective, few if any of these "modernizing" elites escaped being beholden to the emperor and his regime. Conversely, as Chapter 2 demonstrated, such apparent cooptation weakened the independent political legitimacy such embryonic classes might otherwise have asserted based on shared economic interest in influencing Ethiopia's economy in a capitalist direction. To empower such bourgeois interests, the *derg* appeared to reason, would undermine the very socioeconomic revolution it sought to effect.

For the *derg*, therefore, there were few if any legitimate civilian successors to the elites of the old order. Its implicit argument was that only they, as middle- and lower-ranking officers, had escaped being compromised by Haile Selassie's government and therefore upon their shoulders fell the task of transforming the socioeconomic order in preparation for the reconstitution of the state itself. For the military regime also, the means used to effect the transformation were not necessarily to be synonymous with methods of rule that would obtain under the transformed state.

For civilian constituencies such as CELU, enjoyment of modest socioeconomic benefits under the old regime did not entail their political cooptation, as attested (from their perspective) by their participation in the events of the February Revolution. Implicitly for CELU and its associated constituencies, political empowerment and forms of democratic participation were natural concomitants of economic and educational advancement—the essence of and inseparable from processes of state transformation. Theirs was a vision of the state different in concept from the institutions of government as they experienced them at the hands of the military regime. For them also the processes of state transformation were to be consistent with those later to form the basic law of the new state itself. From their perspective the regime's use of military force represented a rejection of their concept of both the process and the end of state transformation.

To those whose alienation became apparent during the first year of its rule, the military regime offered concessions in its vision of the transformed state rather more than in the structure of what it claimed was only transitional rule. It ended the association of the regime with Ethiopian Orthodox Christianity, a hallmark of the old regime, by introducing an equal number of official Islamic, Orthodox, and Western Roman Catholic and Protestant holidays, in addition to traditional patriotic holidays plus May Day. It replaced the patriarch and senior officials of the Orthodox Church while in general not interfering with the practice of religion; it drastically reduced the number of official religious holidays ostensibly in the interests of productivity without greatly interfering with the continued informal observance of such occasions.

The military government's decision to invite civilian participation in its government produced the most fundamental, costly, and enduring conflict between the regime and its opponents. Rather than pursuing the alternative of returning to its barracks, the *derg* invited civilians from the ranks of those who opposed military rule to assume cabinet and other important governmental positions. This initiative badly divided the ranks of civilian critics of military rule, engendering an intense debate within their ranks on the merits of cooperating with a government they wished to replace. In general terms those who responded to the regime's call to return from self-imposed exile were more likely to accept its offer to participate in government and in the formation of Meison, which became the "government" party until summer 1977. Those who declined to participate were characteristically more likely to be individuals who had been in the country for some time on the eve of the old regime's fall. They were to form the backbone of the principal opposition party, the Ethiopian People's Revolutionary Party (EPRP).[66]

The alliance of Meison with the military regime was tactical and proved to be short-lived, though its consequences were far more enduring. Those who formed Meison appear to have believed the momentum of the revolution to be endangered without some civilian support and to see in such an "alliance" with the military an opportunity to entrench themselves as the eventual civilian successors to the military government.[67] The basis of this working relationship appears to have been forged in the fall of 1975 and to have brought forth as its first fruit an initially unpublicized agreement to form a "politburo" to improve the political consciousness and organization of the "broad masses" whom the regime sought to liberate.[68]

Thus, at least partly as a result of its own tactics, the *derg* appeared to change from being a temporary regime above politics to one that appeared to the "opposition" party as a partisan government whose term appeared increasingly indefinite. In this context the military government's promulgation of its National Democratic Revolutionary Program (NDRP) in April 1976 defined its concept of the state for which the preceding socioeconomic reforms had been the foundation.[69] At least as significant were the ground rules it laid down for what was to have been peaceful progress toward that objective. However, what had begun as a basic disagreement over revolutionary tactics escalated into three years of violent confrontation over both the ends and means of revolutionizing the Ethiopian state and, indeed, over the nature of the existing Ethiopian state itself.

The State Transformation Crisis

The essence of the National Democratic Revolutionary Program was its contemplation of an inclusive struggle by the "broad masses" against enemies left behind by the old regime, which were identified as bureaucratic capitalism, feudalism, and imperialism. Introduced in a speech by Mengistu that reflected his increasingly public leadership of what had been a largely anonymous military committee, the NDRP left vague how these enemies and the proponents of the revolution were to be recognized and distinguished from each other.[70] The struggle against these enemies was, however, to cement a common identity among the "broad masses" of Ethiopians of all regional, ethnic, religious, linguistic, and economic attachments who saw the replacement of the old regime as in their interests. Such political identity, the NDRP suggested, was being further established by shared economic liberation from the shackles of the old order through the rural land reform. This economic and political mobilization of Ethiopians was to find structural expression in comprehensive economic development, improved educational opportunity, and health care facilities—all guided by a "centralized national plan based on socialist principles."

Beneath this umbrella of this common identity, the NDRP stipulated that the "right to self-determination of all nationalities will be recognized and fully respected" and that their "equal recognition" was an aspect of the regime's conception of socialism. On this basis each nationality was to enjoy "regional autonomy" to decide on matters concerning its internal affairs.[71] Special attention was to be devoted to nationalities resident along the country's borders whom the regime counted as victims of long-term subjugation. It might have added that these remained communities of strategic importance to preserving the existing boundaries of the Ethiopian state.[72] Accordingly, each nationality was to be able to "determine the content of its political, economic, and social life," and to that end each would be empowered to "elect its own leaders and administrators to head its internal organs." Implementation of such autonomy of nationalities was to be "in accordance with all democratic procedures and principles."[73]

Of central importance in the National Democratic Revolutionary Program was the process it outlined for arriving at the new Ethiopian state to be identified as a people's democratic republic. All Ethiopians not associated with the evil trinity of the *ancien regime*—feudalism, imperialism, and bureaucratic capitalism—were to be permitted to establish political parties. While the ultimate leadership of the new republic was to rest in proletarian hands, others such as farmers and petit bourgeois cadres were to collaborate with the proletariat in building the new state. The NDRP envisaged such parties eventually coalescing in an all-encompassing congress-like party under working-class leadership. The military would turn over to such a party the government of the country while reserving to itself guardianship and developmental roles in the new order.

To oversee and facilitate the process of party building, the NDRP made public the creation of the People's Organizing Provisional Office (POPO), later known as the Provisional Office for Mass Organizational Affairs (POMOA), or simply the "politburo." This politburo was to serve a number of critical and potentially contradictory objectives: fostering the emergence of political parties within the stipulated guidelines, providing political education for those who would staff and lead such parties, and maintaining liaison between the military regime itself and the evolving parties. In addition, POMOA was to provide political analysis of the revolution's political dimensions, issue directives for the enforcement of mandated political changes, and generally "aid in the creation of the necessary conditions for the establishment of a People's Democratic Republic."[74] The potential contradiction, soon realized, lay in the same juxtaposition of grass roots revolutionary political mobilization and central management of the process that afflicted the rural land reform.

Weeks of relatively untrammeled political expression without either precedent or sequel followed promulgation of the National Revolutionary Democratic Program. In addition to party formation, the *derg* initiated biweekly discussion forums in all government departments, including the university and schools, that were designed to raise political consciousness and nurture revolutionary leadership cadres. During this period a remarkable debate published in *Addis Zemen* elucidated the theoretical positions of Meison and the EPRP.[75] This debate, in combination with their published manifestos, outlined the parties' respective positions on the nature of the state the parties hoped to establish. Of more immediate concern at the time, the debate presented the parties' concepts of the process of transforming the state. The same debate revealed the extent to which the National Democratic Revolutionary Program appeared to reflect elements of both parties' positions.

The military government, the NDRP, and both of the two principal parties sketched in broad outline the structure of the post-imperial state toward which each professed to be working. Both parties committed themselves to formation of a state reflecting principles of scientific socialism, signaling a significant shift from the policy of Ethiopian socialism first enunciated by the *derg* in December 1975.[76] In retrospect, however, there appear to have been significant ambiguities and subtle differences in their positions on the introduction of scientific socialism.

First, EPRP appeared to emphasize a state founded upon elections and popular sovereignty, while Meison's rhetoric suggested a greater emphasis on national unity, perhaps at the expense of popular participation. The NDRP, Meison, and EPRP all spoke of a state under proletarian leadership. However, Meison's platform outlined a "National Democratic Republic" that would exercise "National Dictatorship" whereas EPRP's platform identified the goal as a "Proletarian Dictatorship" of a "People's Democratic Republic," and it spoke more in terms of a "new" democratic revolution than of a "national" democratic revolution.[77]

Second, the EPRP stated a greater commitment to elections than did the Meison manifesto. Meison indicated that the leadership of the new state, a national committee, might be elected either directly or indirectly and would be accountable to "the public *or the organization* that elected these committee members" (italics added).[78] Meison promised, rather vaguely, publicly elected organizations in "several places," but made no direct reference to local government, elected or otherwise. With respect to nationalities Meison spoke only of their right to cultural identity rather than to the manner in which they might govern or be governed. By contrast, EPRP forthrightly asserted that "in all regions and at all levels, the people concerned have the right to recall if necessary their administrators," and it spoke without qualification concerning the election of a People's government at the national level.

The NDRP appeared to strike a compromise between the positions of the Meison and EPRP. It made no reference to either a national or a proletarian dictatorship envisaged by Meison and EPRP. It said nothing about elections at any level, but it did confirm that nationalities would have the right to self-government as well as to their cultural identity, albeit only on internal matters.

Third, EPRP envisaged more extensive self-determination for the country's component nationalities than did Meison. The EPRP manifesto anticipated a post-imperial Ethiopia premised on recognition and enhancement of many nationalities united by commitment to peaceful and democratic processes of conflict resolution and self-determination. Meison, while recognizing the principle of self-determination, appeared to endorse a far more unitary post-imperial state. Meison specifically recognized the right of nationalities to decide their own future, "even to the point of secession," but then made recognition of the integrity of nationalities *remaining* within Ethiopia dependent upon their peaceful deportment towards one another. It said no more about how nationalities would relate to one another in the new Ethiopia. By contrast EPRP defined a far more pluralistic vision of postindependence Ethiopia. Though it did not explicitly recognize the right of secession, EPRP did call for "full rights to the peoples of the various Ethiopian nationalities to determine their own destiny." More importantly, EPRP recognized the role and value of self-determination for nationalities *within* Ethiopia. It honored their right to campaign peacefully for changing the basis of their relationship to the polity through "a peaceful struggle for a voluntary union of the type they choose on the basis of equality and brotherhood." Moreover, it specifically called for an end to the military campaign against the Eritreans and for an end to the "forcible Amharicization" of nationalities. It honored the claims of self-determination for minorities concentrated in particular geographical areas, and it called for development of the country's many languages and enhancement of their respective cultural traditions.

Recognition of self-determination for Ethiopia's component nationalities was a centerpiece of the National Democratic Revolutionary Program. It appeared to go further than Meison in its endorsement of such self-determination. However, it placed more emphasis upon the objective of unifying the country's diverse nationalities: the struggle to expunge vestiges of feudalism, imperialism, and bureaucratic capitalism remaining from the old regime.

Fourth, while the objectives of the two parties in terms of socioeconomic development were broadly similar, the EPRP manifesto gave relatively greater emphasis than Meison or the military government's initiatives to the political and social entitlements of peasants and, particularly, proletarians. EPRP emphasized that land "come under the full control of the broad peasant masses in PRACTICE"; it proposed to help "poor and middle peasants" to organize themselves for such control; and it proposed that they be permitted to arm themselves and organize "revolutionary peasant militias within peasant associations." The provision for actual peasant control of their means of production was a clear indictment of the military regime for not living up to the potential for local self-administration implied in the rural land reform. Similarly, EPRP appeared to challenge the government's contention that it was simply governing until the rural poor were organized to defend their own interests. At the same time, the EPRP endorsed a wide panoply of entitlements for the urban working classes.[79]

Thus, behind the important difference between EPRP and Meison on the proper structure of a transitional administration lay significant and corresponding differences in the two parties' concept of the state to be established.[80] The EPRP's commitment to a transitional regime based on a civilian government broadly representative of all classes opposed to the old regime reflected its commitment to a post-imperial state emphasizing local self-determination, popular sovereignty and class collaboration under proletarian-led governments. Meison's support of a centralized military regime resistant to popular participation in its theoretically transitional administration appeared to find reflection in its manifesto, which gave relatively greater emphasis to a unitary state and an administration asserting its relative autonomy vis-à-vis existing classes, progressive and reactionary, weak and strong.

In the abstract, the National Democratic Revolutionary Program might have been a basis for reconciling national liberation movements and alienated civilian constituencies to mutually agreeable processes for working out differences in design and for establishing a post-imperial Ethiopian state. The manifestos of the "government" and "opposition" parties defined subtle but important differences in their respective visions of the post-imperial state that the NDRP, however, appeared to make a reasonable attempt to bridge. In practice, however, the NDRP failed to mediate the profound differences among the parties on how to build the new state. EPRP was unalterably opposed to military leadership of the transition, believing instead in a broadly based civilian regime composed of representatives of all classes not identified with the overthrown imperial government. Meison appeared to share the military regime's insistence that revolutionary and implicitly military leadership was required to prevent classes organized under the old regime from dominating the embryonic organizations of the poor, particularly in the context of rural and urban land reforms.

A fundamental irony underlay the conflict between the "government" and the "opposition" coalitions over the process of building the new state. Despite their manifest agreement on the oppression of the working classes under the old regime, the parties could not agree on the *identity* of the working class, specifically the requisite *political credentials* for membership in the working class and thereby eligibility to lead the revolution. Did the working class consist exclusively of peasants, tenants, and lumpen proletariat as the military regime and Meison appeared to suggest? Alternatively, were organized labor, students, civil servants, and teachers also oppressed under the emperors, as EPRP contended, and therefore entitled to membership in the working class and destined to rule the new state? The NDRP represented what proved to be a politically futile attempt to allow a broad range of classes to participate in the state building process while retaining a relatively restrictive definition of the working class for purposes of eventual leadership.

The issue of which classes should participate, and when, in a revolution predicated on scientific socialism is a familiar one in Marxist theory, and its replication in the Ethiopian setting was not surprising. What was distinctive and of critical importance in the Ethiopian setting was the question of who possessed *political credentials* for membership in the working classes for purposes of revolutionary leadership. The issue appeared to arise in the Ethiopian setting because (a) class formation of the kind characteristic of advanced capitalism was only embryonic in Ethiopia, rendering objective determination of class membership more difficult; and (b) constituency-based organizations under the old regime gave the appearance of having been successfully coopted by the emperor. The two problems were interrelated. Organizations appearing to represent real albeit embryonic classes, but which were in fact coopted by the regime, blurred the very *identity* of such classes as well as delaying and making more difficult their genuine organization. Thus, the constituents of EPRP's coalition were relatively but also modestly privileged under the old order; they were favored by the emperor's government but their political freedom was severely restricted; and they were organized but their cooptation prevented their exercising power under the regime. Were these classes sufficiently oppressed to legitimize them as "working classes" under the new order? EPRP and its constituent groups thought so; the military regime thought not, based upon their degree of organization and their relationships to the emperor's government rather than upon their economic circumstances.

A central problem of state transformation in the Ethiopian context was not only specification of legitimate forms of political expression for identifiable socioeconomic classes but the *eligibility* of embryonic classes for whom the revolution was ostensibly launched in their interests to be organized *for* as well as *in* themselves. For the military regime wholly new structures needed to be created for this purpose, especially for peasants and tenants whose lack of organization under the old order it thought indicated lack of political maturity. On the argument that they lacked such maturity, the *derg* seemed to take the position that they were *ineligible* for representative organizations under their own control. It did not even trust the projected primary beneficiaries of revolution—

peasants, tenants, and proletarians—to protect the new structures created for their benefit from the residual influence of reactionary cadres. For EPRP, by contrast, participation by such classes when the transformation began in February 1974 had ipso facto constituted their rite of passage to true class consciousness. It had purged organizations like CELU through which they participated of guilt through previous cooptation by the old regime. EPRP suspected that underlying the regime's distrust of all such structures, new as well as old, lay a fear of any organizations it could not itself control, a fear reminiscent of the regime it displaced.

The military regime itself *did* represent a unique political form in the Ethiopian context as an elected body of 120 junior officers and enlisted men. But it remained shadowy and anonymous during the process of deposing the emperor, and as EPRP was quick to observe, it became progressively less uniquely democratic and more characteristically militarily hierarchical when it turned from overthrowing the old regime to transforming the Ethiopian state.[81] Thus from EPRP's perspective the *derg* in form as well as in method of ruling came increasingly to resemble the imperial regime it had taken the lead in deposing.

The NDRP precipitated an enlargement and a deepening of the state transformation crisis by bringing to the fore the issue of revolutionary political legitimacy. The military regime asserted the power to prepare and approve the credentials of groups and organizations for participation in the formation of the post-imperial state, but the regime in the days following promulgation of the NDRP in effect allowed its own credentials for this role to be debated. This debate over revolutionary credentials and process became a debate over the nature of the Ethiopian state itself, for each party saw in the other's positions continuation of rather than processes to transform the Ethiopian state bequeathed them by the old regime they had joined in overthrowing.

The depth of conflict over these issues was such that developments over the next two years, from mid-1976 to mid-1978, entrenched the parties in their positions, leading to more serious conflict. Whatever indications of changes of heart appeared in either camp produced not efforts at mediation but only further conflict. The complexity of the issues and their effect on the problem of organizational legitimacy hindered each "side" in disciplining its cadres. Moreover, conflict over the issues was muddied by the settling of personal scores, personal power struggles, and other seemingly extraneous issues. Thus, when the *derg* found itself unable to control prices within the city or to use price policies to ensure marketing of sufficient food supplies from countryside to the cities, it responded by blaming the difficulties on merchants whom it alleged had hoarded for subversive and counterrevolutionary purposes. The execution of a number of merchants on such grounds in concert with adjusted official prices did produce increased food supplies in Addis Ababa markets, but it also reinforced opponents' convictions that the regime's heavy-handed methods reflected political continuity with the imperial past rather than the promise of liberation under a new socialist order.

The military government quickly became unhappy with the substance of the political discussions in all government departments that were to raise the revolutionary consciousness of their employees. It found that topics for discussion ranged over economic matters and matters of freedom of expression that were in its view unrelated or counterproductive to the purposes of the discussion groups. The regime therefore acted to instill more control and orthodoxy in these discussion groups, with the result that civil servants, teachers, and other constituencies already alienated from the military regime and perhaps for that reason sympathetic to EPRP became more so. The government's response dramatized the underlying contradiction of the NDRP from its perspective: By establishing the discussion groups it made its own revolutionary credentials a subject of discussion, while clamping down on them diminished the regime's already limited reservoir of political legitimacy and antagonized further those already uncomfortable with its leadership.

The prosecution of the war in Eritrea did more than weaken the legitimacy of the military regime: It undermined the legitimacy of the concept of the post-imperial Ethiopian state as reflected in the National Democratic Revolutionary Program and, in general, also in the manifestos of both Meison and EPRP. In May 1976, shortly after the promulgation of the NDRP, the *derg* issued a nine-point plan for its application to Eritrea. The key provision recognized the "difficulties existing in the Administration Region of Eritrea and the urgency of overcoming them." As a consequence, in order to realize the national self-determination promised in NDRP, the government offered to "discuss and exchange views with the progressive groups and organizations in Eritrea which are not in collusion with feudalists, reactionary forces in the neighborhood, and imperialists."[82] In practice this appeared to represent an appeal to the EPLP to break ranks with the Eritrean Liberation Front (ELF) with which it had been allied since August 1975.[83] The EPLP rejected the offer out of distrust of the military government based on two years of conflict with it on top of fifteen years of struggle against an imperial government in Addis Ababa, and because it was unwilling to risk loss of its political base to the ELF.

The military regime responded almost immediately by organizing a Red March on Eritrea. Promising participants land for their efforts, the *derg* relied upon peasant associations to mobilize companies for the campaign. The rousting up of armies of poor, poorly trained, primitively equipped peasants against an enemy with the hope of gaining the most important and traditional of spoils—land—was reminiscent of imperial armies of Menelik's time and much earlier. It was a strikingly traditional venture resented by at least some elements of a professionally trained army possessing modern equipment and military technology. However, tens of thousands of ragtag peasant draftees sallied north, only to be savagely cut down by liberation armies even before they reached Eritrea.

The 1976 peasant march was a disaster in human terms and in political terms for the military regime. It must have provoked disillusionment and anger in the rural communities from which the militiamen were drawn, whatever their feelings concerning the liberation movements and those supporting them. In addition to testing the patience of the armed forces itself, the peasant march signaled the failure of the policy of accommodating nationalities' self determination envisaged by the NDRP, and it served to reunite rather than further divide Eritrean opposition to negotiations with an Addis Ababa government. An ominous portent for the future was the participation of the Tigrean People's Liberation Front in the defeat of the peasant armies. Though long restive and, on one occasion, in open revolt against imperial rule, the emergence of the TPLF represented the beginning of sustained opposition of a region far more unambiguously a part of the historical Ethiopian polity than Eritrea. Most important of all, the peasant march and its failure attacked the heart of the National Democratic Revolutionary Program and thus the military regime's own design and those of both major parties for the post-imperial Ethiopian state.

The failure of the peasant march ignited what appears to have been gradually deepening dissent within the military government itself. As such it inflamed dissent already festering as a result of many factors: the failure of the *zemecha* in political terms and the return of alienated students to the cities, the restiveness of the armed forces at the design as well as the consequences of the march, the regimentation of civil servants' discussion groups, the attacks on merchants already struggling in a sagging economy, the purging of the labor movement, and the competition of EPRP for control of *kebelles* created by the regime's own urban land reform.

Against this background, dissension surfaced inside the *derg*. Captain Sissay Habte, who chaired its political and foreign affairs committee, Captain Kiros Alemayeheu, who had run the *zemetcha* campaign, and Brigadier General Getachew Nadew, sometime military commander and martial law administrator of war-torn Eritrea, attempted a coup against Mengistu. They were arrested, publicly accused of being EPRP and/or CIA agents, and executed (Kiros allegedly committed suicide in prison). The deeper reasons for their insurgency appear to have been related to the official responsibilities each had held. These led them individually to a common conviction that the military regime's manner of governing the country had endangered not only the survival of the regime but the well-being of the country as a whole.

The ranks of the Ethiopian People's Revolutionary Party grew dramatically in 1976 to include large numbers of virtually all the disaffected constituencies. Even large merchants, as the regime was quick to observe, joined its ranks. More worrisome to the government, there were indications that even some elements of the armed forces themselves were sympathetic to EPRP, while within the *derg* some were reported to have questioned the value of Meison as a civilian ally in the light of growing EPRP strength.[84] The EPRP used the occasion of the third anniversary of the emperor's dethronement to attempt a general strike and disrupt the official celebrations. Some observers claimed the demonstration indicated EPRP's special strength among white collar workers.

The *derg* responded by immediately declaring the EPRP an enemy of the revolution. Immediately afterward Mengistu was slightly wounded in an assassination attempt. Two weeks later Fikre Merid, a leading Meison figure and head of POMOA, was assassinated, precipitating open, armed urban civil war known as the period of the White Terror (the regime's response was dubbed the Red Terror) that was to continue for over a year. Its trademarks were assassination and counterassassination, demonstrations, attempted disruption of facilities, and bloody struggles for control of all urban organizations such as *kebelles* and unions. Thousands of Ethiopians lost their lives in this urban civil war.

While the parties committed to the revolution fought each other, ephemeral and moderate counterrevolutionary opposition to the military regime appeared in the form of the Ethiopian Democratic Union (EDU). It gained support in certain northern precincts for a combination of regional, ethnic, and religious as well as political reasons. Sudan appeared for a time to support EDU as a useful means of weakening a regime in Addis Ababa that it suspected of aiding opponents of its own regime notwithstanding the accord of 1972. There were three principal founders of EDU. One was a popular commander of Mengistu's own division who was transferred against his will to the governorship of his native Gondar province. Another was the heir to a royal line descended from Johannes IV who had ruled Tigre prior to 1974. Last, there was the sultan of the northern Afar pastoralists whose ambivalent relationship to Haile Selassie's government included representing his people's claims for loss of grazing lands to plantations run by a transnational corporation while at the same time serving on its board of directors.

The EDU was not strictly a royalist party, but it did oppose the socialism of both the military regime and its major opponents. Though its appeal was never widespread, the EDU did keep a portion of northern

Ethiopia unsettled for at least two years. Its most important military victory, at Setit Humera in January 1977, occurred at a time when Eritrean liberation forces had obtained extensive control in the countryside and in all but the most important cities and political struggle with the EPRP had turned to open civil war.

The military government's escalating wars with its growing numbers of adversaries prompted a movement for reform within the *derg* itself, directed in large measure at its increasing domination by Mengistu. Mengistu's political vulnerability became particularly apparent during the latter part of 1976 as he bore responsibility for his government's deteriorating political circumstances and for the country's economic doldrums. The outcome was a plan to reform the organization of the *derg* to restore some measure of the support it appeared to enjoy in the early months when the land reform was announced, while strengthening its capacity to act decisively. The *derg* established a committee under the chairmanship of Captain Moges Woldemichael, ostensibly to heal a reported growing breach between Mengistu and his deputy, Atnafu Abate, that had apparently intensified over the latter's enthusiasm for the peasant march.[85]

The committee gained regime approval for a three-tiered combination legislative-executive structure including a congress of the entire *derg* that would assume responsibility for broad domestic and foreign policy, a smaller central committee to implement the decisions of the congress, and a standing committee of seventeen to act on behalf of the central committee, particularly in the area of foreign affairs and defense and in supervising POMOA. General Teferri Bente, who had succeeded Aman Andom, gained increased executive authority of the kind that had been a factor in Aman's overthrow: chairman of the standing and central committees as commander in chief of the armed forces. Captain Moges replaced the principal Meison figure in the government, Haile Fida, as chair of the political committee. Captain Alemayehu Haile acquired the potentially important post of secretary general. While Mengistu remained vice-chairman of the *derg*, he became chair of the Council of Ministers; and the reform made the council and thus Mengistu directly subordinate to the *derg*. Particularly remarkable was General Teferri's speech at the end of January 1977 introducing the reforms, in which he called for negotiations with the Eritrean liberation forces and invited all parties to join the regime in a government of national unity.

Three days later Mengistu engineered a countercoup, assassinating Teferri, Mogus, and Alemayehu. He assumed Teferri's post of head of state and head of the *derg*. The internal reforms were otherwise maintained but the size of the committees was reduced. General Teferri's invitation to the regime's adversaries was withdrawn, and Mengistu proclaimed the

"Red Terror" to a mass meeting of Addis Ababa's dispossessed and uprooted. Thus, the military government declared open war on the EPRP, which with the assassination of Fikre Merid and the attempt on Mengistu had already begun "White Terror." Terror and counterterror accompanied the political education campaigns and countercampaigns of POMOA and its foes, especially the students. While most dramatic in the capital city, the civil war extended to the countryside, where peasant association defense committees were mobilized to fight all manner of opponents: vestigial opposition from local notables of the old order, those seeking to settle personal scores, those supporting liberation movements, and elements of EPRP.

In the course of the campaign, the military regime continued to experience difficulty in maintaining orthodoxy in its own ranks. Later that spring several members of Meison were executed for alleged collaboration with the country's "enemies." In November 1977 Atnafu Abate himself, long the second man in the government behind Mengistu, abandoned his commitment to the military suppression of EPRP and the liberation movements and was executed.

Meanwhile Meison drafted the proclamations clarifying and increasing the responsibilities of peasant associations and *kebelles* in the urban and rural land reforms respectively for preparing for the formation of higher-level workers and peasants organizations. At the national level, these were the All-Ethiopia Trade Union and the All-Ethiopian Peasants Association respectively.[86] POMOA supervised the creation of revolution and development committees not only to hasten development processes but to support the government's domestic war effort and later the war effort in the Ogaden. Meison increasingly concentrated its energies on strengthening grass roots organizations created under the reforms by POMOA. As the guerrilla war increasingly centered on the urban *kebelles,* Meison came to favor arming them, which the military regime staunchly resisted perhaps because it lacked confidence in their political loyalty. This issue caused paralysis within the military government and became the precipitating factor in the fall of Meison as the "government" party a few months later in August 1977. Meison then went underground and may have eventually reached some form of rapprochement with its former adversaries in the EPRP.

Other parties did gain legitimacy under the terms of the National Democratic Revolutionary Program. Foremost among these was Abyot Seded (revolutionary flame). Though never exclusively military in membership, military men predominated in its leadership and its base was in the military. Its most visible leader became then Master Sergeant Legesse Asfaw. Organized in late 1977, Seded's ascendancy represented the military regime's increasing reliance for political support on the military itself, which was reflected in the growing influx of military personnel within the ranks of the normally all-civilian civil service. It appears to have been organized within the ranks of the *derg* itself, perhaps as a response to the increasing failure of the regime through Meison to reach an accommodation with proponents of civilian rule.[87]

Seded gained influence initially through participation in a coalition of remaining socialist parties. Most notable of these were Maleride, which sought to link military and civilian cadres around Marxist-Leninist principles, and Wasleague, which sought support within the ranks of the proletariat. Seded entered both the civilian competition for control of *kebelles* and other institutions and the civil war, and it did so not only in opposition to EPRP but to Meison, thereby contributing heavily to forcing the latter out of the government by late summer 1977. The other parties in the coalition quickly faded, leaving Seded as the sole official party as well as effectively the "government party."

Seded's rising star foretold a successful military campaign against both EPRP and Meison and the effective end of the experiment of multiple parties representing alternative approaches to the socialist revolution. Where military regimes elsewhere in Africa have often adopted the ways of civilian politicians in the running of their countries, the *derg* moved in the opposite direction.[88] During the Ogaden campaign against Somalia and into 1978, the military regime increasingly subordinated civilian structures of its own creation to the structures and methods of military governance, including a notable increase in the posting of military officers to civil service responsibilities.

Thus, by 1978 the National Democratic Revolutionary Program was effectively a dead letter. Its essential initiatives were the promotion of self-determination for nationalities within a socialist Ethiopia and recognition of civilian parties as steps in the formation with the assistance of the regime of a working-class-led Ethiopian state. Despite broad agreement on the principal objective of a socialist Ethiopian state, civil war broke out over inability of the government and opposition coalitions to establish legitimacy of any political structure through which the building of the post-imperial Ethiopian state could begin to occur. Moreover, the peasant march and its failure signified the removal of another cornerstone of the design for a post-imperial Ethiopian state: nationalities' self-determination within the rubric of common attachment to socialism.

The formation of a socialist post-imperial Ethiopian state neared the abyss of collapse in 1977. The near-failure transformed the military government from its self-proclaimed role as prophet, midwife, and servant of the new state to its de facto and, to most civilian leadership cadres outside the military establishment, illegitimate embodiment. Its relative

The Crisis of the Post-Imperial State

autonomy had become de facto absolute and had brought with it not the fruition of the social revolution it had designed, and with which all parties were in broad agreement, but its frustration for all parties, including the *derg* itself. Yet to be determined, however, was the long-term impact of the military regime's rule, opposition to it, and the resulting civil wars on the "broad masses" whose advancement was the military government's self-proclaimed raison d'être. This will be the subject of Chapter 6.

The Crisis of the Horn of Africa

The crisis of the Ethiopian state prepared the way for a larger crisis of the Horn of Africa.[89] Between mid-1977 and mid-1978 the political definition of not only Ethiopia but the entire region known as the Horn of Africa was at stake. Within at least Africa, nowhere have the colonially imposed political definitions of an entire region been so broadly and fundamentally challenged.

The Horn of Africa has seen the conjunction of both African and European empires. In the twentieth century the legitimacy of all of these imperial impositions have been fundamentally challenged and none have been definitively resolved. Somalia's historical claims to Djibouti, parts of northeastern Kenya, and the Ogaden region of Ethiopia reflect not only Somalia's rejection of colonial rule but rejection of the boundaries its agents established. The Eritrean civil war bears witness to an unresolved historical issue concerning the border between the Italian and Ethiopian empires. The distinctiveness of such disputes in the Horn may have arisen in part because Ethiopia did not participate in the congress of imperial powers at Berlin in 1884 and, more recently, because the superimposition of French and British rule undermined de facto validity and historical precedent for the earlier imperial impositions of Italy. The 1977–1978 crisis of the Horn of Africa represented the most recent such challenge to the existence of imperial boundaries as they were established by the conquests of Menelik and enlarged by Haile Selassie's cashiering of federation with Eritrea.

The border between colonial Somaliland and imperial Ethiopia was never accepted by the latter, which weakened its political defenses against Somali claims to suzerainty over ethnic Somalis resident within the Ogaden. Like most pastoralists, the peoples of the Ogaden were unconcerned with internationally imposed boundaries, and they wandered back and forth across the line in accord with the seasonal rhythms of their economies. Moreover, the ethnic roots of President Siad Barre of Somalia were in the Ogaden. The Ethiopian crisis provided Somalia a perceived opportunity to make good its historical claims to the region and emboldened it not only to support insurgents but to invade Ethiopia in their behalf. The ramifications for Ethiopia were ominous and profound. A Somali victory in the Ogaden combined with Eritrean liberation armies' success in the north threatened to greatly impede Ethiopia's rail and road access to the Red Sea ports of Massawa and Djibouti. More fundamental, the Somali offensive reverberated beyond the Ogaden, creating resonance in a far larger region of southern and eastern Ethiopia and the potential for balkanization of the entire Horn of Africa through the unraveling of the expanded empire established by the conquests of Menelik II.

However, the very vagueness in the imperial political definition of the Horn of Africa also complicated the development of the insurgencies and liberation movements bent upon the removal of empires from the region. The spheres of self-determination movements were not well established by contrast to those elsewhere on the continent, however arbitrary they have been at the outset. Thus, the linkages of self-determination insurgencies to one another were ambivalent and uncertain. The key unanswered question was: How would the peoples of the region define their borders and their relationships to one another if given a free choice? This already difficult question became far more complex given the professed objective of the military regime in Addis Ababa to transform imperially established political and socioeconomic relations into ones founded on equity and national self-determination *within* the preexisting boundaries.

Ethiopia required the massive military assistance of the Soviet Union and Cuba to overcome the Somali invasion and stabilize the military balance of power in Eritrea. The political map of the Horn of Africa thus changed dramatically. The Soviet Union changed clients in the region from Somalia to Ethiopia. In cautious, sharply qualified fashion the United States gravitated to the support of Somalia after a quarter-century's military and economic patronage of Ethiopia. The Soviet Union and, to a lesser extent Cuba, subsequently extended their "international" defense of the Mengistu government to the "domestic" arena as well, i.e., Eritrea and provision of security for the *derg* in Addis Ababa.

Ethiopia's change of international patrons was a dramatic and traumatic external extension of its state transformation crisis. After World War II Haile Selassie exhibited again his passion for collective security, undeterred by the failure of the League of Nations to come to Ethiopia's defense against the Italian invasion in 1936. Conversely, Ethiopia became an important collaborator of the United States with respect to the Cold War and in the Middle Eastern theater, not least because of the Kagnew base in Asmara from which the United States monitored Middle Eastern activities and Soviet behavior. In encouraging Haile Selassie's "modernization" initiatives in education and agriculture, the United States was subject to criticism for supporting illusory development masking continued traditional autocracy and of being a patron of the imperialism, bureaucratic capitalism, and feudalism later decried by the military government. But the reduction of U.S. provision of military assistance in the early 1970s, at least in part because of new approaches to the Arab world in the wake of the oil crisis, was received by many Ethiopians of many persuasions as indifference to the country's political integrity at a time of major Soviet presence in Somalia. Some even considered the crisis in U.S.-Ethiopian relations as a precipitating factor in the collapse of Haile Selassie's government, while others treated the phasing down of U.S. military assistance as an effort to destabilize the revolution.

These resentments, as well as the military regime's ideological directions and the U.S. role in supporting Haile Selassie's government, have contributed to long-term strained relations between Ethiopia and the United States since 1975. Thus, the issues over which the countries sparred during this period, compensation for nationalization of firms owned by U.S. citizens and the human rights issue, did not reflect all the underlying issues between them. Nevertheless, throughout this period the United States remained the largest contributor of famine relief support, thereby in a sense helping to underwrite the ecological viability of the Ethiopian state while the *derg* and its adversaries warred over its transformation.

The perpetuation of Ethiopia's territorial integrity has depended upon more than military superiority with external assistance; it has rested upon the underlying political ambivalence of many communities in the region based in turn upon the absence of settled geographical expressions of historical political identity. The Western Somalia Liberation Front (WSLF), the principal vehicle of Ogaden Somalis, favored union with Somalia on ethnic grounds, but became estranged from Somalia in the wake of the invasions. The WSLF did not wish to exchange one militarily established empire for another. The Oromo Liberation Front (OLF) has continued to mount insurgencies in parts of southern and western Ethiopia against what it regards as a perpetuation of imperial rule from Addis Ababa. But OLF-WSLF cooperation foundered over the latter's original association with Somalia, which was not to the taste of the OLF. The OLF and WSLF shared with the Eritrean and Tigrean liberation fronts a common resistance to military-sustained imperial rule, but the OLF in particular has appeared to be less than entirely convinced that the northern liberation movements fully disavow colonization of the south as fully as they have that which they themselves suffered. It is likely that such ambivalences are replicated many times at more local levels.[90]

Thus, the hypothesis emerges that the political fabric of the Horn of Africa and therefore of Ethiopia is founded upon multidimensional political ambivalence arising at least in part from the complex modern imperial history of the region. Ethiopia's military victory in the Ogaden and improved military posture in Eritrea by mid–1978 suggested that the Ethiopian polity might survive, but the longer-term political ambivalences of the region suggested also the preconditions for its successful nurturing within the imperially established boundaries. These parameters would appear to continue to include broad recognition of impulses to self-determination.

Conclusion

This chapter has portrayed the crisis of the Ethiopian state induced by the imposition of military rule on civilian processes of revolutionary political and socioeconomic change, aggravated by adverse consequences of imperial rule outlasting the *ancien regime* itself. Viewed in the larger context of the Horn of Africa, the possible outcomes of the crisis would appear to be neither a unitary state nor unbridled anarchy but rather the relative magnitude of centrifugal and centripetal tendencies within the region. With the consolidation of military rule in Ethiopia, this balance of forces and the larger question of the significance of the Ethiopian transformation began to turn increasingly upon the quality of military rule. This is the subject of the following chapter.

Notes

1. Throughout this discussion the state is conceived along lines discussed in Chapter 1, i.e., as the fundamental, working organizing principles that define and limit the practice of politics by governments (or regimes) and citizens.
2. "Post-imperial" in this and the remaining chapters refers to the long-term objective the *derg* and its opponents seek, however differently they conceive it in substance. Use of the term does not imply that in fact, or in the view of the *derg* or its opponents, Ethiopia has ceased to be an empire.
3. Addis Ababa: Government of Ethiopia, Proclamation No. 1 of 1974.
4. 2 *Ethiopia Mirror*, 4, July 1974.
5. Proclamation No. 1, *op. cit.*
6. CELU statement September 16, 1974.
7. References to "legitimacy" do not imply a value judgment by the author but his estimate of how the *derg* and its opponents are regarded by each other and by the peoples of the country.
8. Proclamation No. 1, *op. cit.*
9. Interviews.
10. See Blair Thomson, *Ethiopia: The Country That Cut Off Its Head*. London: Robson Books, 1975.
11. *Ethiopia Herald*, December 20, 1974.

12. *Declaration of Economic Policy for Socialist Ethiopia.* Addis Ababa: Government Printer, 1974.

13. In recent years a number of those cases have been quietly settled after more than a decade during which they placed a continuing strain on relations between the two governments.

14. Addis Ababa: Government Printer, Proclamation No. 31 of 1975.

15. On the abortive coup see Christopher Clapham, "The December 1960 Coup d'état," 6 *Journal of Modern African Studies,* 4, 1968, pp. 495–507

16. *Ibid.*

17. See discussion of Chilalo Agricultural Development Unit in Chapter 3.

18. See for example Abdul M. Hussein, "The Political Economy of Famine in Ethiopia" in his (ed.) *Drought and Famine in Ethiopia.* London: International African Institute, 1976.

19. Interviews.

20. *op. cit.*

21. *Ibid.*

22. John M. Cohen and Peter Koehn, "Rural and Urban Land Reform in Ethiopia," 14 *African Law Studies,* 1, 1977 pp. 3–62

23. John Bruce, "Ethiopia: Nationalization of Rural Lands Proclamation," *Land Tenure Center Newsletter,* No. 47, January-March, 1975. Land Tenure Center, University of Wisconsin, Madison.

24. Proclamation No. 1, *op. cit.*

25. One of the best initial analyses of the implementation of the land reform was by Marina Ottaway in her "Land Reform and Peasant Associations: A Preliminary Analysis," *Rural Africana,* No. 28, 1975, pp. 39–54, and her "Land Reform in Ethiopia, 1974–77," 20 *African Studies Review,* 3, 1977, pp. 79–90.

26. Proclamation No. 31, *op. cit.*

27. *Ibid.*

28. *Ibid.*

29. Proclamation No. 31, *op. cit.*

30. Addis Ababa: Government Printer, Proclamation No. 142 of 1978 subsequently supplanted by creation of Ministry of State Farm Development, May 1983.

31. *op. cit.*

32. *op. cit.*

33. *Ibid.* and Proclamations No. 71 of 1976.

34. Proclamations No. 31 and No. 71, *op. cit.*

35. Proclamation No. 31, *op. cit.*

36. *Ibid.*

37. *Ibid.*

38. *Ibid.*

39. The best account of land tenure practices in *rist* areas is Allan Hoben, *Land Tenure Among the Amhara of Ethiopia.* Chicago: University of Chicago Press, 1973.

40. Cohen and Koehn, *op. cit.*

41. Kenya undertook a major land consolidation program in the 1950s. See M.P.K. Sorrenson, *Land Reform in the Kikuyu Country.* Oxford: Oxford University

Press, 1967. However, more recently the efficacy of consolidation has come under question. See C. Leys, *Underdevelopment in Kenya: The Political Economy of Neocolonialism*. Berkeley: University of California, 1975; and Judith Heyer, J. K. Maitha, and W. M. Senga (eds.), *Agricultural Development in Kenya*. Oxford: Oxford University Press, 1976.

42. Proclamation No. 31, *op. cit.*
43. *Ibid.*
44. John Bruce, "Legal Consideration-Nomadic Lands," Memorandum, Ministry of Land Reform and Administration, May 20, 1962.
45. *Ibid.*
46. On the transition of Afar pastoralists to settled agriculture see L. Bondestam, "People and Capitalism in the North-Eastern Lowlands of Ethiopia," 12 *Journal of Modern African Studies*, 2, 1974, pp. 423–39; John W. Harbeson, "Afar Pastoralists and Ethiopian Rural Development," 28 *Rural Africana*, 1975, pp. 71–87; and John W. Harbeson, "Territorial and Development Politics Among the Afar of Ethiopia," 77 *African Affairs*, 309, pp. 479–498.
47. Cohen and Koehn, *op. cit.*
48. Mesfin Wolde Mariam, "Problems of Urbanization," *Proceedings of the Third International Conference of Ethiopian Studies*. Addis Ababa: Haile Selassie I University, 1970.
49. *Ethiopia Herald*, July 25, 1975
50. *Ethiopia Herald*, July 17 and July 24, 1975
51. Addis Ababa: Government of Ethiopia, Proclamation No. 47 of 1975.
52. Interviews.
53. Proclamation No. 47, *op. cit.*
54. *Ibid.*
55. Cohen and Koehn, *op. cit.*
56. Interviews.
57. For example, some Tigrean leaders never accepted that the imperial throne passed to Shoa after the death of Johannes IV in 1886.
58. M. Ottaway, *op. cit.*
59. Interviews.
60. M. Ottaway, "Land Reform," *op. cit.*
61. Interviews.
62. *Ibid.*
63. Provisional Military Administrative Council memorandum to ministries of land reform, interior, agriculture, community development and social affairs, and *zemecha* administration, May 20, 1975.
64. Addis Ababa: Government of Ethiopia, January 4, 1976.
65. *Ethiopia Herald*, December 6, 1975.
66. Rene Lefort, *Ethiopia: An Heretical Revolution?* London: Zed Press, 1983.
67. *Ibid.* and interviews.
68. *Ibid.*
69. Addis Ababa: Government Printer, April 1976.
70. *Ibid.*
71. *Ibid.*

72. *Ibid.*
73. *Ibid.*
74. *Ibid.* and Addis Ababa: Government Printer, Proclamation No. 91 of 1976 and Proclamation No. 119 of 1977. At the same time the Yekatit 66 Political School was established, Proclamation No. 120 of 1977.
75. Marina Ottaway, "Democracy and New Democracy: The Ideological Debate in the Ethiopian Revolution," 21 *African Studies Review*, No. 1, April 1978, pp. 19–31.
76. Unpublished manifestos of EPRP, August 1975, and Meison (1976).
77. *Ibid.*
78. *Ibid.*
79. *Ibid.*
80. *Ibid.*
81. Lefort, *op. cit.*
82. Lefort, *op. cit.* and Fred Halliday and Maxine Molyneux, *The Ethiopian Revolution*. London: Verso, 1981. There is a substantial literature analyzing the Eritrean situation in the context of the Ethiopian transformation. It includes Richard Sherman, *Eritrea: The Unfinished Revolution*. New York: Praeger, 1980; Haggai Erlich, *The Struggle Over Eritreat 1962-1978*. Stanford, California: Hoover Institution, Stanford University, 1980; Berekhet Habte Selassie, *Conflict and Intervention in the Horn of Africa*. London: Monthly Review, 1980; Pliny the Middle-Aged, "Eclectic Notes on the Eritrean Liberation Movement: E Pluribus Unum?" 2 *Ethiopianist Notes*, No. 1, 1978, pp. 37–46; Richard Lobban, "The Eritrean War: Issues and Implications," 10 *Canadian Journal of African Studies*, 2, 1976 pp. 335–46; and Tom J. Farer, *War Clouds on the Horn of Africa*. 2d ed. Washington: Carnegie Endowment for International Peace, 1979.
83. Lefort, *op. cit.* and interviews.
84. Lefort, *op. cit.*
85. Interviews.
86. Proclamation No. 130 of 1978.
87. Interviews.
88. Harbeson (ed.), *The Military, op. cit.*
89. Farer, *op. cit.*; J. Harbeson, "Multilateral Approaches to Multidimensional Conflict Resolution: Lessons from the Horn of Africa," in Arthur Day and Michael W. Doyle (eds.), *Escalation and Intervention: Multilateral Security and Its Alternatives*. Boulder, Colorado: Westview, 1986.
90. Harbeson, "Multilateral Approaches to Multidimensional Conflict Resolution: Lessons from the Horn of Africa," *op. cit.*

6

Military Rule and the Transformation of State and Society

The Mengistu regime achieved militarily stable control of Ethiopia by mid-1978, having overcome direct challenges to its survival and returned to a standoff the war with Eritrean liberation forces. Since then, it has sought to (1) consolidate its ostensibly transitional rule, (2) extend, implement, and promote development under the reforms instituted at the outset of its tenure, and (3) effect the transition to the people's democratic republic it prophesied upon liquidating Haile Selassie's imperial order.

The preceding chapter explained how the *derg's* very initiatives in these areas provoked multifaceted crises over the transformation, objectives, and even existence of a post-imperial state, crises that resulted in the several theaters of war. The central question since 1979 has therefore become how, if at all, the extent of the military regime's success in combat has affected subsequent disposition of fundamental questions concerning the nature, leadership, and future of the Ethiopian state that provoked or enlarged these wars in the first place. These questions have fallen into two categories: those concerning the constitution of a post-imperial Ethiopian state and those relating to processes of preserving while also transforming the Ethiopian state with this end in view.[1]

The constitutional issues have been

1. The survival of an Ethiopian state within the preexisting boundaries, following the dismantling of the institutions of the *ancien regime*
2. The design and realization of a transformed Ethiopian state as the People's Democratic Republic (PDR)

The process issues have been

1. The military regime's rule as midwife and architect of the transformation of the Ethiopian state
2. The regime's implementation of the social and economic reforms, specifically including further rural collectivization[2]
3. The military's transfer of power to the Workers' Party of Ethiopia (WPE)
4. The ratification and inauguration of the PDR

The thesis of this chapter is that the inauguration of the People's Democratic Republic in 1987 represented a symbolic rather than a substantial further transformation of the Ethiopian state. Similarly, the infusion of civilian cadres in the governing Workers Party of Ethiopia reflected more a ceremonial than a real transfer of power from an ostensibly provisional military administration to a permanent civilian one. The de facto transformations these events confirmed were the permanence of a once transitional Mengistu regime and the equation of the regime with the new Ethiopian state for which it was once to be but the midwife. These de facto transformations of the Ethiopian state underlay the regime's failure to manage effectively the parallel socioeconomic transformation in ways consistent with its own vision of its purposes. Thus, the fruits of these violent struggles between the regime and its opponents were postponements rather than confirmations of the long-term goals initially espoused by both the Mengistu regime and its opponents. In early 1988 it remained to be seen whether the WPE government of the PDR would attempt or eventually succeed in building on its existing power base to transform these institutional symbols of regime change and state transformation into substance.

The Mengistu regime contributed to this result by concentrating since 1979 on the consolidation of its own authority at the expense of cultivating the political and socioeconomic foundations of a post-imperial state, the ostensible purpose underlying its own successive party formation and socioeconomic reform measures. The regime followed this course by addressing state transformation issues as extensions of its wars and the political insurgencies preceding them, i.e., as challenges to its survival. One visible result has been liquidation of the institutions of the old regime. A second has been a de facto capacity of the Mengistu regime to impinge fundamentally on the lives of its subjects to a degree greatly exceeding anything the the emperors even attempted except perhaps in their mobilizations for war. In this process the regime's shift from essentially African socialism to scientific socialism has been at issue not in and of itself but as interpreted in the Ethiopian context by the Mengistu regime in support of its approaches to the state transformation issues.

However, a third consequence has been a poor return in political as well as socioeconomic terms on the regime's investment in socioeconomic transformation. The land reform has been managed in such a fashion as to discourage rather than cultivate political engagement in the regime's state transformation strategy. Similarly, such management has failed to date to promote broadly the economic advancement of the 80 percent of the population that draws its livelihood from the land. Underlying the regime's approach to the management of these reforms has been a disposition to treat those at the grass roots who manifestly suffered under the old regime as ineligible for significant political participation in the transformation. Thus, the regime has treated those who were to be among the major beneficiaries of revolution in much the same way as it dealt with other constituencies whose leaders it considered to have been coopted by the old regime.

This chapter will consider this thesis by tracing the regime's consolidation of power after 1979, the formation of the Workers' Party of Ethiopia and the People's Democratic Republic, and the impact of these political transitions on implementation of rural reform.

Toward a Command Economy

With the assistance of Soviet and Cuban legions Ethiopia repulsed the Somali invasion, reoccupied the Ogaden, and exploited insurgency within Somalia the better to keep the regime of President Siad Barre off balance. Liberation movements of south and southeastern Ethiopia, while by no means reconciled to the Addis Ababa regime, were to become sufficiently ambivalent in their relationships with each other, toward Somalia, and toward those of the north that coordination of sustained, strong insurgencies for self-determination in the region were forestalled at least for the time being.[3] External military assistance did not enable the *derg* to defeat Eritrean and Tigrean liberation armies, but did permit it to break the siege of Asmara, retake several key cities, and render more distant and speculative the liberation armies' prospects for achieving militarily sustainable independence.

The fragile distinction between "domestic" and "international" spheres in the Horn of Africa, dramatized by the Eritrean and Ogaden challenges to imperially defined boundaries, magnified the Ethiopian military regime's task in seeking to forge a people's democratic republic. The issues posed by these wars could not but impinge heavily upon the character of a "domestic" Ethiopian society already torn by civil war over the processes of constructing a post-imperial state. On the one hand, rule by military means had been precisely the issue that provoked civil war between the *derg*, with its civilian collaborators, and its civilian opponents.

Some of these opponents perceived their cause of self-determination to be parallel to that of the Western Somalia Liberation Front supported by the Somali armies, even if their relationships with each other were at best troubled. On the other hand, the same blending of "national" and "international" struggles encouraged the *derg* to pursue its objectives by similar means in these related theaters, i.e., to pursue the domestic tasks of state transformation and implementation of social and econopmic reforms by martial means.

The rise of the military-based Abyot Seded party terminated the *derg's* collaboration with the civilian-based Meison, leading it forcibly to suppress the civil war between Meison and the Ethiopian People's Revolutionary Party and driving both underground. Abyot Seded's ascendancy also corresponded with the subordination to the regular military establishment of militias mobilized by peasant associations and *kebelles* created under the land reforms. Thus, the fears and claims of the *derg's* opponents became self-fulfilling: a military regime ruled increasingly by military means. The Ogaden war magnified this reality of de facto Ethiopian military rule as the *derg* struggled to mobilize men and material, including food production, to sustain its armies. After the war, the *derg* articulated plans, policies, and structures for promoting development that purported to define fundamental rights and obligations of all Ethiopian citizens as well as to establish structures for the management of development processes. In fact, however, it sought to legitimize rule by decree, tightly centralized authority, command-based development, and civic obligations sanctioned by criminal penalties accompanied by few rights or privileges and little room in practice for individual, local, or regional self-determination.

The realities of war heavily influenced not only the *derg's* strategy for effecting development, based upon the reforms it previously promulgated, but the de facto foundations of the post-imperial state laid down in the process. In 1977 the *derg* established a National Revolutionary Operations Command (NROC), which treated as interdependent the military struggles against its "domestic" and "international" enemies and the fight to overcome poverty and underdevelopment. It stated that "poverty and economic dependence cannot be seen in isolation from the (domestic and foreign) enemies."[4] At the national level the NROC joined military commanders, heads of development ministries, and *derg* officials to coordinate this "two front war." At the local level defense committees and militias, formed to combat not only residual royalist-landlord opposition and opponents of the *derg's* rule, were made officially subordinate to regular military commanders at the insistence of the military establishment. This centralization of military authority was to be applied not only in the prosecution of the Somali war but in the development effort as well.

The *derg's* linkage of military and development "combat" reappeared a year later when it proclaimed the National Revolutionary Development Campaign (NRDC) on the fourth anniversary of its accession to power in September 1978.[5] In announcing the new initiative, Mengistu conceded that despite the liberating effects of social and economic revolution, war and revolutionary conflict itself had inhibited and restricted efforts to translate those opportunities into real achievement.

> Even if the control of the economy which is the foundation for the existence of any society, has in the main been freed from the control of the exploiters and has been put to serve the interests of the broad masses, we have had no peaceful interval to be able to develop it. Forced by our enemies to concentrate on the political and military spheres, we could not attend to the economy as much as we would have liked. In fact in some areas economic activities had virtually come to a standstill because of the escalation of the struggle from political to primarily military confrontation. Even today we cannot say economic activities have fully resumed. The wound which the war has left on the economy has not yet healed.[6]

While recognizing the efforts of state farms, settlers, and peasant farmers as well as afforestation, fishing, and water development programs, Mengistu conceded the existence of "a frightening situation in urban areas regarding the shortage of food items." He admitted, further, that the government had not been able to establish proper marketing structures and that military campaigns had heightened food shortages.

Mengistu attributed much of the economic crisis accompanying the war effort to continued peasant individualism, notwithstanding membership of most rural households in theoretically more-collectivized peasant associations under the terms of the 1975 land reform. His criticism appeared to reflect either tacit recognition of substantially incomplete implementation of the reform and/or denial of the political legitimacy of a peasantry reorganized under a reform his regime itself had sponsored. He found the root of the production problem not just in circumstances but in structure. In his view the heart of the problem was "individualism on the part of the peasant producer . . . the old anarchic relationship between the buyer and the seller." Such behavior (which he considered reactionary) consisted he said, in acting "to produce only what is sufficient for one's own family, to refuse to bring crops to market until prices rise, and to underproduce in order to maintain prices at a very high level." Because such actions rendered the war effort more difficult, Mengistu found the structure of peasant individualism itself to be a challenge to the integrity of the nation as well as an obstacle to more efficient economic development. For these ills Mengistu prescribed a combination of intensified political consciousness-raising, increased reliance upon state farms, collectivization, and new marketing structures for which the NRDC was to be the instrument.[7]

The National Revolutionary Development Campaign conceived of "development" in martial terms. Development plans were to be formulated, human and material resources mobilized, and directives formulated at the national level. Plans and directives were to be disaggregated and implemented at regional, provincial, district, and local levels. These bodies were to meet according to procedures and with a frequency determined by the campaign's leadership. All Ethiopian citizens and organizations were to give priority to implementation of directives issued them and to maintain strict discipline in discharging these obligations. The campaign appeared to rest upon the premise that the "broad masses" would set aside individualistic tendencies for national economic mobilization as they had been expected to in the past in response to calls to arms.[8] The NRDC created a Central Planning Supreme Council (CPSC) and vested overall authority for directing the national development campaign in an executive committee led by the chair of the PMAC, Mengistu. The merging of development and military campaigns was further expressed in the creation of a congress of the CPSC, which included both armed forces and police commanders as well as members of the *derg* itself, cabinet members, and senior civil servants. Significantly, only four places were assigned to representatives of the "broad masses," the leaders of the All-Ethiopia Peasant Association, the All Ethiopia Trade Union, the Revolutionary Ethiopian Women's Association, and the Revolutionary Ethiopian Youth Association. However, apart from Mengistu and a representative of the *derg's* standing committee, the executive committee was composed exclusively of ministers and civil servants.

The NRDC's military conception of the development process was particularly evident in the functions assigned to the executive committee of the CPSC.[9] Indeed, the congress of the CPSC was charged with setting guidelines for the executive committee, but it was the latter that was to be responsible for actually planning and implementing the "campaign." The functions given the executive committee repeated the military motif of the campaign. The NRDC extended the authority of the executive committee beyond constituted leadership to enable it to "assign any Ethiopian to participate in any field of activity."[10] Moreover, it emphasized development by command in empowering the executive committee to ensure "strict adherence to discipline in any organization or association with a view to assuring that the development campaign achieves its objectives . . ." and to "take all measures necessary to implement the development campaign and the plan with efficiency and strict discipline."[11] Every citizen and organization was obliged to cooperate with the campaign by giving priority to CPSC orders, an obligation backed up with civil and criminal penalties.

Entirely absent from the NRDC were any provisions for consulting those who were to be the beneficiaries of its prodigious efforts, apart from a single reference to the need "to study the problems of the peasant" at the district level. The NRDC did not seek to organize below the level of the district, but the NRDC charge clearly implied substantial limits on the autonomy of local peasant associations and their service cooperatives. Urban dwellers associations were specifically denied the power to collect voluntary contributions from their constituents for their own local projects without prior ministry approval. Peasant leaders were to be included in the district, provincial, and regional level congresses but not in the executive committees except by invitation.[12]

The NRDC structure challenged at least one important Marxist-Leninist orthodoxy. The rationale of the NRDC appeared to lie in the military regime's reliance upon a blending of the *theory* of military organization and the *practice* of Leninist democratic centralism. The theory of democratic centralism calls for a degree of participatory deliberation before decisions are reached that has only rarely occured in practice at least in the Soviet Union. However, such participation has been altogether absent even in the *designs* of the regime's measures to promote development since at least 1979 let alone in their implementation. Instead, the command structures the *derg* established bear a closer resemblance to those theoretically found in the armed forces. One might well argue that, in a regime so conscious of ideology, this distortion of Marxist-Leninist *theory* indicated the relatively greater importance of the military imperatives in designing the development campaigns. The strategy also appeared to place regime consolidation above development concerns, given that it ran directly contrary to a wealth of empirical evidence supporting the importance of local organizational participation in development processes.[13]

The NRDC established a continuing strategy of, first, attacking persistent peasant individualism and independence through a campaign of collectivization and, second, retreating from dependence upon the smallholder sector for production marketed through official channels by promoting a state farm sector. On the one hand, it determined that the country could not be fed by the efforts of smallholder agriculture alone. In May 1978, therefore, it announced the formation of a state farms development authority on the premise that crop shortfalls "arising from the failure of peasant associations to produce them on a scale commensurate with their demand due to natural disasters or other causes can be overcome on the basis of self-reliance only when the State establishes large-scale farms and produces such crops."[14] The military regime has persisted in this course, announcing in the Ten Year Plan in 1984 the goal of dramatically increasing the number of state farms and their share of the agriculture market by the mid-1990s.

On the other hand, the government decided to challenge directly what it considered the root cause of the country's agricultural stagnation—peasant individualism and independence—through a three-pronged campaign: further collectivization, villagization, and resettlement. First, the *derg* decided in June 1979 to mobilize the requisite organizational resources to collectivize the smallholder sector.[15] The justification and objective of the measure was to curb not only the observed tendency of peasant association members to concentrate on the acquisition of personal wealth but the form in which it took place: in small, isolated hamlets beyond the reach of planned, technologically sophisticated production. Although such collectivization had been envisaged much earlier and had been informally encouraged, this proclamation made collectivization of the smallholder sector an explicit and official priority of the government.

The regime prescribed producer cooperatives as a scientific socialist remedy for peasant households' allegedly unpatriotic preoccupation with the acquisition of personal wealth. In so doing, the regime gave priority to further collectivization over consolidation of the first phase of land inaugurated in 1975 with which a number of practical problems had surfaced.[16] Moreover, while acknowledging the existence of traditional forms of rural cooperation, the regime rejected these as models because producer cooperatives, unlike traditional forms of collaboration, were "not only to help the majority to provide for themselves but also to contribute to the the national economy and rid the country of poverty and backwardness by means of a modern administrative state."[17] By implication, peasant associations established by the original 1975 proclamation and service cooperatives established to facilitate their marketing and input distribution functions shared the inability of "traditional" cooperative forms to promote national as distinct from local political and economic interests.

Based on a tour of several provinces, Mengistu candidly addressed what he considered to be the adverse consequences of peasant economic individualism for the economic well-being of the country as a whole by its undermining of state enterprises established for such larger purposes. Shortly thereafter, he chaired a meeting with representatives of the armed forces, "who are fighting on the battlefields, [and] demand[ed] of the Ethiopian masses in the rear" that they form themselves into producer cooperatives and increase productivity so that the armies' costly military campaigns would not have been conducted in vain.[18] Though not stated explicitly, a further motivation for such collectivization was doubtless the political imperatives of feeding not only the cities but the armed forces, from whence came the initial rumblings that toppled Haile Selassie's government.

The *derg* envisaged the process of building producer cooperatives as an extended three-stage process, an important tacit official acknowledgment that the campaign for smallholder collectivization would not be easily won. The first stage, known as *melba,* would permit every family to retain up to 2,000 square meters of land for private exploitation, with any remaining lands merged. No more than one such association would be permitted within the jurisdiction of any peasant association. Farm implements and plow animals left to individuals in this first phase passed to collective ownership under second-stage cooperatives (*welba*). In this second phase individual families were to retain no more than 1,000 square meters for their personal use, with the remaining lands devoted to the collectivity. At this stage individual income was to be largely a function of the extent of individuals' contributions in labor to the cooperative. The degree of collectivization was assumed to be sufficient at this stage to permit the introduction of increased mechanization and also increased occupational specialization. At this point members of the collective were to become a commune (*weland*) involving full collectivization with legal status acquired from the parent peasant association, which would accordingly be dissolved. To encourage this transition to increased collectivization, producer cooperatives were to be provided a range of financial incentives by the government.

The second prong in the government's attack on peasant individualism, villagization, originated in its attempt (1) to militarily secure parts of Bale and Hararghe provinces from secessionists' attacks during and after the Ogaden war, and (2) to alleviate political tensions in the Wabe Shebelle valley arising from displacement of smallholders by new state farms believed necessary to feed the army and the cities. Gradually the government came to believe that villagization was a needed means to the creation of producer cooperatives.[19] Thus, the government relied upon villagization models evolved to ameliorate politico-military threats to mount a microlevel campaign against the corrosive economic effects on its other struggles of what it viewed as persistent peasant individualism.

The villagization policy has been a particularly striking example of a prominent motif in the regime's development campaigns: its seeming indisposition to draw on the development experience of other countries, even that of neighbors with which it has maintained good relations. The *derg's* stated commitment to scientific socialism represented a departure from African socialist thinking characteristic of newly independent African countries, of which Tanzania has been a premier example.[20] However, the military regime's villagization policy appears to have resembled Tanzania's villagization program in concept, application, and also in its pitfalls. It has been designed to end rural households' isolation, in some cases by involuntary means, and it has been managed by a highly centralized bureaucracy. Several lessons the regime might have drawn from the testimony of Tanzania's own leaders have apparently not been drawn: the need for careful planning, the importance of real decentralization, and the folly of taking for granted dutiful full participation rural agricultural economies in the national-level public sector economy.[21] One must hypothesize that the reasons lie in neither ignorance of nor indifference to these lessons. Rather, they are to be found in the distinctive political circumstances attending the constitution of the post-imperial Ethiopian state, which, at least from the military regime's perspective, have rendered the development lessons of these experiments inappropriate to its immediate political purposes.

The third dimension of the *derg's* effort to restructure the lives of Ethiopia's rural millions has been its resettlement of whole communities from overcrowded and drought-stricken rural areas, as well as urban unemployed, in relatively less densely populated areas of southern and western Ethiopia. By contrast to the collectivization and villagization programs, the military regime's resettlement program carried ample precedent in Ethiopia's recent past.[22] Agriculturalists had long recommended resettlement of individuals from the overcrowded northern provinces to less densely cultivated areas in south and southwestern Ethiopia. Missionaries and others established experimental settlements with varying degrees of official encouragement. Unofficial migration also occurred. In 1979 responsibility for resettlement was transferred from the Ministry of Agriculture to the Relief and Rehabilitation Commission. When the 1984–1985 famine struck, the government ordered the commission to resettle 1.5 million people from affected areas to relatively underutilized lands in southwestern Ethiopia. However, many of these same affected areas were at least partially controlled by insurgents opposed to the regime and its reforms and seeking greater autonomy. In these circumstances the dimensions, timing, haste, and frequent involuntariness of the resettlement project has aroused suspicions, particularly on the part of external donors, that the regime's working motivations for the resettlement were military and political rather than humanitarian and socioeconomic.[23]

Such centralized and comprehensive control and such collectivization of economic life at the grass roots were virtually without precedent in prior Ethiopian history. The three facets of the military government's campaign to eliminate the independence and individualism of peasant households, at least in organizational terms, constituted a genuine Ethiopian revolution in and of themselves. The initial rural land reform proclamation of 1975 had contemplated fundamental socioeconomic reordering of the rural areas, but suggested a substantial degree of local responsibility for its implementation. During the military regime's period of collaboration with Meison, follow-up proclamations had appeared to reinforce the concept of such local responsibility. However, the postwar initiatives of the military regime have made implementation of the land reforms and development unambiguously the responsibility of the central government to be accomplished by directives to the apparent exclusion of any negotiation or consultation.

The *derg* further extended centralized direction of all aspects of the economy in 1984 by decreeing establishment of the National Committee for Central Planning (NCCP).[24] Its effect was to reinforce the regime's concept of planned development by command. The NCCP's plans were to be formulated on the basis of those submitted by other central and local bodies and mass organizations. However, whereas the NRDC plans were to be given "priority" over other initiatives by all public and private organizations, the final plans the NCCP decreed were *orders* that commanded "proper, efficient, and strictly disciplined implementation in the various sectors of the economy and in the different regions." The penal code continued to apply to any person violating the provisions of the proclamation. In addition, the only short-, medium-, or long-term development initiatives that could be undertaken by anyone were those "consented to and recognized by the Office of the National Committee" unless approved by a "superior organ," presumably Mengistu and his closest associates.

Noteworthy in the centralization of development responsibility has been the downgrading of the authority of cabinet ministers in favor of not only military and party officials but of civil servants. The membership of the NCCP, for example, included only one representative of the Council of Ministers, the minister for finance, but it did provide for the inclusion of several unnamed "civil servants" as well as party officials and "anyone else coopted by the Chairman," i.e., Colonel Mengistu.

The imposition of centralized, command-based development and fundamental transformation of life at the grass roots for millions of rural households effectively replaced the rural development hierarchy envisioned in the original 1975 land reform proclamation. It overlaid and superseded the pyramid of regional and provincial peasant associations that were to be elected from the grass roots under the provisions of the 1975 rural land reform with a hierarchy of military, civil service, and party officials charged with carrying out directives of the military high command in Addis Ababa. Representatives of the elective peasant association pyramid were included in the hierarchy of centrally directed officials but only as a minority and without leadership responsibility. The structure of the official hierarchy at regional, provincial and lower levels clearly revealed the military regime's expectation that peasant associations would serve primarily as instruments of its authority at the lowest level rather than as a principal vehicle of peasants' initiative and political expression at the grass roots.

The centralized command economy has been of fundamental importance not only to the *derg's* strategy for revolutionary economic development but to its consolidation of political power. Its organizational structure for development could no longer be disguised as the work of a transitional regime seeking only to remove the vestiges of the *ancien regime* in order to prepare a tabula rasa for the civilian political order of the future. Instead, the extensive political and administrative control it sought to exert over all Ethiopians from the capital to the most remote villages was the work of a regime that would establish enduring political foundations upon which the prophesied people's democratic republic would rest. The initial land reforms and other nationalizations liquidated the socioeconomic structures of the feudal order and established the foundations of socialism, but without dictating the political uses to which those structures should be put by their participants. The measures promulgated with the NRDC and afterward undertook the political organization of the reform's beneficiaries through the imposition of extensive controls on their economic activities.

Political Development from Above

The military regime's first effort to organize Ethiopia politically in preparation for formation of a post-imperial state, the National Democratic Revolutionary Program, ended in failure. To have been established upon the foundations of the regime's major socioeconomic reforms, initial implementation of those reforms in fact exacerbated previously unresolved basic conflict over the legitimacy of the regime's determination to guide the transition from empire to republic. As a consequence the NDRP dissolved, leading to civil war between the EPRP and the military regime's temporary collaborator, Meison; the breakup of Meison's coalition with the regime; and violent conflict within the *derg* itself, precipitated in part by the disastrous peasant march on Eritrean liberation forces. The rise of the military party, Abyot Seded, and the outbreak of the Ogaden war terminated this first unsuccessful effort at revolutionary political development.

Two years later the military regime made a second attempt, albeit on very different terms from the first one. Mengistu had by then consolidated his position as the increasingly unchallenged leader of the military government. Military victory with Soviet and Cuban help in the Ogaden and the further application of this assistance to the Eritrean front effectively silenced open debate or conflict inside or outside the *derg* over its military answer to national liberation insurgencies within the former empire.[25] Similarly, the military regime had addressed the problem of "domestic" postreform development in the same martial terms it had prosecuted the "international" war against Somalia in the Ogaden.

These measures resolved an early tension between decentralized and centralized management in favor of the latter. There had been a marked emphasis on the local responsibilities of peasant associations in the early land reform proclamations and on spontaneous multiple party formation in the National Democratic Revolutionary Program of 1976. The NORC, NRDC and NCCP re-established unbounded central direction in the management of socioeconomic transformation, and the COPWE did likewise in the area of party formation. In so doing, the Mengistu government confirmed the fears of its opponents that had sparked civil strife over the process of transforming an empire into a republic in the first place. It appeared to abandon any pretense that its role in both the socioeconomic and political transformations was the transitional one of midwife. Through such centralization, the *derg* established that it was indeed upon martial foundations and under its management that the superstructure of the long-anticipated people's democratic republic would be built. Whether such recentralization was inevitable and would have occurred in any event is a matter of speculation. That the military regime in this case viewed further socioeconomic and political transformation as extensions of its military campaigns is strongly suggested by the available evidence.

The military government announced the formation of a Commission for Organizing the Party of the Working People of Ethiopia (COPWE) on December 18, 1979.[26] COPWE was the military regime's second effort to establish a ruling Workers' Party. The first, POMOA, became embroiled in the civil war between EPRP and Meison, which aborted the regime's effort to base its rule on some form of civilian support. COPWE, by contrast, was launched on the foundation of unambiguous, centralized, and command-based military rule. Where POMOA had been a means of basing military rule on civilian support, COPWE was an instrument for introducing some measure of civilian rule on the basis of established military foundations.

Mengistu's speech announcing the formation of COPWE, which was to function along Marxist-Leninist lines, dwelt heavily upon the lessons of the previous five years of revolutionary struggle and conflict, as distinct from abstract requirements of a socialist revolution. Mengistu candidly recognized and addressed the issue of the new commission's legitimacy against the background of previous civilian opposition to party formation via POMOA and the collapse of the military government's collaboration with Meison, which he did not mention by name. In the light of this unhappy history, how, he inquired, could the country have confidence in those responsible for the new effort? He acknowledged the problem, saying, "Even today we cannot fully reply to this question."[27] His answer appeared to be that lack of centralized leadership allowed these so-called (but not named) false prophets to engage in their mischief and that the structure of COPWE would prevent that mistake from being made a second time. Those who were true revolutionaries were to be defined and identified by their adherence to COPWE guidelines, over which Mengistu, as its chair, would have a great deal to say.

The primary objectives of COPWE were (1) to "disseminate Marxist-Leninist philosophy and inculcate it into government and mass organizations, cooperative unions and the Ethiopian broad masses in general" and (2) to establish a political party to lead in the establishment of socialism and a People's Democratic Republic of Ethiopia.[28] The enabling Proclamation No. 174 enjoined the organizing commission to establish means of spreading Marxist-Leninist philosophy, including the formation of political schools, discussion forums in government and mass organizations, bans of nonscientific and technical literature from "imperialist" countries alien to Marxist-Leninist teachings, and means of strengthening "useful" cultures and traditions with the goal of a socialist society in view. At the same time, COPWE was to assume responsibility for creating local organizations "which will execute the directives of the Workers' Party," and for assisting the government in implementing its laws and regulations faithfully "without distorting their class and ideological essence" and without interfering in matters of detail.[29]

The proclamation of COPWE created a structure for party organization that a careful reading makes clear formalized the broad and largely unbounded powers of its chairman. The proclamation explicitly vested in the chairman control of the leadership of COPWE and indirectly of its membership as well. Mengistu became chairman with little evident discussion or controversy. He was given the power to "select, assign, transfer, suspend, and dismiss members of the Central and Executive Committees [and to] select, assign, transfer, suspend, and dismiss officials and members of the COPWE leadership."[30] He was also to prepare regulations concerning the recruitment of members and candidate members to which subordinate bodies of COPWE were to be obliged to adhere. There was no direct indication that either the executive committee or the general assembly would have any power of review and approval of these guidelines. Moreover, he was placed in charge of the relationship between COPWE and the *derg* and given the power to "determine the agenda of the General Assembly, Central Committee, and the executive committee."[31] He was also given broad power to "take the necessary measures to resolve any antirevolutionary situation or a situation which affects the pride and well-being of the people arising while efforts are being made to form the [Workers Party of Ethiopia]."[32]

The proclamation did not vest all of COPWE's authority in the chairman. The general assembly was given the power to approve the general program and internal regulations of COPWE, and local organizations were permitted to offer recommendations on the deployment of new and candidate members. With these exceptions, however, the proclamation vested no power to initiate regulations, proposals, or recommendations in any COPWE organization it established. Though perhaps an implied power, nothing in the proclamation suggested the right or responsibility of any structure within COPWE even to report to higher authorities on its accomplishments and problems. The proclamation confined membership in COPWE exclusively to individuals who were adherents of the NDRP and of Marxist-Leninist principles and who had made "concrete contributions" to advancing the revolution. But such individuals acquired no power of initiative within COPWE, only the power to follow directions issued them.

All members of COPWE were to pay monthly dues, the apportionment of which was not specified. Criminal penalties were to be visited upon anyone, member or nonmember, interfering with the work of COPWE in any fashion. Any person who "obstructs or attempts to obstruct any COPWE activity by means of force, threat or conspiracy *or by any other means*" (emphasis added) would be sentenced to ten years at hard labor. Similar penalties were to be imposed on any person who "infringes or obstructs the implementation" of the proclamation itself or any "regulations, guidelines, decisions, or directives" issued as a result of the proclamation.[33] By contrast to the previous NDRP no other parties were to be permitted to form in the transition to an overarching workers party. COPWE under Mengistu's largely omnipotent chairmanship was to have sole responsibility for defining a future single-party, workers-led state. The parallel between the illusion of structure and the reality of personal rule in the old regime and in the military government was no longer invisible or a matter of conjecture.

In the first years of its existence COPWE established itself at the grass roots through the formation of approximately 6,500 cells whose total membership was uncertain. In the process of building at the grass roots as well as at the central level, COPWE has drawn heavily on the ranks of the military. The seven members of the the executive committee of COPWE at the beginning were military men, and all were members of the PMAC's own standing committee. The other members of the standing committee, all military men found places on the central committee. Moreover, 79 of the 123 standing and alternate members of COPWE were drawn from the ranks of the military or the police. All the commanders of the military sectors, who were promoted to brigadier general on the occasion, became members. The dominance of military officers extended to COPWE subcommittees and to subnational levels, even as they have also been appointed to fill most of the governorships at regional and lower levels.[34]

The converse of military preeminence in COPWE was the underrepresentation of other important constituencies, especially in the executive committee and the central committee. No representatives of youth organizations were included, and there were only two women. Labor unions and peasant associations were included in the large COPWE congresses but not in the two leadership committees. Moreover, the ethnic composition of the two committees allegedly overrepresented Amhara and Tigre at the expense of the many other communities that had expected the revolution to produce liberation from the effects of imperial conquest wrought by the emperors.[35]

Increasingly, Mengistu and his government came to see individualism at the grass roots, especially in rural areas, as more than predictable peasant stubbornness; he viewed such behavior as part of a syndrome of antirevolutionary behavior, including hoarding, corruption, and unresponsiveness to directives, all of which signified antirevolutionary allegiance. The organization of the urban *kebelles* and, in March 1982, of the All-Ethiopia Peasants Association and All-Ethiopia Trade Union were both substantially tightened on the premise that antirevolutionary attitudes and behavior had corroded the development efforts. A Revolutionary Ethiopian Women's Association and a Revolutionary Ethiopian Youth Association, both of which were initially organized at the grass roots, were brought under central government direction in 1980.[36] More explicit still was the creation in September 1981 of special courts and workers committees to control such "opposition campaigns."[37] Said the *derg* of this problem in creating the special courts:

> For some time now these enemies of our revolution have changed their methods of struggle and have started the very dangerous but final plan of hatching covert plots to challenge our revolution. The covert plot of antipeople elements against our revolution is expressed today in the form of exploitation, wastefulness, extortion, bribery, pilfering and individualism.[38]

The Mengistu government's concerns were not without foundation. Its campaigns, military and quasi-military, against "domestic" and "international" opponents in pursuit of military and development targets did not eliminate opposition. Reports of the activities of a labyrinth of opposition groups were necessarily shadowy, imprecise, and difficult to verify. Nor could the extent of their inroads on the loyalties of the government's subjects be ascertained easily or clearly. However, the Eritrean liberation movements have by no means been defeated. As of January 1988 the Eritrean People's Liberation Front appeared to have achieved preeminence among its rivals, which have alternately collaborated, fought, and made separate overtures to Addis Ababa. The Tigrean People's Liberation Front appears to have survived and gained increasing strength, and as such it represents a new extension of the area effectively lost to control from Addis Ababa since 1974. In the southern provinces the Oromo Liberation Front remains an active force, apparently joined by many members of the once-powerful Somali-Abo Liberation Front, as is the Western Somalia Liberation Front.

The Ethiopian People's Revolutionary Party, Meison, and the Ethiopian Democratic Union have all suffered military defeat at the hands of the Mengistu government, but they continue to exist and have been reported to have joined in the creation of a shadowy Ethiopian National Democratic Front (ENDF). To date, Mengistu has survived known unhappiness within the ranks of his own military establishment. Among the sources of such discontent have been the role of the militias established by *kebelles* and peasant associations, loss of access to land which had been a reward for service in the emperor's armies, the role of the Soviets and Cubans, and the effect of militarization of the revolution in allegedly dissipating and deprofessionalizing the ranks of the armed forces at the cost of the country's security—precisely the regime's reason for politicizing them.

The strength of opposition has been very difficult to gauge. It has been the Mengistu government's evident supposition that these residual animosities, military at times, have expressed themselves through economic foot-dragging and noncooperation. Indeed, some regime opponents in exile have suggested that such economic guerrilla warfare exists and is the best available means for destabilizing the regime's rule and the de facto state it has sought to institutionalize. One possible measure of political as well as economic protest is increased growing of *chat* in place of coffee on which the country's export economy is if anything even more dependent than before.

The Mengistu regime sought relief from such continued opposition to its rule by the creation of a special penal code and a special court system to hear cases falling under the code. The proclamation establishing the court enabled it to block any economic transaction pending a hearing on its legitimacy and to subpoena any person or document necessary for the conduct of such hearings. The head of state, Mengistu, assumed personal authority to appoint judges, prosecutors, and other personnel for these courts. One level of appeal was permitted. The courts were to function in accordance with procedures codified in existing civil and criminal codes. Penalties up to and including life imprisonment and execution were within the competence of the court, with these most extreme penalties made the subject of personal review by the head of state.

The workers control committees were established to eradicate unlawful practices such as abuse of authority, carelessness, cheating, giving and taking bribes, and hooliganism as well as inefficiency and overbureaucratization.[39] The Workers National Control Committee was to be a centralized body with responsibility to oversee the accounts of any organization or individual private or public, the implementation of all rules and guidelines, prosecution of individuals found to be in criminal default in the performance of their duties, protection against the misuse of natural resources, investigation of possible misdeeds, and ways to "control inefficiency and work delays." The committee was to establish subordinate committees at all subnational levels.

The military government reemphasized extension of military institutions to the society at large and the blending of military and development campaigns as different forms of combat to be organized in similar ways through the National Military Service Proclamation.[40] All Ethiopian citizens aged 18 to 50 were rendered liable to military service for terms of up to 24 months, which could be extended in war, during which time the government undertook the major responsibility of providing all their material needs. A principal justification of the new law was that "the youth of the country can contribute to the economic and social development of the country" in the process of national military service.[41] At about the same time, the *derg* also established a National Defense and Security Council whose mandate extended not only to defense concerns but to a range of nonmilitary crises, e.g., those of an ecological nature.

The PMAC statement introducing the national military service edict provided a striking rationale for this further militarization of Ethiopian life. "Military aptitude," it said, "was ingrained in the nation's culture" and had been instrumental in preserving the country's unity. Remarkably, furthermore, it cited with approval military exploits of the modern founders of the empire it had overthrown—Tewodros, Johannes, and Menelik—that had preserved the country against its external enemies. By contrast it scored Haile Selassie and his entourage for abandoning the field of battle during the Italian invasion of 1936. Thus, in one of its first retrospective quests for historical sources for its own legitimacy, the *derg* seemed to conclude that it was military campaigns that had preserved Ethiopia's unity as much or more than broader political and cultural factors cited by scholars of Ethiopian history.[42] The military government drew the conclusion that "the national military service will cement class solidarity between the armed forces and the broad masses."[43]

On these foundations the military government sponsored the formation of a single ruling workers' party, which officially became the government of the country in September 1984, the tenth anniversary of the overthrow of Haile Selassie's government. However, the Provisional Military Administrative Council did not dissolve but continued in a vaguely articulated role as a partner of the WPE. Both were chaired by Mengistu. At its inception the leadership of the party closely resembled that of COPWE. The politburo included all of COPWE's executive committee, all of whom were also officers of the Provisional Military Administrative Council though they generally dropped references to their military rank. Although many civilians were included in the central committee, 17 generals, 12 other officers, and 45 individuals no longer using their military rank constituted 55 percent its membership. All of the PMAC's standing and central committees and most of the officers in charge of the universal military service were included in the central committee.

Over the next three years this Workers' Party of Ethiopia in turn promulgated (1) its own program for the future of the country, (2) a draft constitution of a People's Democratic Republic pledged to establishment of a socialist society, and (3) a ten-year plan to encompass the second decade of post-imperial Ethiopia. Included in the WPE program were outlines of a comprehensive policy toward the country's component nationalities reflected in the new constitution approved in February 1987 and formally inaugurated six months later. Only then was the PMAC formally dissolved.

The WPE government hailed each of these developments as critical milestones rather than as end products in the process of bringing to fruition a socialist revolution in Ethiopia led by an alliance of workers and peasants with the participation of the army as well as other "democratic" elements of society. The government continued to consider this political reorganization consistent with the 1976 National Democratic Revolutionary Program (NDRP), the blueprint for the new order, although in fact civil war and international conflict produced had tolled its collapse and set in motion de facto processes of state formation bearing little resemblance to those publicly envisaged by the *derg* or its opponents.

Thus, from September 1984 to September 1987 the obvious question became whether and to what extent the transition from provisional military to Workers' Party rule would become more than symbolic. The fundamental and underlying issue became how far, if at all, the WPE government would undertake to depart from the military regime's de facto constitution of the post-imperial state as synonymous with itself. To what extent would it undertake to constitute a post-imperial Ethiopian state that in fact as well as theory accommodated political participation by those other constituencies whose credentials for leadership in the transformation of the state had been denied by the *derg*, symbolic adherence to the National Democratic Revolution of 1976 to the contrary notwithstanding? Would the WPE regime recognize that peasants, proletarians, youth, women, professionals, small-business people, and civil servants had come of age politically? Would it consider that these groups had been legitimately organized for participation in the post-imperial state as they demanded in the February Revolution and as they appeared to be promised in the NDRP?

The evidence suggests such a momentous transition occurred more in symbolic than real terms between late 1984 and early 1988. Mengistu Haile Mariam assumed the position of general secretary of the WPE as well as the roles of chairman of the PMAC and commander in chief of the armed forces. The dropping of military titles in favor of the universal "comrade" made less apparent but no less real the prevalence of military people in the power structure of the party, especially in the upper reaches. Moreover, the PMAC was not abolished but remained formally in existence as Mengistu's titles attested. To judge from who ruled Ethiopia, the succession to power of the WPE was a change of form more than of substance and, by itself, seemed to portend an intention of less rather than more transformation in the character of the regime. Representation of other constituencies within the WPE appeared to be on the basis of strict subordination within a hierarchy controlled at the apex by Mengistu that continued to rest upon rather than relax the foundations of martial rule outlined above. The formation of national and regional *shengoes,* or assemblies, represented the renewed promise and large potential, but in early 1988 not yet the reality, of a long-sought and much-heralded reconstitution of the state on foundations broader than the military and martial rule.

The Program of the Workers' Party of Ethiopia set forth the goal of socialism "and ultimately of communism."[44] Candidly, the Program recognized that the socialized sphere of the economy was small vis-à-vis the private sectors. The Program pledged to expand the sphere of the socialized sector and to strengthen its organization. It recognized that the socialized and private sectors were in competition and that regulation of the private sector would be required to prevent it undermining the socialized public sector. To further the organization of the public sector, the Program postulated further strengthened organization of the WPE itself as a first requisite.

The proposed strengthening of the WPE drew upon Marxist-Leninist imagery to legitimize establishment of the dictatorship the *derg* had previously established de facto in its struggle to survive. To this end, the Program argued for the necessity of a transition from a broad alliance of working-class cadres, the peasantry, the armed forces, the "revolutionary intelligentsia, small business men and office workers" toward an eventual proletarian dictatorship. However, nothing in the Program recognized the de facto existence of a military dictatorship, the task of effecting a transition from military to working-class dictatorship, or the fact that the "broad alliance" and its pre-dictatorship working-class leadership had never been achieved—all as a result of the civil and regional wars and the Mengistu regime's struggle to prevail in them.

To support the stated political objective of proletarian dictatorship, the Program attributed great importance to mass organizations in agriculture and all sectors of the economy. These, it argued, "must not be based on spontaneity" but on "mutual support and complementarity of activities."[45] An important application of this policy was to be the reorganization and relocation of the peasantry from peasant associations based on scattered households to producer cooperatives organized on the basis of rural producers' resettlement in villages.

While foreseeing a transition from an agriculturally to an industrially based economy, the Program emphasized the primacy of agriculture in the short to medium term. The Program's central strategy in agriculture was to "change the agriculture of the country into modern and large scale farms stage by stage" within which more advanced technology and strengthened organization of production would be possible. The corollaries of the strategy were to be redoubled efforts to establish state farms and to transform peasant associations into producer cooperatives facilitating not only stronger organization and more advanced technology but better social and production services and increasingly socialized trade and distribution facilities. Pastoral populations were also to be settled. The Program recognized that in this process care must be taken to conserve and nurture the country's eroding natural resource base.

To these ends the Program pledged creation of an efficient system of economic management based on principles of democratic centralism and strong central and regional planning, but it stated no intention to alter the departures from Marxist-Leninist orthodoxy even in the *design* of democratic centralism discussed above. Rather the implementation provisions appeared to reinforce instead of modify the command-based economic organization previously established by the *derg*. This emphasis was reflected in the stated intention that in order "to help control plan implementation and the observance of planning discipline, the periodic plans will be formulated in the form of laws."[46] The Program placed considerable reliance upon the previously established workers control committees to ensure sound management and appropriate responses, thereby avoiding waste and inefficiency that it associated with the old regime.

The Program recognized the existence of nationalities and pledged equality of treatment for nationalities within the new Ethiopia. However, it made clear that the primary expression of such equality would be in the economic sphere. "Since economic relations are the basis for the oppression of nationalities," it said, "it is in this sphere more than in any other that the expression of their equality has to be guaranteed."[47] The influence of civil and regional war in the Mengistu government's de facto departure from the nationalities policies contained in the National Democratic Revolutionary Program was apparent, for the Program was clear that national self-determination was not to be perverted by the enemies of revolution into secession and would be expressed particularly in economic cooperation.

The Program seemed to rationalize the existing political structure by setting forth economic objectives whose achievement by legally enforceable legislation could only be approached by continuation or reinforcement of existing draconian measures. Having made strong economic performance an important measure of progress toward socialism and vanquishing residual influences of the old regime and/or its allies, the military government proceeded to set extremely high standards for itself in meeting those objectives in the Ten Year Plan (TYP). External economic analysts of the Ten Year Plan have been virtually unanimous in thinking the Plan unrealizable and imprudent.[48] The Plan set a target of 6.5 percent per annum increase in gross domestic product GDP, including 4.3 percent in agriculture, 10.6 percent in industry and 6.5 percent in services. It recognized that to achieve an increase in savings as percentage of GDP from 3.0 percent to 15.0 percent would mean that the "effort to restrain consumption and stimulate the growth of savings will be considerable."[49] It pledged a "tremendous effort" to increase export earnings from 13.2 percent to 15.4 percent of GDP during the Plan period.

In agriculture the Plan goals were food self-sufficiency and greatly expanded productive capacity to be accomplished through socialist reorganization of production. This reorganization was to accomplish more than a *thirteen*fold increase in the number of producer cooperatives to embrace more than 50 percent of rural households from the present 1.2 percent. It planned to double the cultivated area encompassed by state farms and to "hasten the socialization of the trade and transport sectors of the economy."

In addition, the Plan anticipated major expansion in human resource development to eradicate literacy still variously estimated at from 40 to 60 percent of the population in 1984, to expand health services to reach 85 percent of the population, to create an additional five million jobs, half a million new houses, to eliminate or substantially modify regional disparities in income and standards of living, and to meet the requirements of war victims requiring rehabilitation.

A central feature of the Plan and the TYP was the contrast between reiteration of the renewed objectives with respect to the working classes and continued reliance on structures just established to compel their obedience. Both the Plan and the TYP foresaw reorganized modes of production, increased production from the working classes, and improvement in their standards of living and their leadership. Yet the structures set in place by the military government since 1978, and endorsed by the Plan and the TYP, did little even formally to suggest that such classes should assume greater control over their own circumstances let alone assert nationwide leadership. To the extent that the military men in the government regarded themselves as belonging to the working classes, the issue then became the extent to which the military would share leadership with other segments of the working class. To a remarkable extent, however, the WPE leadership of the country treated very lightly the issue of its own legitimacy within the framework of the prescribed adherence to the teachings of Marx and Lenin.

On these political and economic foundations the WPE government proposed to establish a constitution for the People's Democratic Republic.[50] The draft constitution enshrined the leading role of the WPE itself, which would nominate members for election to the national *shengo* (or National Council) and, in a revolutionary break with historical precedent, shengos also at local levels.[51] The national *shengo* was in turn to elect the president and a council of state chaired by the president. The council was to supervise the council of ministers, the courts, and—another important innovation—a procurator general responsible for ensuring adherence to state regulations in very much the role of the *derg*, at least prior to the creation of the WPE. The draft lent constitutional legitimacy to the broad outlines of the WPE economic program while guaranteeing a broad panoply of individual rights. The new constitution did not indicate how such constitutional rights would be reconciled with the martial organization of the country established by the military regime before its promulgation.

The draft constitution was ambivalent on the question of nationalities. While emphasizing "the realization of autonomy," it nonetheless stated unequivocally that Ethiopia "is a unitary state in which all nationalities live in equality."[52] Based on the Plan, the implication was that the equality would be expressed more in economic than in political terms.

It did, however, emphasize the development of the languages of the nationalities.[53]

A principal issue posed by the constitution draft was whether its institutionalization would result in even the appearance of transformation or confirmation of the de facto military structure of rule greatly reinforced by the *derg* since 1979. There was little evidence that the military regime's continuing adversaries found even such appearances. In one official response, the Eritrean People's Liberation Front saw no commitment to recognize or make financially feasible the political autonomy of nationalities within boundaries they themselves considered legitimate. It questioned the extent to which the array of individual rights set forth in the constitution would in fact be honored, given the regime's past history.[54]

The launching of the WPE government and the ratification and inauguration of the new constitution appeared to bring to fruition a thirteen-year struggle to erect a people's democratic republic on foundations of an Ethiopian state assumed to have survived the demise of the institutions of feudal-imperial rule. The preceding analysis has suggested, however, that the new republic rested on continuing rather than temporary structures of martial rule established by the Mengistu regime to (1) consolidate in the political and economic spheres its progress in quelling military challenges to its rule and (2) preserve the existing perimeters of the Ethiopian state as established by the emperors. The regime has appeared to rely on the *practice* of Marxism-Leninism, e.g., democratic centralization, as a *theoretical* ideological rationale for its exertions. The fruits of its initiatives appear to have been (1) abolition of the institutions of the old regime more than transformation of the foundations of the state on which they rested by enhancing the economic and political power of classes previously oppressed and (2) a de facto shrinking of the effective boundaries of the preexisting state as a result primarily of broadened insurgency in the north.

Military Rule and Socioeconomic Transformation

In the military's management of development efforts based on its revolutionary reforms, the temporal and the spatial dimensions of the quest for the post-imperial Ethiopian state have converged, especially in the agrarian sector that in turn is central to the health of the country's economy as a whole. There have been some good years, spurred in large part by good rains and/or favorable international prices for the country's agricultural exports. These years have been the exception proving the rule that the country's agrarian crisis has continued largely unabated, notwithstanding the comprehensive reforms undertaken by the military regime. Poverty, ecological degradation, age-old land tenure insecurities restated in new forms, periodic famine, and heavy impositions by the country's power structure (albeit because of revolutionary rather than reactionary intentions) continue to afflict rural households as before.

Prior to 1974 these elements of agrarian crisis reflected the nature and contradictions of an *ancien regime* whose institutions continued to define the Ethiopian state in feudal-imperial terms while purporting to strengthen it through more rapid economic development. An important thesis of this chapter is that underlying the continued Ethiopian agrarian crisis are not only unwise official policies but grass roots expressions of the macro-level contrast between the symbolic and substantial transformation of that inherited state structure just described. This section will also argue that the military regime's martial approach to development, deriving in the first instance from its struggles to preserve and transform the Ethiopian state in macro terms, is neither necessary nor appropriate in pursuing the same ends at the grass roots. Improving the country's general poor economic performance since 1974 and realizing the socioeconomic promise of its would-be revolution would appear to depend upon not only policy changes but improved management. To a significant degree, however, such alterations depend in turn upon progress in transforming the Ethiopian state at the grass roots along lines envisaged but so far elusive at the macro level. Finally, the chapter suggests that opportunity for such transformation at the micro level may not only be greater than but, more speculatively, the foundation for similar results in macro terms.

The Transformation of the Peasantry

The Mengistu regime and its adversaries, who have fought over the ends and processes of transforming the Ethiopian state, have shared the conviction that a major objective of the transformation should be socioeconomic liberation of peasants and tenants shackled by primordial feudal-imperial relations of production. At the macro level the regime and its challengers have exposed fundamental issues of state transformation through their struggles over the political credentials of particular classes or class fragments to lead the transformation. Their shared recognition that all but the few had been oppressed under the old order was dissipated by conflict over whether their respective political credentials to lead the transformation had been tarnished through material cooptation *through their organizations* by the old regime. Largely overlooked in the course of this conflict has been the condition of the classes *themselves* and how their reorganization might prepare and strengthen them for revolutionary leadership.

At the micro level, however, the transformation of the peasantry as a class as well as liberation of rural producers' productive capacities has been a central objective of the regime's reforms. However, the regime's agrarian management has in fact betrayed at best ambivalence toward not only the organizations for peasant revolutionary participation but also the transformation of the peasantry itself. The underlying reason has been that agrarian management processes, billed and perhaps intended by the regime as means of liberating the peasantry, have in fact been extensions of its macro-level struggle with its adversaries over leadership in transforming the Ethiopian state.

The stated objectives of and asserted progress achieved by the regime's agrarian policies and management have been clearly set forth (emphasis added):

> Thanks to the radical changes that have been effected in the rural areas, the peasants are no more *an ignorant mass on which the idle parasitic landlords and usurers flourish.* They are ridding themselves of illiteracy, ill-health, and domination of any sort. Instead of being a double object of exploitation the peasants have become a conscious and organized power to reckon with.[55]

This remarkable glimpse into the mind of the military leadership revealed its perception that the rural poor were no more prepared for partnership with the military in advancing the social revolution, at the time of its initiation, than were other civilian constituencies with which it warred. Moreover, as recounted above, the military in effect defined the peasantry as lacking due patriotism in failing to produce for the market during the height of the civil and regional wars. Thus, continued submission by peasants and tenants to exploitation under the old regime disqualified them, in the military government's view, at least for immediate full partnership in a social revolution launched in large part for their own advancement. But the military asserted that through its comprehensive and thorough efforts to control rural peoples, their political organizational and socioeconomic liberation had begun to come to pass. The facts, however, seem not to justify such an assertion even in terms of the regime's own stated objectives and criteria.

Haile Selassie effectively applied internationally fashionable economic wisdom favoring import substitution strategies to his own political purposes of regime support. So, too, the military's Ten Year Plan appeared to rationalize its objectives through reliance on two elements of conventional wisdom concerning agricultural development: predictable decreases in the size of the agricultural vis-à-vis the industrial sector and industrialization and gradual progression from smaller, more atomistic units of production and social organization to larger, more corporate ones—including in this case, collectivized ones. First, the military regime has invested very lightly in agriculture, as though it were of secondary or tertiary importance to manufacturing or service sectors, when in fact it is the primary one for the foreseeable future. Despite its evident priority in the short to medium term, agriculture and settlement continued to account for only 3 percent of central government current expenditure in 1985–1986, although it did claim about one-third of capital expenditure in the same year or approximately 15 percent of total expenditure.[56] Meanwhile agriculture continued to contribute nearly 50 percent of gross domestic product and provide a living for 80 percent of the work force.[57]

Second, the government has been true to its announced intention of encouraging larger-scale and more collectivized units of production over those of smallholders who acquired individual usufructuary rights within peasant associations under the terms of the 1975 reform. The government has engineered a nearly fivefold increase in the acreage under state farms, from about 67,000 hectares in 1974 to nearly 330,000 hectares by the early 1980s, with plans to further double the hectarage by 1994. Similarly, although only 1.2 percent of agricultural households had been mobilized into producer cooperatives in the first five years of the program, the military regime pledged to incorporate over 50 percent during the next ten. The regime's rationale was familiar and clearly articulated in its Ten Year Plan: the pooling of labor and other resources in rural areas was to support the introduction of advanced technology with resulting increases in production and productivity.[58]

To support its strategy the regime has heavily channeled productive resources assigned to agriculture toward the state farms and producer cooperatives. Occupying but 3.2 percent of agricultural land in 1984, state farms received 85 percent of agricultural credit and nearly 75 percent of improved seeds. Moreover, the regime has required the peasant associations to support the formation of producer cooperatives. Service cooperatives, initially established to process peasant association output and agricultural inputs, have been required to contribute 25 percent of their profits to the formation of producer cooperatives and to give the producer cooperatives priority in all their operations. Producer cooperative members have been given preferential tax treatment, jurisdiction over any common lands held by peasant associations within which they form, and producer cooperative members are to have been represented prominently on the governing committees of their corresponding peasant associations. At least in Arusi, peasant associations have often been chaired by members of producer cooperatives formed within their midst.[59]

Producer cooperatives have received first priority in the sale of any oxen within a peasant association, the shortage of which has been a critical constraint in post-land reform development. They have been guaranteed access to fertile land within peasant associations and priority in distribution of fertilizer, improved seeds, the time of extension agents, and innovations in cattle breeding. Producer cooperatives have received greater inducements to participate in the official economy through priority access to consumer goods, farmgate prices from the Agricultural Marketing Corporation above those paid by the service cooperatives, and more opportunities for training in agricultural skills. According to Cohen and Isaksson, the regime has made the spread of producer cooperatives the primary objective of the service cooperatives.[60]

Minimal resources for the agricultural sector and their concentration on state farms and producer cooperatives have combined to exclude the great majority of rural households from participation in the reformed rural political economy prophesied in the declaration of the 1975 land reform proclamation. The regime's actions have effectively denied the country's own economic and by extension political base of power in the rural areas where most Ethiopians continue to live and work. The stark facts are that 95 percent of production and 65 percent of marketed production have continued to originate from the smallholder sector notwithstanding the government's concentration of resources on state farms. Moreover, within the small-farm sector, producer cooperatives have not yet begun to challenge the size, production, or productivity of the peasant association subsector despite the advantages offered them. Virtually all the marketed production upon which the country as a whole depends has emanated from four provinces: Gondar, Gojjam, Shoa, and Arusi representing only 38 percent of the rural population. Most of the marketed surplus of these four regions is sold to the government and distributed by it to four principal cities plus the military. Despite the axiomatic efficiency of small producers, the government relies heavily on the production of very inefficient state farms to distribute grain within this very restricted sphere.

Thus, the military government's attempt to generate rural development by control and command has excluded a large body of producers whose economic behavior it has been unable to control by such means. It has yet to succeed in bringing economic results commensurate with the concentration of official resources in those subsectors and regions wherein its writ has run on such terms. The result has been to shrink in scope and diminish in strength the effective size of the rural economic sector upon which the regime may rely as bases for telescoping officially sponsored industrialization and agricultural production on an enlarged, technologically sophisticated scale. It has left relatively unattended the interests of substantially larger communities of rural producers in accomplishing development for its own sake and as a protection against recurrent drought and famine through land reform measures created by the military government ostensibly for such purposes. A historically fundamental purpose of the state has been to defend its citizens' physical security against external attack and internal violence. Perhaps today that purposes should be broadened to include defense against ecological catastrophe as well. In that case, the regime's practice has objectively tended to weaken the foundations of a modern Ethiopian state itself.

In political terms, moreover, the regime's approach to effecting rural transformation has risked continuation of the very disinheritance of the peasantry that fueled demands for revolutionary change before 1974 by excluding rather than engaging rural producers. Having gone to war to defend the geographical integrity of the Ethiopian polity as defined by its imperial predecessor, the regime has risked shrinking the effective perimeters of the agricultural sector upon which the economy of the post-imperial state depends in at least the medium term.

The disengagement of the peasantry in the regime's allocation of resources to agriculture has been matched in management of the agrarian reforms it has instituted. One of the clearest recent pictures of the nature and profoundly disturbing impact of the government's management of the rural socioeconomic transformation appeared in a paper by Dessalegn Rahmato on a resettlement project in Gojjam.[61] The settlement in Mettekel district was hastily chosen to accommodate land-poor drought victims from neighboring Wollo and Tigre provinces, though it in fact drew from overcrowded but less drought-afflicted Kambatta district. The settlement was hastily organized at the outset, and several attempts, costly in both human and economic terms, were necessary before it was actually established. Even then it was located in an area known to be waterlogged and unhealthy and easily accessible only by helicopter. The site was chosen on the inaccurate assumption that the land was unused by the resident Begga peoples, who practice shifting cultivation and whose interests received no consideration. The settlement prompted overcultivation of marginal lands both by the settlers themselves and by the Begga within their diminished domain. The delicate balance between people and environment was thus upset, posing an ecological and economic threat to the viability of both the new and the host communities, not to mention the unlikelihood that either would be in a position to contribute to the country's economic development. According to the account, these difficulties were greeted by managing officials with nothing but indifference. The medium of structural change was the message, its significance for underlying processes of social and ecological change remaining unheard.

An important issue is the relative contributions of the two major parameters of the government's rural development management, telescoping and enlarging socioeconomic structures of production, to the outcomes achieved. Serious charges were leveled against the government for its precipitous decision in 1984 to resettle 1.5 million Ethiopians from drought-affected areas of the north to more fertile, less populous regions in the south within the space of less than two years. The government did halt this campaign after some 600,000 were settled in the face of international outcries that the hasty, unplanned, poorly supported, and largely involuntary relocations had produced tens of thousands of deaths, while many who survived were reduced to brigandage in a desperate effort to survive.[62] Some have argued, perhaps with some justification, that the numbers of deaths have been exaggerated, that the government did issue a rare admission of error, and that the problem was not the concept of resettlement long-recommended by agricultural exports but the haste and poor preparation accompanying the efforts.[63] The adverse human consequences for the people involved, however, were enormous regardless of the relative contributions of inappropriate management and poor design.

An in-depth study of 84 settlement schemes undertaken *prior* to the famine-induced resettlement campaign and with somewhat less drama and urgency has suggested that inadequate planning and implementation, not just haste per se, left the ecological and economic viability of most schemes in doubt.[64] The study observed a failure to plan the schemes carefully and implement them according to published specifications. Interview data included in the study suggested that management shortcomings, in the eyes of the settlers, were the most pervasive of the difficulties they experienced. Many lacked schools, clinics, and other infrastructure. High land and labor costs have yielded returns far below expectations. The major long-term consequence, however, has been the losing struggle of the settlement communities themselves to achieve viability. Some settlers have deserted because they were brought to the schemes involuntarily, while many others have left because they were not permitted to bring their families with them. Producer cooperatives established on most schemes have not succeeded in instituting procedures for mediating ethnic and other social conflicts. Only a handful of the settlement communities were prepared to be locally self-supporting after the three years allotted to achieve that objective.

Settlement scheme results may not always fairly measure the achievements of a rural social revolution, for they characteristically bring together strangers, urban unemployed, transplanted pastoralists, and families suffering from the stresses of the settlement process itself. Moreover, other countries with regimes of a very different character have experienced comparable results. By contrast, villagization, a more distinctive hallmark of the Ethiopian rural transformation, is analytically distinct from other forms of resettlement in that it has brought together established farming households within the same precincts they have historically cultivated.

Those assembled together are not necessarily restricted to the poor and destitute from a variety of economic sectors, but may include more experienced and established farming households. The major change, however, is a pattern of residence facilitating community organization and economies of scale in the delivery of social services, agricultural support, and the introduction of more sophisticated production technologies. These objectives are in themselves not necessarily uncontroversial. Far more controversial, however, is the government's resort to villagization as a means of denying producers access to private markets and price competition with the government, controlling their consumption and accumulation, and dictating their form of social organization, i.e., the establishment of producer cooperatives.

Cohen and Isaksson's study was the most thorough examination of the process of villagization prior to 1988, though the authors were careful to emphasize the dangers of generalization from the special circumstances of the Arusi region in which they conducted their investigations.[65] While they found little evidence of farmers being compelled to move to villages without regard to their preferences or timing in terms of the agricultural production cycle, they did conclude that "despite the government's statement that the major reason for promoting villages is to make it easier for rural people to get basic human services, the mission found little evidence that there is a coherent, financially realistic plan for achieving that objective."[66] At the same time, the government administrative resources, disproportionately concentrated on villages and producer cooperatives, have been heavily devoted to tasks of enforcing villagization itself and compelling village support for regime policies largely to the exclusion of realizing development purposes and potential used to justify such rural restructuring. As of early 1988, it remained to be seen when and whether the regime would turn from the processes of collectivization itself to these development purposes. In February 1988, however, in response to World Bank and other donor pressures, the regime did agree to increase prices to producers and relax restrictions on private trade in agricultural produce. It was not clear then to what extent this signaled relaxation of pressure for further collectivization.

The deployment of agricultural extension personnel has also dramatized the regime's working priorities. Several studies have noted the lack of emphasis on promotion and dissemination of agricultural research and improved technical training for extension agents. They have observed the government's reliance instead upon extension personnel to establish producer cooperatives, enforce adherence to government directions, and extract contributions in cash and in kind for official campaigns such as famine relief and drought protection.[67] An important irony is that while the regime is to be commended for addressing long-term ecological requirements, e.g., tree-planting and small-scale irrigation, official priorities in the planning and implementation of villages and producer cooperatives may have served to undermine these laudable campaigns. These campaigns have often failed to take account of and plan for possibly adverse the ecological consequences of such rural reorganization, e.g., soil depletion and erosion.

More generally, the available reports have suggested that the government has yet to treat those peasants who have participated in its campaigns for villagization, collectivization and resettlement as the liberated rural citizenry it has claimed as the objects of its labors. A 1986 International Labor Organization survey reported that "The interaction between the community and the government appears in general to be bureaucratic in style, dominating over people, instructing and teaching 'ignorant' peasants what to do and treating peasants as objects to be acted upon rather than subjects of change. Such interventions stifle the initiative of peasants."[68] Other accounts have suggested that peasant association and producer cooperative meetings have been dominated by government officials issuing instructions and demanding adherence to them at the expense of these bodies' deliberative functions. The preliminary indications have been, thus, that the government has so far employed structural change to implement rural reforms as a vehicle for regime maintenance, for directing and controlling the lives of rural Ethiopians at the expense not only of development but of the socioeconomic and political transformation of the peasantry as a class.

Given the highly centralized decision making in Addis Ababa and the critical importance of skilled development management at the grass roots in promoting the success of collectivization through villagization and resettlement, much depends upon effective lines of communication between the capital and periphery. Yet there have been indications that serious administrative shortcomings continue to exist despite official efforts to revamp the administrative structures and reorient civil service personnel. Many such deficiencies are endemic to development management, but some appear particularly to have been functions of the regime's struggle for power and its resultant approaches to administering development processes.

First, administrative entropy has adversely affected those working within the regime's management structures in ways analogous to the effects of these structures upon their clients, the rural producers. Symptoms have been found particularly in the management of the state farms. An in-house appraisal of the state farm sector by the Ministry of State Farms has suggested that decision-making authority and material rewards have been excessively centralized within a complex, multitiered bureaucratic structure.[69] Conversely, resources, information for administrative decision-making, and incentives to make decisions optimally have been absent the closer one gets to the level of the individual state farm firms. A principal and ironic consequence has been that the administrative resources concentrated on state farms, upon which the cities and the regime have been so dependent economically, have diminished rather than enhanced the regime's ability to control them and maximize their service to the regime and its *raison d'état* for deploying them.

Second, if agrarian reform management in Ethiopia has been diminished by diversion of human resources from their appropriate purposes and by administrative entropy, an important corollary has been that the regime's demands upon these resources have frequently exceeded their capacity to respond. The Agricultural Marketing Corporation has been a salient example. A 1983 joint government-World Bank study concluded that the AMC's capacity to function within the parameters established by fairly rigid government directives had been stretched to the limit.[70] The AMC is obliged to handle *all* grain sales in four provinces in addition to all the output of the state farms. It must purchase 50 percent of grain from the other regions at prices set by the government and, in principle, in volumes established by quotas issued by the government. But AMC has lacked the trucks, storage facilities, and staff for collection stations to purchase and deliver all the grain available in surplus areas in timely fashion.[71] At the same time, officially mandated uniform and fixed prices have prevented AMC from offering remunerative prices to farmers in the surplus areas, upon which the official economy depends, though the AMC nevertheless remains under continuing official pressure to increase its share of marketed production.

Third, literacy along with land reform has been one of the twin pillars of the military regime's strategy for liberating Ethiopia's rural poor. Despite their success, however, the literacy campaigns have illustrated another dimension of the regime's misdirection of finite administrative resources. On the one hand, the result of the several campaigns has been a geometric increase in the country's literacy levels. One study remarked that one effect had been to moderate considerably a prevalent preexisting belief that nonformal education is the poor relation of formal classroom instruction. Nevertheless, the study also observed that "the most conspicuous feature of the operation of the National Literacy Campaign (has been) its monolithic, hierarchical committee structure and uniform *modus operandi*," and that literacy campaigns had been enmeshed in a committee structure of "staggering" proportions.[72] The same study suggested that the literacy results were to a considerable measure achieved in spite of rather than because of the educational hierarchy, and that results were "more dependent upon initiative and leadership at the grass roots level than on structural formalities."⁷³ Several reports have suggested that primary schools have experienced little official contact with ministry officials and have been forced to fall back upon their own resources and initiative. The government's pursuit of comprehensive control of rural socialization through the literacy campaign, the study implied, had proven counterproductive and self-defeating by in effect delegating the real work of educational development involved to those peripheral to the formal structures.

Fourth, the government has sought to overcome these administrative inadequacies through increased investment in the training of professional personnel and through the mechanism of the Workers' Party of Ethiopia. University enrollment has risen sharply since 1974, the number of campuses has expanded, and emphasis upon professional curricula has become more pronounced. In mid-1987, moreover, the government was in the midst of negotiations for substantial external support to further upgrade higher education. Through better and locally trained personnel, the regime legitimately aspires, *inter alia,* to improve the quality of development management across a variety of sectors. Meanwhile, with the creation of the Workers' Party of Ethiopia, a new instrument has come into existence to strengthen and preserve the focus of the public sector on such key objectives. The open question, however, has been the extent to which the regime will allow these potential sources of development strength to be used optimally. A hallmark of the *ancien regime* was its success in coopting dissident university graduates to its purposes simply by employing them. Yet to be determined is the extent to which the successor regime will follow a different course, i.e., "liberating" its skilled work force by allowing it collectively to apply its expertise to the identification and amelioration of development problems. The fragmentary evidence to date, however, has strongly suggested that the regime's determination to impose control on its own administrative cadres, as it has upon its adversaries, has stifled application of such expertise to improve management in the interests of the regime's own command effectiveness as well strengthened economic performance.

If the regime's preoccupation with control in the wake of its struggles for survival is one apparent contributor to its administrative pathology, an important political consequence has been the isolation of the regime from its constituents or, conversely, its constituents' increased political peripheralization. Specifically, this syndrome has made more difficult removal of obstacles to the engagement of a previously peripheralized peasantry, notwithstanding any existing recognition and concern over its circumstances.

The Peasantry and the Transformation of the State

Goren Hyden's study of Tanzania elucidated peasant capacity to thwart a comprehensive rural transformation on which a regime has staked its own reputation as well as a country's economy.[74] Chapter 1 suggested, however, both a need for greater clarity concerning what a peasantry may be resisting and exploration of a wider range of choices that both regimes and peasants might be prepared to consider in dealing with each other.[75] Indeed, the Ethiopian evidence suggests that the peasantry did not reject the Ethiopian *state* or its transformation, despite ageless exploitation by successive feudal regimes. Rather, it opted broadly to participate at least partially in agrarian reform conceived as an integral component of state transformation. Moreover, rural households do not appear to have rejected transitional military rule in principle, despite the macro-level struggle over that issue. Perhaps most important, the continued peripheralization of most rural households in political and economic terms appeared to have reflected not peasant utilization of the "exit option" but their being "driven out the door" by the regime's management. The reason, as previously described, has been the regime's treatment of agrarian reform management as another theater of conflict with those it has engaged in the country's civil wars, possibly in part because of the military training of its leaders.

Thus, it is on the anvil of agrarian reform management and peasant responses, as well as of agrarian policies themselves, that linkage between macro-level and micro-level quests for the post-imperial Ethiopian state has been forged. As the Ethiopian transformation extended into its second decade, the regime's policies in implementing and extending the agrarian reform and peasant responses have produced not only economic stagnation but, if anything, weakened foundations of the Ethiopian state itself in the process of its transformation.

However, if more appropriate management and wiser policies are required to reverse stagnation in the midst of what was to have been socioeconomic transformation, opportunities as well as a necessity for closing an underlying gap between promised and actual state transformation at the micro level may be present. Whether pursuit of such opportunities at the micro level could establish a stronger foundation for corresponding further macro-level transformation remained a matter of conjecture in early 1988. The pages that follow explore this hypothesis in the context of at least some of the presently defining, and generally discouraging, features of agrarian reform. Because 80 percent of the population is involved, these features are also characteristic of the socioeconomic transformation as a whole.

Acceptance of Land Reform Structures. Rural Ethiopians clearly accepted voluntarily the structure of the rural transformation as outlined in the original 1975 proclamation. In mid-1985, 20,157 peasant associations had been formed embracing approximately 5.6 million households, or perhaps 75 percent of all rural households. Moreover, nearly 80 percent of the peasant associations and their members have joined in the formation of service cooperatives whose functions include marketing of crops, distribution of agricultural inputs, and retailing of consumer goods. Through service cooperatives peasant associations exhibited a distinct, if by 1988 still embryonic, proclivity for building stores, mills, schools, and clinics. Through 1985 slightly fewer than 4,000 service cooperatives had on average accumulated approximately $20,000 of capital apiece, a not insignificant figure given the degree of poverty prevalent in the Ethiopian countryside.

It is not clear, however, how peasant association members have understood the terms of their tenure on the land. There is little evidence to indicate, for example, the extent to which peasant association members recognize and accept that their associations, not they themselves, possess legal jurisdiction over their lands under the terms of Proclamation No. 31. Transfer, subdivision, redistribution, and succession practices offer some clues in this regard. Dessalegn Rahmato, in his 1981 study of land reform in four districts, found that although no land transfers were to occur except via the peasant associations, members had in fact been left on their own to subdivide and redistribute land.[76] They have done so in response to population pressures within the individual associations themselves, since redrawing of peasant association boundaries has not occurred widely, rather than on the basis of any comprehensive officially sanctioned plans. A host of questions have remained almost entirely unanswered, however, in terms of the criteria evolved to effect such adjustments and how they have related to the published criteria contained in Proclamation No. 31. Similarly, little if any evidence has yet been garnered concerning informal patterns of land inheritance. Even the amount of usable land available to rural families is open to question in some areas because of lack of standardized measurement systems.[77]

Thus, one may hypothesize that the Ethiopian peasantry has accepted the formal structures and tenure arrangements imposed by the 1975 proclamation as a framework for economic liberation with the implications for state transformation they implied. However, greater attention to the role of the less collectivized peasant associations in managing peasant socioeconomic change within their jurisdictions would appear to be required. At the same time, slow peasant response to greater collectivization via producer cooperatives would appear to dictate the necessity of compromise. In addition, the differences in the rate of such greater collectivization point to a need for more locally tailored management in the interests of economic performance and the regime's own stated objective of a politically organized revolutionary peasantry. The February 1988 agreement with the World Bank on higher prices for producers and lifting of some restrictions on private trade in grain may have signaled some first steps toward such compromise.

Though acceptance of slower-paced collectivization and more attention to the consolidation of the first phase of land reform need not imply abandonment of the ultimate goal of full collectivization, it would appear to require alteration of the regime's approach to the peasantry. Concentration of the regime's resources on accelerating second-phase collectivization before the first has been consolidated would appear to require treatment of the peasantry less as the objects and more as the subjects of such transformation. That is to say, it would require treatment of peasants less as unprepared for greater control over their own affairs because their transition to full collectivization is incomplete and more as qualified for such empowerment by virtue of having reached an important intermediate stage of transformation. It would involve treatment of the peasant sector less as another theater of war the regime has fought in order to survive and more as one in which critical first steps have been taken toward realizing in practice the regime's postulated design for the post-imperial state. It would appear to involve less regime assertion of arms-length autonomy and more direct involvement with the conditions and circumstances of a class that is a major partner in an evolving Ethiopian state.

Passive Participation. Peasant associations appear to have become instruments for transmission of official directives rather than institutions through which members' interests and concerns are articulated to government. The existing fragmentary evidence suggests that leadership within the associations has been impermanent in duration as well as variable in perceived quality and that the associations have been executive-dominant, with the constituent assemblies playing weak, intermittent, and passive roles. They have been weakly institutionalized: Operating procedures have not been widely discussed and established on the basis of consensus, elections have been held irregularly, and members have rarely used the associations effectively to articulate their concerns and those of their fellows. Alleged "corruption" within the associations becomes a problematic concept given such weakly institutionalized operating norms and procedures. Members have, as a result, appeared to harbor some resentment at the interference with work on their farms of association meetings over which they have little influence.[78]

At the same time, associations have responded to government demands through some combination of fear, resignation, and genuine interest. Defense squads have been formed, recruitment for military campaigns has occurred, schools have been built, taxes have been collected, and official directives received within the framework of the associations. Service cooperatives and producer cooperatives have been formed on the basis of peasant association structures. Moreover, during the period of discussion prior to the ratification of the 1987 constitution, both urban *kebelles* and some peasant associations appear to have been forums for vigorous discussions of some of its provisions: notably one effectively outlawing polygamy, which the government eventually saw fit to withdraw.

The hypothesis emerges that rural households find membership within the associations to continue to be in their interests, notwithstanding confirmation within such frameworks of their traditional political subservience to government officials. One principal issue for arbitration is whether peasant association—and producer cooperative—members will assert and/or the regime will permit such associations to become a forum for the resolution of grievances and arbitration of differences over development management in local settings. A second major issue is whether members will assert and/or government will permit these associations to become vehicles of local self-administration and manifestations of rural people's political and economic expression.

The preliminary evidence has suggested negative answers to both sets of questions. At the same time, however, pressure on the regime for policy changes has appeared virtually to exclude such consideration of management issues, notwithstanding the strong evidence of a correlation between strength of local producer organizations and economic productivity.[79] The possibility exists, therefore, that the regime might be able to encourage strengthened producer economic productivity by encouraging their local organizations to raise and address concerns, many of which might not necessarily involve challenge to overall regime policies. Similarly, external donors might also concentrate on such concerns more than they appear to have done so to date.

Qualified, Reluctant Collectivization. Six years after the government's decision actively to seek the formation of producer cooperatives, only 1,856 had been formed representing but 2 percent of peasant association households, despite all the economic incentives the government has made available to encourage their formation.[80] Few if any producer cooperatives have advanced to second and third stages of producer cooperative formation envisaged by the 1979 policy. At the same time, while Arsi region may have many unique characteristics facilitating villagization that are not to be found elsewhere, at least 1.5 times as many households were villagized in this one province in two years as participated in producer cooperatives throughout the country in the preceding eight, as a result of government pressure.[81]

This contrast between progress in villagization and progress in collectivization suggests the hypothesis that rural Ethiopians may be more prepared to accept community living than communal production. This apparent greater peasant receptivity to the villagization initiative itself may also testify to the relative importance rural peoples place on proximity to schools, clinics, and other social services—discounted by the inconvenience of traveling between village homes and "suburban" farms. These priorities may differ somewhat from those assumed by the regime in its provision of tangible economic incentives to promote producer cooperatives.

However, the regime appears to have concentrated on the objective of collectivization itself largely to the exclusion of the reasons why at least some rural producers have been prepared to travel partway down this road. The government appears to have conceived both villagization and resettlement as means to formation of producer cooperatives on the apparent assumptions that villages will be easier to pressure into forming collectives and that village living will by itself diminish peasant resistance to them. Moreover, villagization alone has enabled the government more easily to restrict producers' access to private markets dominated, in the regime's view, by those still hostile to the transformation as the regime has defined it. At the same time, however, peasant movement into villages has in and of itself begun to put pressure on the government, in terms of its own priorities, to provide the anticipated social services, moderate overt political pressures on the villagers, and help them institutionalize community life against the risk that villagers will otherwise desert. The extent to which the government could forcibly prevent desertions or in fact bring sufficient pressure on villagers to form producer cooperatives remains open to conjecture.

The objective of producer cooperative formation appears to be one on which most rural households and the government remain at odds with each other. Fragmentary data suggest not only that cooperatives remain unpopular with nonmembers, but that members themselves regard the benefits as mixed. One commentary based on a study of producer cooperatives in one northern and one southern district suggested that some members think they are treated as tenants, pressured into joining and obliged to remain even if they wish to leave.[82]

The preliminary and fragmentary evidence therefore suggests the hypothesis that rural families and the government may have a basis for dialogue with each other over the question of diminished peasant individualism in social and economic terms. The real issue need not necessarily be framed in terms of individualism versus collectivism, as the government and many of its critics portray it, for rural peoples in Ethiopia as elsewhere have many established traditions for cooperation and mutual assistance. Rather the issue may be what *form* such cooperation should take and at what stage. Their movement into villages has indicated at least some rural peoples' disposition to accept new forms of communal existence without necessarily being prepared to allow their exit options to be closed off. At the same time, the government appears generally to have limited the extent of its coercion of rural households to establish villages and cooperatives without backing away from its commitment to establishing these new institutions. Once again, such a state of affairs seems to suggest the basis of an accommodation between rural producers and the regime with potentially favorable consequences for production and grass roots regime support. However, one underlying precondition for such an accommodation is regime reappraisal of the revolutionary credentials of the peasantry at stages *during the course* of a prolonged transformation.

Languishing Productive Capacity. On balance, the regime's reforms have failed to elicit the anticipated, broadly based liberation of rural productive energies and a corresponding quantum increase in the rate of the country's economic development. The World Bank has estimated that the agricultural production grew at an average annual rate of only 1.2 percent during the first post-imperial decade, slightly more than half the rate of the preceding ten years and less than half the 2.8 percent rate of population growth over the same period.[83] Between 1980 and 1985 overall production increased at an annual rate of only 0.3 percent while growth in agriculture actually declined −3.4 percent.[84] And agricultural production continued to account for 40% of gross domestic product and over 80 percent of both export income and individual work force incomes. In the six years between the regime's de facto consolidation of its rule and the outbreak of the 1984–1985 famine, production and yields of major crops showed a pattern of gradual decline after an initial spurt in 1979–1980. This has occurred despite the fact that the abolition of feudal dues, discounted by taxes introduced by the military regime, has appeared to result in a substantial net resource transfer to rural producers.[85]

Productivity in peasant associations has continued to exceed that of producer cooperatives despite the resource investment in the latter. The government's reliance on state farms has in fact appeared to expand, though it has not been cost-effective vis-à-vis either producer cooperatives or peasant associations. And state farms have consistently absorbed more than 60 percent of capital investment in agriculture.[86]

The net effect of these agricultural trends has been to confirm, perhaps increase, the country's vulnerability to periodic outbreaks of drought and famine that wreak lasting destruction on the country's productive capacity and the well-being of its peoples. Even during 1986–1987, when good rains promised to help restore the country's production, five million Ethiopians—more than ten percent of the population—required famine relief assistance. The loss of life in the famines, and the diminished physical and mental capacities of those who live through their devastating effects, make the country's recovery slower and more difficult and leave it more vulnerable to future such catastrophes.

The underlying causes of the country's languishing productive capacity extend well beyond increasing farmgate prices and reallocating and improving the delivery of agricultural support services. The World Bank, whose negotiations with the government for an extension of agricultural support begun under the Minimum Package Program, has contended that removal of restrictions on private marketing (including trade across district borders), a reduced role for the AMC, strengthened agricultural research, and reorientation of extension agents' activities to center on development rather than collectivization would (in addition to improved farmgate prices) bring forth the desired smallholder production response. Others have insisted that the government must reorient its development promotion from state farms and producer cooperatives to individual peasants.

Such steps might well appeal to producers, to judge from a great deal of experience elsewhere, but they fail to take account of the regime's political interests asserted through its existing agricultural policies. For the regime the problem is which concessions, if any, it might make to gain both needed international development assistance and satisfactory agricultural performance while still avoiding a slippery slope toward abandonment of the political and socioeconomic transformations that have been its well-publicized raison d'être. The February 1988 agreement with the World Bank on increased agricultural prices and lifting of restrictions on private grain trade without abandonment of collectivization may have gained the regime just such a compromise. Not yet clear is whether this agreement also signaled relaxation of what one analyst has termed the regime's "garrison socialism"—in this instance in reliance on state farms and collectives. Such "garrison socialism" has been reflected in the belief, based on the regime's military struggles, that those outside these spheres are prey to those who have continued to subvert its hard-won grasp on power.

The February 1988 break in the impasse between the World Bank and the government over policy conditions precedent for resumption of Bank assistance to the agricultural sector may encourage similar flexibility at the macro level. The formal inauguration of the People's Democratic Republic and examples of experimentation with alternative approaches to socialist agriculture in other countries of Marxist-Leninist persuasion would appear to allow room for the regime to adapt without appearing to capitulate. A study of the Ethiopian economy by a team of Soviet advisers quoted Lenin at length in support of policy changes very similar to those advocated by the World Bank.[87] While embarrassing the government in the short run, the report did afford a Marxist-Leninist-oriented regime ideological justification for such flexibility. Moreover, there would appear to be room for mutual recognition by the regime, external donors, and the peasantry itself on the need to consolidate existing reforms, both at the peasant association and producer cooperative stage. Meanwhile, there may be room for experimenting with alternative means of agricultural organization in the name of agrarian socialism. Acceptance of the collectivization explicit in the first stage of the land reform (following the example of the International Labor Organization) rather than appearing to insist on a return to an individualized peasant sector, might promote such dialogue as well.

Dependence upon Private Sector Marketing. Despite or perhaps because of its energetic pursuit of large-scale industrial and agricultural production and rapid rural collectivization through resettlement and villagization, the regime has continued to remain heavily dependent upon the private sector for marketing of official produce. This has been the case notwithstanding the regime's determined effort to curb or eliminate such dependence.

Most observers agree that as is common with other African countries, notably Tanzania, a large volume of Ethiopian agricultural surplus is traded through an informal sector, official prohibitions notwithstanding. In possible contrast to other countries, however, the Mengistu government has been dependent upon private traders as intermediaries within the official agricultural sector itself. Although perhaps declining, in 1982–1983 approximately 30 percent of the produce purchased by the AMC was provided by private traders.[88] The government has resorted to high quotas, bans on cross-district trading prior to February 1988, and licensing of traders to control this dependence. The dependence is a practical necessity, for the AMC has continued to lack the administrative capacity and resources to replace the traders, let alone increase its share of marketed produce above the present estimated 30 percent. Underlying that seemingly inescapable cooperation, at least in the short run, is the reality of a central government that since imperial times has been more centralized in theory than in practice. This has been a reality that continues to frustrate the pretensions of the successor regime, notwithstanding marked progess in strengthening central government capacity within certain sectors and geographical areas.

Little explored is the possibility that the regime's unwanted interdependence with the private sectors in agricultural marketing, difficult though it has often been, might serve as a rough model for such collaboration within a larger sphere. Might the regime, which is deeply suspicious of private traders, conclude that regulation rather than elimination of them is consistent with its objectives and represents a prudent deployment of its resources? Would the regime be prepared to orient the public sector's share of marketing in such a direction? Such accommodation with private traders might enable the regime to loosen its burdensome market quota requirements on producers with accompanying economic and political benefits in peasant engagement.

This possibility raises a largely unexplored research issue, i.e., who *are* the private traders involved? To what extent are they remnants of the old order who have shifted from landholding to trade and who therefore are unreconstructed opponents of all that the regime has sought to effect? On the other hand, to what extent do they constitute a petit bourgeoisie for which legitimate roles in the transition to scientific socialism can be defined and defended? The nature and economic strength of this private sector and its relationship to the regime have been largely hidden by the regime's official national control of the agricultural economy, but these questions demand further investigation. This is an area where the regime appears not to have fully explored its own basic position with respect to processes and ends of state transformation.

Restricted Integration. A major theme of Chapter 3 was the presence of geographical, sociocultural, and economic foundations for an historically evolving state more durable than the feudal institutions through which it was maintained. The issue is how these foundations have been strengthened, changed, or weakened by a decade of development based upon design and implementation of comprehensive reforms. The hypothesis is that the course of the rural economic transformation, like that of the political transformation, has at least failed to build upon these underlying foundations for political integration.

The most prominent evidence is that the regime's development campaigns have been effectively excluded by civil strife in the northern regions of Tigre and Eritrea. One indicator of this reality is that virtually all government economic survey data broken down by region have omitted data from those two regions. While especially the rural areas of these two regions have been largely beyond the government's effective jurisdiction, smaller sections of others have also been sufficiently insecure to substantially inhibit officially sponsored development efforts. These areas have included parts of the northern provinces of Gondar and Welo, the southwestern province of Welega, and the southeastern regions of Bale and Hararghe. The reasons for such persistent political dissidence have been explored in earlier chapters. The continued existence of such challenges to the regime's asserted "constitutional" settlement have contributed to keeping a military regime on a military footing in its development efforts, not least because of the geographical diffuseness and apparently variable and shifting strength of Oromo resistance to the regime in the south. Further stark evidence of the reality these challenges is the govenrment's continued to allocation of over 50 percent of current public expenditure to defense, well above what the emperor's regime spent in its last years.[89]

There are other important examples. These have included restrictions on interdistrict trade in agricultural products, the barriers to adjusting the boundaries of peasant associations to reflect demographic trends, a possible decision to make Amharic the sole language of government and all public instruction, the continued rudimentary communications and transport infrastructure, conflicts between settlements and communities surrounding them, and of course the effects of the military campaigns themselves. More limited have been the steps taken to counteract the country's centrifugal tendencies. These have included recognition of a variety of languages and religious persuasions. At least in principle, moreover, some new structures such as the party and the hierarchy of rural and urban cooperatives from the grass roots to the center offer potential bases for increased integration.

Again, the regime may find it possible to place more emphasis upon the organizational potential of the newly inaugurated institutions of the PDR to create genuine integration and to rely less upon surrogates in the form of the martially imposed restrictions upon the public at large. Some of these barriers to economic and political integration would appear amenable to treatment within the new institutions without major reorientation of regime policies. Others, however, such as the conflict with liberation movements, would appear to require the regime to rethink its whole concept of the Ethiopian state to accommodate the de facto pluralism that appears to have been one of its major historical characteristics.

Standards of Living: Limited Progress. By conventional indicators, the standards of living of Ethiopian peoples have on balance improved only modestly since 1974. Per capita income in 1984 was the lowest in the world, estimated at U.S.$110. Thus, Ethiopia has slipped from being among the poorest to being *the* poorest country in the world. All Ethiopians have suffered from the effects of inflation, but these have been accentuated in the urban areas by a freeze on incomes above U.S.$300 for more than a decade. There have been persistent rumors of a *reduction* of these frozen incomes in the interests of greater equality. One study of urban household economies demonstrated that a high proportion of urban peoples remained at or below the poverty line.[90] In rural areas nonavailability of consumer goods in adequate volume and of appropriate quality has been a continuing barrier to rural economic development. For hundreds of thousands of rural Ethiopians, moreover, the return of drought and famine conditions has wiped out what marginal capacity for survival they may have possessed.

Life expectancy has remained essentially unchanged at one of the lowest levels in the world. Infant mortality has continued at a similar level. Both rural and urban housing facilities are substantially unchanged in quality and availability from what they were in 1974. Much of the stock of urban housing, in particular, has remained of deplorable quality even by the standards of major cities in other impoverished African countries. The availability of doctors has actually diminished over what it was on the eve of the revolution, though their distribution within the country may have improved. Prior to 1974 approximately two-thirds of all doctors were believed to practice in Addis Ababa. The availability of health stations and of nurses and medical assistants appears to have improved modestly. These comparisons do not take account of the effects of famine in 1984–1985 which placed the country once again utterly at the mercy of international humanitarian aid groups. Access to clean water for household purposes appears to have improved only modestly, though UNICEF and other donors have embarked with some success on projects to upgrade it.[91]

The real transformation in standards of living has occurred in increased opportunity for education at all levels. Literacy campaigns have raised the percentage of those able to read and write at primary school level from beneath 10 percent to more than 50 percent. The literacy campaigns have lent legitimacy to nonformal education, increased emphasis on which helped to spark the February 1974 revolutionary uprising.[92] The percentages of school-age children enrolled in primary, secondary, and higher education have also been expanded fivefold. On the other hand, formal educational opportunity has expanded more rapidly than educational quality. Primary and secondary schools have been obliged to resort to double and triple shifts for lack of teachers, and availability of books has been a continuing serious problem. At the same time, postliteracy programs to sustain newly won reading and writing skills and apply them constructively are in short supply within the country.

Structural Inequalities. It is no surprise and it is no reflection on the quality of the socioeconomic transformation that pronounced inequalities continue to characterize Ethiopian society. What is important is that new if less dramatic inequalities have been introduced by the reform structures, even as those primordially sanctioned by the structures of feudal-imperial Ethiopia have in many ways been liquidated.

In rural areas these structured inequalities are incipient rather than full-blown, but they are nevertheless important for what they portend. First, among the most important of these inequalities has been access to oxen. Small but significant income differences in rural household income appear to be closely related to access to oxen. At the same time, a major feature of the formation of producer cooperatives has been the eventual collectivization of these critical means of production, while outside these organizations patterns of sharing such essentials as oxen appeared to have emerged or continued. Second, inequalities in landholding and in productive capacities appear to have resulted from demographic changes that are difficult to accommodate within the framework of the land reform. Family size remains unequal within associations, and population growth patterns remain unequal across the countryside. The result has been that unequal access to landholding continues because of the structure of the land reform, even as its major effect was to abolish the inequalities of imperial rural economy. Moreover, within the producer cooperatives significant inequalities in income distribution have begun to appear based on accumulations within the workpoint system the cooperatives employ.[93]

Third, women and pastoralists have not participated in what was to be a socialist revolution on an equal basis with men and agriculturalists respectively. Peasant association membership is vested in households, whose representative is normally the household head and in most cases a male. Moreover, the land reform did not directly address traditional informal land tenure rules that survived in the interstices of the feudal order, rules that also in many cases discriminated against women. The Revolutionary Ethiopian Women's Association (REWA) appears to have had little impact in pushing for changes in the status of women in rural or urban areas. One consequence of military rule has been that the government of the country continues to be overwhelmingly in the hands of men at all levels throughout the country.

Pastoralists, excluded from prime riverine grazing areas in the Awash Valley, continue to be so as a 10,000-hectare river basin development project has replaced the private and joint venture estates that displaced the pastoralists in the first place. With the exception of small experimental schemes for pastoralists at Amibara in the middle valley and Dubti in the lower valley, essentially nothing has been done to address the now long-standing grievances of the pastoralists. In fact the number of pastoralists at Amibara was itself reduced when the government discovered that most pastoralists had not been satisfactorily integrated into production work on the scheme. Research at the nearby Institute for Agricultural Research, however, has effectively dispelled the myth that Afar pastoralists cannot become efficient agriculturalists, and the government now contemplates the development of a further extension of the river development project specifically for pastoralists.[94]

Fourth, though it is difficult to document, it appears that private traders and the military have been victimized less than others by the consequences of inflation, income freezes, and unacceptable terms of trade. The volume of private trade in agricultural goods beyond the control of the government suggests the possibility that considerable accumulation has been possible in this sector. The building of some new churches has been fragmentary evidence suggesting suppressed investment and liquidity outside the reach of government. Moreover, for evident reasons, military officers have been among those who through promotions have been able to escape the effects of the wage freeze. While ostentatious display of wealth is rare in Ethiopia today, there is some reason to suspect that for these two groups the burden of enforced austerity has been less than for others.

A major purpose of Ethiopia's political and socioeconomic transformations has been the elimination of profound inequalities entrenched under the regimes of the emperors. Much less clear is the extent to which surviving inequalities, including those resulting directly from the structures of reform, are acceptable or matters of concern to either the regime or its constituents.

Unchanged Ecological Vulnerability. The recurrence of serious drought and famine indelibly recorded Ethiopia's continued vulnerability to ecological disasters. The February revolutionary uprising was sparked in large part by the conviction that governments bear responsibility for relieving and attempting to prevent such disasters through promoting broadly based development. This chapter has recorded that socioeconomic transformation based on revolutionary rural reconstruction has so far failed measurably to diminish the country's vulnerability to ecological disasters.

A key issue is the relationship of the country's ecological vulnerability to the design and implementation of the several stages of land reform and associated development efforts. The available evidence would appear to suggest the following: The 1984–1985 drought and famine cannot be attributed to the 1975 land reform proclamation, which was in part the regime's response to the hypothesis that land tenure inequities had contributed to the outbreak of the 1972–1973 famine.[95] The reason is that the 1984–1985 famine occurred in districts where implementation of the proclamation has been most resisted and least accomplished, in part because of political resistance to the military regime itself. While there are known ecological risks in villagization, they are ones that might be controlled with the careful planning and management that have not necessarily generally been in evidence. The allocation of resources to producer cooperatives at the expense of households remaining in the peasant association subsector, the diversion of existing agricultural extension staff from agricultural to regime support activities (including the formation of producer cooperatives), and the weak support given agricultural research all represent steps not calculated to diminish rural vulnerability to ecological catastrophe. Counterbalancing this negative record are the regime's efforts to promote tree-planting and vigorous albeit unpopular efforts to restrict further diminution of the country's dwindling forest resources, currently placed at only about 3 percent of land area. These efforts have been applauded by at least some international donors.[96]

Conclusion

These generalizations are, once again, based on limited, fragmentary, and incomplete evidence. Together, however, they suggest a struggling socioeconomic transformation, one grievously damaged by war and by the effects of famine. While the structures of social change and opportunity have been effectively installed, they have yet to produce the economic and social liberation that has been their raison d'être. Beneath the structures themselves lie historical-political realities of both ancient and more recent origin that impede converting promise into performance. Prominent among these have been the weaknesses of central government inherited from imperial times and the profound conflict over the political transformation whose effects have been evident in the government's approaches to implementing a socioeconomic transformation at the grass roots. However, despite these circumstances, the foregoing account suggests possible bases for even a historically oppressed peasantry and a martially inclined authoritarian regime to reach some accommodation on some of the fundamental obstacles to realizing the promise of the long-awaited socioeconomic transformation. Such accommodations may presume but also be the foundation for bringing the regime's own promise of state transformation closer to reality.

Notes

1. The emphasis on constitutionalism refers not primarily to constitutional documents per se but to the actual working fundamental parameters of political life that documents express with varying but always only partial fidelity.

2. Since the institutions established under the land reform are clearly of great importance locally, they are treated as having constitutional significance in fact even though they are not treated as such in the country's formal constitutional document.

3. John W. Harbeson, "Multilateral Approaches to Multidimensional Conflict Resolution: Lessons from the Horn of Africa," in Arthur R. Day and Michael W. Doyle (eds.), *Escalation and Intervention: Multilateral Security and Its Alternatives*. Boulder, Colorado: Westview, 1986.

4. Addis Ababa: Government of Ethiopia, Proclamation No. 129 of 1977.

5. Addis Ababa: Government of Ethiopia, Proclamation No. 156 of 1978.

6. *Ethiopian Herald,* September 12, 1978.

7. All these were implicit in the original land reform proclamation, No. 31 of 1975, but were made explicit and given official impetus at this time.

8. The voluntariness of the "response" to drafts by local peasant associations and their subsequent responsiveness given the disastrous Peasant March were open to question.

9. Proclamation No. 156 *op.cit.*

10. *Ibid.*

11. *Ibid.*

12. *Ibid.*

13. Among the many important sources see particularly Norman Uphoff and Milton Esman, *Local Organization in Rural Development*. Ithaca: Cornell University Press, 1984.

14. Addis Ababa: Government of Ethiopia, Proclamation No. 142 of 1978. Subsequently supplanted by a Ministry of State Farm Development in 1983.

15. *Ethiopian Herald*, June 26, 1979.

16. The practical problems of implementing the original 1975 proclamation are discussed later in this chapter.

17. *Ibid.*

18. July 2, 1979.

19. John M. Cohen and Nils-Ivar Isaksson, *Villagization in the Arsi Region of Ethiopia*. Report prepared by Swedish International Development Authority (SIDA) Consultants to the Ethio-Swedish Mission on Villagization in Arsi Region, December 1–14, 1986. Uppsala: Swedish University of Agricultural Sciences, International Rural Development Centre, February 1987.

20. For general analyses of African socialism see Carl Rosberg and Thomas Callaghy, *Socialism in Sub-Saharan Africa: A New Assessment*. Berkeley: University of California Institute for International Studies, 1979. Also a much earlier work by Carl Rosberg and William Friedland (eds.), *African Socialism*. Berkeley: University of California, 1964.

21. Major analyses of Tanzanian socialism have included Goran Hyden, *Beyond Ujamaa: Underdevelopment and an Uncaptured Peasantry*. Berkeley: University of California, 1980; Andrew Coulson, *Tanzania: A Political Economy*. Oxford: Clarendon Press, 1982; and Michaela von Freyhold, *Ujamaa Villages: Analysis of a Social Experiment*. New York: Monthly Review Press, 1979. See also the author's "Tanzanian Socialism in Transition: Agricultural Crisis and Policy Reform," Hanover, New Hampshire: Universities Field Staff International, *Reports*, No. 30, 1983.

22. A survey of Ethiopia's resettlement experience was prepared by Gail Simpson, "Socio-Political Aspects of Settlement Schemes in Ethiopia and Their Contribution to Development," in *Land Reform, Land Settlement and Cooperatives*. 2, 1976, pp. 22–40. Also Eshetu Chole and Teshome Mulat, *Land Settlement in Ethiopia: A Review of Developments*. Addis Ababa, Ethiopia: Institute for Development Research, Addis Ababa University, December 1984.

23. Interviews with donor officials.

24. Addis Ababa: Government of Ethiopia, Proclamation No. 262 of 1984. Government Printer.

25. Though difficult to document, there have been repeated indications that Soviet and Cuban delegations, especially the latter, have had reservations about the wisdom of the government's military approach to the Eritrean problem. One reason is that some considerable proportion of the Eritrean liberation leadership had reputedly been trained at some point by Cubans.

26. *Ethiopian Herald,* December 18, 1979.
27. *Ibid.*
28. *Ibid.*
29. *Ibid.*
30. Addis Ababa: Government of Ethiopia, Proclamation No. 174, 1979–80.
31. *Ibid.*
32. *Ibid.*
33. *Ibid.*
34. "Ethiopia: New Party," 23 *Africa Confidential,* No. 18, September 15, 1983.
35. Interviews.
36. Marina Ottaway, "The Ethiopian Land Reform: From Political Change to Economic Development," footnote 7, paper presented to International Congress of Ethiopian Studies, Addis Ababa Studies, November 1984.
37. Addis Ababa: Government of Ethiopia, Proclamations No. 215 and No. 213 respectively.
38. Addis Ababa, September 7, 1981.
39. Proclamation 213, *op.cit.*
40. Addis Ababa: Government of Ethiopia, Proclamation No. 236 of 1983.
41. *Ethiopian Herald,* April 6, 1983.
42. *Ibid.*
43. *Ibid.*
44. Addis Ababa, Ethiopia: Government Printer, September 1984.
45. *Ibid.*
46. *Ibid.*
47. *Ibid.*
48. Report (at one time very closely held) in Ethiopia entitled *Socialism from the Grass Roots: Accumulation, Employment and Equity in Ethiopia.* Geneva: International Labor Organization, September 1982.
49. *Ibid.*
50. Addis Ababa, Ethiopia: Government Printer, June 1986.
51. The most exact English rendering of the Amharic term *shengo* is "council of elders."
52. *Ibid.,* Article 2.1.
53. *Ibid.,* Article 2.5.
54. Interviews.
55. *Ethiopia: Decade of Revolutionary Transformation.* Addis Ababa, 1984, n.d.
56. *Socialism from the Grass Roots, op. cit.*
57. International Monetary Fund, *Recent Economic Developments.* Washington: July 15, 1986.
58. Ten Year Plan, *op. cit.*

59. Cohen and Isaksson, *op. cit.*
60. *Ibid.*
61. Dessalegn Rahmato, "Notes on Settlement in Mettekel Awraja," International Conference of Ethiopian Studies, Moscow, 1984.
62. Jason W. Clay and Bonnie K. Holcombe, *Politics and the Ethiopian Famine 1984–1985*. Cambridge, Massachusetts: Cultural Survival, Inc., 1986.
63. Mary Kay Magistad, "On the Razor's Edge," 32 *Africa Report*, 3, May-June 1987, pp. 61–65.
64. Eshetu Chole and Teshome Mulat, *op. cit.*
65. Cohen and Isaksson, *op. cit.*
66. *Ibid.*, p. 33.
67. *Ibid.*, plus a proposal for Second Minimum Package Project (Credit–1088 ET/Loan 40-ET), 1983.
68. International Labor Organization, *From Crisis to Sustained Development: A Programme of Action*, 1986.
69. Ministry of State Farm Development, *Toward a Strategy for the Development of State Farms*, Volume 1, Main Report, Part 6, Overall Performance and Strategic Options. Addis Ababa, Ethiopia: 1986.
70. Joint Government of Ethiopia-International Bank for Reconstruction and Development Mission, *Review of Farmers' Incentives and Agricultural Marketing and Distribution Efficiency*. Addis Ababa, Ethiopia: March 17, 1983.
71. International Monetary Fund, *op. cit.*
72. Fassil G. Kiros, *Education for Integrated Rural Development: An Examination of the Problems of Transition*. Addis Ababa, Ethiopia: Addis Ababa University, Institute for Development Research, February 1983.
73. *Ibid.*
74. Hyden, *Beyond Ujamma*, *op. cit.*
75. See Chapter 1.
76. Dessalegn Rahmato, *Agrarian Reform in Ethiopia*. Trenton, N.J.: Red Sea Press, 1985.
77. John M. Cohen and Ingvar Jonnson, "The Size of Peasant Association Holdings and Government Policies: Questions Raised By Recent Research in Arsi Region, Ethiopia," 9 *Northeast African Studies*, 1, 1987, pp. 97–103.
78. *Ibid.*; International Labor Organization, *From Crisis to Sustained Development*, *op. cit.*; U.N. Food and Agricultural Organization, WCARRD-Ethiopia, Mission No. 7, Follow-up Mission, May 3–9, 1982; also Siegfried Pausewang, "Peasants, Organizations, and Markets: Some Observations based on a Study of Achefer (Gojjam) and Shebodino (Sidamo)," Ninth Annual Conference of Ethiopian Studies, Moscow, August 1986.
79. See for example Uphoff and Esman, *op. cit.*
80. Government of Ethiopia, Ministry of Agriculture, 1986.
81. Cohen and Isaksson, *op. cit.*
82. Pausewang, *op. cit.*
83. International Bank for Reconstruction and Development, *World Development Report 1986*, *op. cit.*,
84. IBRD, *World Development Report 1987*. New York: Oxford University Press, 1987.

85. *Socialism from the Grass Roots, op. cit.*
86. Ministry of State Farms, *Toward a Strategy, op. cit.*
87. *Considerations on the Economic Policy of Ethiopia for the Next Few Years.* Report prepared by the team of Soviet consulting advisers attached to the NCCP of socialist Ethiopia, September 1984, n.d.
88. Government of Ethiopia, Agricultural Marketing Corporation, *Grain Marketing Study.* Stockholm: Swedfarm Ab, June 1985.
89. Mulatu Wubneh, "Development Strategy and Growth of the Ethiopian Economy: A Comparative Analysis of Pre- and Post-revolutionary Periods," paper present to conference on Ethiopia held at the Johns Hopkins University School for Advanced International Studies, April 8–9, 1988.
90. *Socialism from the Grass Roots, op. cit.*
91. *Evaluation of the Impact of UNICEF Water Supply Project in Four Administrative Regions.* Addis Ababa, Ethiopia: Addis Ababa University, Institute for Development Research, August 1986.
92. Fassil G. Kiros, *op. cit.*
93. Ministry of Agriculture, Government of Ethiopia, 1986.
94. Interviews, January 1987.
95. See for example Abdul Mejid Hussein (ed.), "Drought and Famine in Ethiopia," African Environment Special Report No. 2. London: International African Institute, 1976
96. Interviews.

7

Conclusions

The Ethiopian transformation has posed issues both of consuming importance to the country itself and of fundamental significance for theoretical inquiry into the political economy of less developed nations. The purposes of this concluding chapter are (1) to review and summarize the working answers evolved over the first thirteen years of the Ethiopian transformation and (2) to consider their contribution to comparative analysis of these larger theoretical issues.

The State of the Ethiopian Transformation

More than a decade of reform, civil war, and international conflict dramatized the most fundamental issues concerning the basis of the Ethiopian polity and the processes of its transformation. First, more than a decade of warfare with domestic, separatist, and international adversaries has exposed dramatically the issue of on what basis, if any, an Ethiopian state survived the demise of time-encrusted feudal and imperial institutions. A summary review of modern Ethiopian political history, presented in Chapter 2, supports the proposition that the Ethiopian empire, even as expanded in the late nineteenth century parallel to the spread of European colonialism, did rest on bases of statehood deeper than conquest per se. The implicit foundations of such statehood, the chapter argued, appeared to center on a stable tension between de facto tolerance of regional diversity and semiautonomy juxtaposed with de jure absolute authority of the emperors. Emperors expressed, but were not themselves synonymous with, an underlying Ethiopian political identity. Chapter 2 argued that in ending Eritrean federation in favor of central imperial rule, Haile Selassie placed the consolidation of his personal regime above the evolving basis of the Ethiopian state, with injurious consequences for its future.

On such underpinnings, Haile Selassie I crafted a superficial overlay of embryonic constitutional monarchy and economic development. Chapter 2 argued that while the emperor was adept in employing such trappings to coopt the support of modernizing elites for the preservation of his regime, the long-term consequences of such policies were in retrospect harmful to prospects for a post-imperial state. On the one hand, he followed his predecessors in seeking to strengthen imperial authority vis-à-vis traditional nobility. On the other hand, in coopting modernizing elites while continuing the tradition of treating his personal rule as synonymous with the state, the emperor compromised virtually all cadres and organizations in each other's eyes as agents of broader processes of political and economic change. By virtue of the training and organization of the armed forces under his regime, junior military officers represented a possible but later vigorously disputed exception to this rule.

Second, the February 1974 uprising, which led not only to the dethronement of the emperor but the liquidation of his entire regime, posed fundamental questions concerning the possibility, processes, and objectives of a post-imperial Ethiopian state. The quest for the post-imperial Ethiopian state was accompanied by comprehensive measures to transform inherited socioeconomic structures to reflect and prepare for realization of the objectives of state transformation. Thus, intertwined with issues concerning the post-imperial state were those concerning its relationship to the socioeconomic transformation. Left unanswered during the dismantling of the imperial regime, these issues confronted both the country as a whole and the successor military regime as soon as it came to power.

Ethiopia's course since the fall of Haile Selassie's government has been one of almost bitter, continual, multifaceted, and in many respects unresolved controversy over the interrelated issues of state and socioeconomic transformation. On the one hand, intensified separatist insurgency in Eritrea has been accompanied by the emergence of Tigrean and Oromo liberation movements and hot and cold wars with Somalia over the future of the Somali-populated Ogaden region. The separatists have demanded the dissolution of the empire into its component nationalities, while the military regime has insisted on its transformation into as Marxist-Leninist people's democratic republic with recognition of separate nationalities under this umbrella. On the other hand, many of those constituencies that followed military leadership in overthrowing the *ancien regime* demanded that the military immediately yield to civilian rule to effect the transformation of the Ethiopian state. The military claimed that as then organized, these constituencies had been coopted by the emperor's regime, disqualifying them for such leadership roles for at least the time being. These same civilian constituencies demanded that state transformation under their leadership should precede and define the nature of accompanying socioeconomic transformation. For its part, the military insisted that socioeconomic transformation must precede and be the foundation for state transformation and claimed for itself the role of midwife and architect of these processes.

The actual outlines of the post-imperial state were hammered out by the course of the conflict between the military regime and its adversaries over these issues. Such pervasive conflict moved the country in directions very different from those implicit in the possibly reconcilable principles over which they fought with each other. In the course of its struggles to survive, the military regime alienated many other civilian constituencies, including those most in favor of the socialist revolution of which the military regime claimed to be the prophet. In the battles to overcome adversaries' challenges to its survival, the regime's priorities gradually evolved from preparing and transferring power to a people's democratic republic to consolidating and entrenching its own rule by martial means. The socioeconomic transformation became less the realization or the foundation of a people's democratic republic than an instrument in the regime's quest to consolidate its rule and, in effect, treat its own rule as synonymous with the post-imperial state. Thus, the formations of the Workers' Party of Ethiopia and the People's Democratic Republic were a superimposition upon, rather more than a transition from, the de facto military state. Not clear in early 1988 was when and to what extent the "new" regime would come to rest on foundations broader than the military after its inauguration more than it did beforehand.

Conflict between the military and its adversaries transformed the processes of state transformation as well as the ends achieved in ways that changed the issues over which they fought. In coming to treat its regime and the post-imperial state as coextensive as a result of its wars of survival, the military regime made self-confirming the fears and suspicions underlying its opponents' attacks. Together the partisans to these struggles caused the quest for the post-imperial state to center less upon its future development and more upon its unresolved historical tensions that their conflicts enlarged. Where earlier these issues centered on regimes, they came to focus on the nature of the state itself. On the one hand, the regime's wars with Eritrean and other liberation movements escalated the issue of centralized versus decentralized feudalism under Haile Selassie to one of whether one state or many should be the legacy of the empire. On the other hand, the military regime's treatment of the state as synonymous with its own rule enlarged the issue of whether and how political economic change might take place within a feudal regime to one of whether the military regime's policies did or did not realize long-held long-held socioeconomic and political visions of the post-imperial state.

Conclusions

The Mengistu regime has brought forth fundamental socioeconomic reforms hailed at their inception as down payments on the liberation of workers and peasants, the central promise of the Ethiopian revolution that was to be. The rural land reform of 1975, in particular, laid the foundations for the deliverance of the rural poor from bonds of tenancy and subservience to landlords entrenched by primordial feudal institutions. Since 1979 the military regime has sought to make this 1975 reform only the first step rather than the culmination of a profound rural socioeconomic transformation. The hallmarks of this transformation were to be increased industrialization; larger units of agricultural production sustained by advanced technology; greater collectivization in the name of equality, efficiencies in service delivery, and economies of scale; greater protection against ecological devastation; and improved standards of living, beginning with improved access to education from literacy formation to higher education.

Progress toward realizing the promise of the socioeconomic transformation has been very modest in its first twelve years. The dominant features of the record to date have been broad acceptance of the initial land reform proclamation but at best a mixed response to its further stages: villagization and producer cooperatives. Rural peoples in at least some areas have demonstrated interest in the benefits anticipated from villagization, but they have shown great reluctance to participate in the formation of producer cooperatives. The cooperatives and associations have become vehicles for the transmission and enforcement of government directives, largely to the exclusion of the articulation of rural peoples' interests and their assertion of local self-reliance. Underlying this posture has been an apparent unwillingness to recognize the political coming of age of a class that was to be a particular beneficiary of revolution; i.e., the peasantry. Similarly, the regime provoked profound conflict by denying the political credentials of other classes, as then organized, to participate in state transformation at the macro level. Their reorganization has not been accompanied by broadened opportunities for participation in realizing the promise of socioeconomic development following the fall of the *ancien regime.*

The implementation of the land reform has yielded generally extremely modest, discouraging results for reasons attributable to an implementation strategy featuring inadequate farmgate prices, diversion of administrative resources from agricultural to regime maintenance purposes, extreme concentration of scarce public resources on state farms and cooperatives at the expense of a majority of the country's rural producers, inadequate support for agricultural research, energetic but only partially effective efforts to restrict the access of rural producers to private traders, and excessive centralization and bureaucratization of administrative machinery.

The larger social consequences of the manner in which the stages of the rural socioeconomic transformation have been implemented have included (1) failure to build upon inherited potential for increased economic and political integration, (2) continued stagnation in economic development by most conventional indicators, (3) standards of living largely unimproved since 1974 except in the area of education, and (4) elimination of gross socioeconomic inequalities synonymous with the old regime and their replacement with incipient but still significant inequalities associated with the manner in which the reforms have been constructed. Women and pastoralists, in addition to noncollectivized rural smallholders, have been among the communities that have made at best only limited progress in escaping inequitable treatment that characterized their lives under the old regime, even though improvement in their circumstances has continued to be official policy. Great strides have been made in literacy formation and access to formal education at all levels, although the country's enduring poverty prevented corresponding increases or even stability in the quality of education offered. If development is the primary vehicle for the country's escape from serious vulnerability to ecological catastrophe, that vulnerability remains durable for many communities representing perhaps a majority of the population. In the circumstances of developing countries the classic purpose of the state, to provide security for its citizens against internal and external threats, may logically extend to defense against ecological threats to the survival of whole communities. If so, the results of twelve years of socioeconomic transformation has been in this respect to undermine rather than to strengthen (let alone transform) the foundations of the Ethiopian state.

Donor agencies and others have been uniformly critical of the regime's development policies, which are often attributed to the country's Marxist-Leninist ideology.[1] The argument of this book, examined in Chapter 6, has been that inappropriate management methods have been at least as important as unwise policies in perpetuating rather than ameliorating the country's historical poverty. Morever, these management methods have been largely attributable to the actual course of state transformation forged in combat rather more than to the regime's ideological predilections. Chapter 6 argued that the regime directly treated its policies and administrative methods as extensions to a new theater of its military struggles for survival. While some of these management approaches might be modified without restructuring of the de facto post-imperial state, others would require such further transformation. Thus, in many respects the Mengistu regime's course of treating its rule as synonymous with the post-imperial state has adversely affected the socioeconomic transformation that was to be its foundation. It follows that more substantive as distinct from symbolic transformation to a post-imperial state envisaged by the country's new constitution, the earlier National Democratic Revolutionary Program and the formal structures of the rural transformation may be an important precondition for more favorable patterns of economic and social progress.

Implicit in this conclusion is the hypothesis, requiring further examination that appropriate development policies and producer-centered management approaches are possible and can bring favorable results *within* the framework of the revolution's original designs. A companion implicit hypothesis is that to the extent the regime feels increasingly secure from threats to its own survival, it may find less reason to oppose such accommodations and more pressure even within its own ranks to take such steps. Specifically within agriculture, more concentrated attention on full implementation of the first or semicollectivized stage of agrarian reform combined with furtherance of a real transition from military rule at the macrolevel may produce more favorable socioeconomic results. Such reorientation may obviate the need for wholesale abandonment of the country's designs for future socioeconomic transformation in more communitarian or collectivist directions. Though many questions remain concerning its implementation, the country's February 1988 agreement with the World Bank to increase prices and lift restrictions on private grain trade without abandoning the rural collectivization campaign may have heralded the beginning of such a compromise.

The foregoing account supports the conclusion that "transformation" is a better term than "revolution" to describe what has transpired in Ethiopia since 1974. For the outcomes have exemplified both meanings of the the term "transformation." On the one hand, real and important change has occurred. An ancient, feudal, and profoundly inegalitarian regime has been overthrown, and reform programs and institutions designed to liberate Ethiopia's millions in socioeconomic and political terms have been established in its place. Marked progress in distribution of land and in promotion of literacy and educational opportunity have been among the country's most important achievements since 1974. Similarly, within the somewhat shrunken perimeters under its effective control the regime has exerted an intensive and comprehensive control over grass roots social and economic behavior almost without precedent in the country's long political history. That these new structures have not brought more favorable socioeconomic results is in part attributable to unwise implementing policies, inappropriate management, and excessively single-minded preoccupation with accelerating further stages of collectivization. But the underlying cause has been de facto reorientations of the processes and directions of the country's political transformation through civil, regional, and international conflict between the regime and its adversaries.

On the other hand there are senses in which a transformation has been restricted to the more mathematical sense of the term, i.e., as change in form without corresponding change in meaning or substance. The conflict between the regime and its adversaries was prepared by policies that strengthened the emperor's personal regime at the expense of the Ethiopian state; i.e., the liquidation of Eritrean federation and the cooptation of modernizing elites to the service of his personal rule. Nevertheless, the resulting wars that engulfed Ethiopia after the fall of Haile Selassie's government in fact produced an unwitting and unacknowledged redirection of the processes and ends of state transformation from a quest for the post-imperial state to a focus on both the nature and contradictions of the inherited imperial state. In his struggle to preserve his regime, Mengistu came de facto to define his regime as synonymous with the Ethiopian state. His regime has thereby continued the pattern of the emperors, denied what has appeared to be the de facto more loosely federated nature of the Ethiopian state within a framework of de jure centralization, and in effect positioned the survival of the regime as an obstacle to more than symbolic transformation of the Ethiopian state and society. The new constitution does recognize the legitimacy of the country's component nationalities but only in a very narrow sense. These provisions and the planned creation of autonomous regions appeared in early 1988 to carry only limited symbolic significance and to have little or no impact on the regime's struggles with liberation movements.

The consequences of such de facto redirection of the Ethiopian transformation are to be seen in the expanded scope of liberation movements restricting the sphere within which the regime's greater control can effectively be exercised, the failure of the institutional reforms to liberate the economic energies of Ethiopian rural producers, substantially increased military expenditure at the expense of realizing the development potential implicit in some of the reforms, and the inequalities and injustices arising from incomplete planning and implementation of the regime's own reforms. Thus, the country remains largely as impoverished and vulnerable to ecological catastrophe as it did before 1974.

Lessons of the Ethiopian Transformation

The Ethiopian transformation has enriched opportunities for exploring fundamental questions of political economy in social science scholarship on developing nations. First, the Ethiopian case has made abundantly clear the importance of conceiving the state as more than synonymous with the institutions of government. The enormous struggle over the formation of the successor state cannot be understood without conceiving the state as a political association based on fundamental understandings or principles recognized over and above institutions of government. It was the state so conceived that the *derg* and its adversaries alike struggled to define and establish. It has been their wars over these principles that have been primarily responsible for postponing realization of this objective, with consequent adverse effects on socioeconomic transformation as well. Particularly in these circumstances, academic analyses of the Ethiopian transformation that treat regime and state as synonymous in effect treat the fundamental and unintended de facto result of the transformation as a norm. In thereby effectively adopting the viewpoint of the military regime, such studies are poorly positioned to examine objectively the underlying issues between the regime and its adversaries over the proper course of state transformation.

More generally, failure to conceive of the state in these larger terms is to deny that African states can work and have worked to evolve, however painfully and however discouraging the contemporary results, constitutional traditions that set standards by which the regimes of the day are to be judged. Conversely, for contemporary research implicitly to make the positivist argument that the state is what the government is and does is to take as given the political misperceptions of history's most notorious authoritarian rulers, who have claimed "l'état c'est moi." Further research on the state as larger and more fundamental than the regimes of the day is, therefore, a central task of contemporary political research on African and other less developed countries.

Second, conceiving of the state in such terms has important implications for the question of the role of the state in processes of economic development, at least in the early stages thereof. Concepts of the *state* as an arena, prize, or relatively autonomous actor in processes of economic development all appear wide of the mark in the Ethiopian case. It is *governments* that are the object of competing economic classes and that may seek to act autonomously, but governments and social classes are in fact engaged together in processes of state formation and transformation whether through conflict or in more peaceful ways. The design and implementation of and responses to the rural land reform clearly suggest the inextricability of processes of state formation and socioeconomic development, although the *derg* sought initially to treat the latter as foundation for the former.

Moreover, the Ethiopian data make a strong case—theoretically as well as practically—for treating the government's assertion of "relative" autonomy as counterproductive to processes of socioeconomic transformation. The converse of such asserted relative autonomy in the Ethiopian case has been the de facto political delegitimization of other classes and constituencies themselves, not just their organized expression, in a transformation ostensibly launched in their name. The resulting conflict over the processes of state transformation has caused the socioeconomic transformation to become neither the precondition for state transformation, as the *derg* envisaged, nor a sure consequence of state transformation, as its opponents argued. Rather it became a means to the regime's process of making itself synonymous with the state, with counterproductive effects on the socioeconomic results obtained.

Third, the autonomy of "the state" has been advanced as a crucial determinant in processes of successful social revolution, most notably and recently by Theda Skocpol in her seminal work, *States and Social Revolutions*.[2] Her study is based upon a careful examination of the French, Soviet, and Chinese revolutions and indeed treats such autonomy as part of the *definition* of a successful social revolution. In a footnote, she suggests that the Ethiopian revolution has followed a comparable course in line with such a definition.[3] Reliance upon Skocpol's criterion of successful social revolution in the Ethiopian case would appear to beg the very issue in dispute between the Mengistu regime and its adversaries, i.e., the nature of the revolution to be launched. Adoption of her definition in the Ethiopian case would be to view the Ethiopian transformation through the lens of one of the major protagonists, the *derg,* and thereby to understate the complexity and significance of the issues the transformation has raised.

A further lesson of the Ethiopian case would thus appear to be the importance of a comparative study not only of the course of "revolutions" but of de facto *definitions* of revolutions, or controversies over them, among those involved. Hence this book has employed the term "transformation" pending more progress in such comparative study.

Fourth, governmental autonomy has also had another important influence on analysis of the political economy of development in Africa. Goren Hyden in his important *Beyond Ujamaa: Underdevelopment and an Uncaptured Peasantry* argued in general terms that at least one socialist state rendered itself irrelevant to a precapitalist peasantry having the capacity and the inclination to employ its exit option, hiding from the state within their economies of affection.[4] Hyden did not subdivide his argument to inquire in what proportions it is the state per se, the government, the socialism of the government, or management by the government that produced this result. Nor is it entirely clear into what the peasants retreat: whether it is always to simple, localized economies of affection or alternatively sometimes into vital, complex, informal economies on a national or even international scale. His subsequent work suggests that accommodation of peasantry through decentralized political structures and/or its economy of affection may prevent the kind of de facto standoff between rural producers and the state he described in

Tanzania.[5] Thus, he has appeared to leave unclear the extent to which the economy of affection is part of the problem or part of the solution.

The lesson of the Ethiopian transformation would appear to be that even in a state within which they have long been oppressed, precapitalist rural producers may be prepared to participate in revolutionary socioeconomic transformation sponsored by a centralized government under certain circumstances. The Ethiopian peasantry did not resist the initial stage of land reform undertaken in the name of a species of socialism akin to that of Tanzania, although it has resisted further collectivization in the name of scientific socialism. Rather, the preliminary evidence from studies of those who have participated in further stages of collectivization, reviewed in Chapter 6, suggests that the quality of the management of agrarian transformation may be as important as the structure of the managing government, or the ideological colors under which it sails, in determining the quality and extent of peasant responses to reforms. However, shortcomings in the Mengistu regime's management of its own reform initiatives suggest that they result from an underlying negative appraisal of peasants' eligibility and capacity to participate in the fulfillment of its revolutionary designs. But such negative appraisal, the Ethiopian evidence suggests, may result less from the nature of the regime's designs themselves than from the nature of the de facto processes of state transformation in which it, along with its adversaries, has been absorbed.

Finally, Ethiopia has been all but ignored in comparative studies of political and economic development in Third World countries, even as students of Ethiopia have themselves often neglected to link their subject to the wider world of struggles to overcome poverty, poor standards of living, and political subjugation. Ethiopia and the comparative study of political economy have been in that respect impoverished by each other. Ethiopia's singularly rich history has given inspiration to other developing nations by its survival as a functioning and independent polity. This book has argued that an understanding of the parameters of Ethiopian political history and of the country's contemporary transformation can be enriched by broader inclusion of this case in comparative inquiries into revolution and the political economy of development, studies that accommodate rather than ignore the significance of the country's singularities. Conversely, the very uniqueness of its history has caused the Ethiopian transformation both to dramatize some fundamental practical and theoretical issues less easily examined in other countries' contexts and to suggest new insights into their nature. Thus, the protagonists in the quest for the post-imperial Ethiopian state have generated important lessons to enrich the understanding and, in many ways, to inspire all who live in and are concerned for the future of developing countries.

Notes

1. An important study of Marxist-Leninist regimes in Africa is Edmund Keller and Donald Rothchild (eds.), *Afro-Marxist Regimes: Ideology and Public Policy*. Boulder, Colorado: Lynne Rienner, 1987. By Foley and Rothchild's criteria, Ethiopia does indeed qualify as an Afro-Marxist regime.
2. Skocpol, *op. cit.*
3. Ibid., p. 350.
4. Hyden, *op. cit.* See his more recent *No Shortcuts to Progress*. Berkeley: University of California, 1984 and also his chapter in the forthcoming D. Olowu and J. Wunsch (eds.) *The Failure of the Centralized State in Africa*. Boulder, Colorado: Westview, 1988.
5. Olowu and Wunsch, *op. cit.*

Select Bibliography

The following select bibliography includes only a few of the most important works that will be valuable to the reader wishing to pursue further the subjects considered in this book. Articles are limited to those addressing the recent history of Ethiopia.

Books

Abir, M. *Ethiopia: The Era of Princes.* London: Longman, Green, 1978.
Bauer, Dan F., *House and Society in Ethiopia.* East Lansing, Michigan: African Studies Center, Michigan State University, 1977.
Clapham, Christopher. *Haile Selassie's Government.* New York: Praeger, 1969.
Cohen, John M., and Dov Weintraub. *Land and Peasants in Imperial Ethiopia: The Social Background to a Revolution.* Assen, Netherlands: Van Gorcum, 1975.
Cohen, John M., and Nils Isaksson. *Villagization in the Arsi Region of Ethiopia.* Uppsala: International Rural Development Centre, Swedish University of Agricultural Sciences, 1987.
Cohen, John M. *Integrated Rural Development: Ethiopian Experience and the Debate.* Uppsala: Scandinavian Institute of African Studies, 1987.
Darkwah, Kofi. *Shewa, Menelik and the Ethiopian Empire 1813-1880.* London: Heinemann, 1975.
Farer, Tom J. *War Clouds on the Horn of Africa: A Crisis for Detente.* 2d ed. New York: Carnegie Endowment for International Peace, 1976.
Gilkes, Patrick. *A Dying Lion: Feudalism and Modernization in Ethiopia.* New York: St. Martin's Press, 1975.
Greenfield, Richard. *Ethiopia: A New Political History.* New York: Praeger, 1965.
Halliday, Fred, and Francine Molyneux. *The Ethiopian Revolution.* London: Verso, 1981.
Hoben, Allan. *Land Tenure Among the Amhara of Ethiopia.* Chicago: University of Chicago Press, 1973.
Jones, A. M., and E. Monroe, *A History of Ethiopia.* London: Clarendon Press, 1955.
Lefort, Rene. *Ethiopia: An Heretical Revolution?* London: Zed Press, 1983.
Levine, Donald. *Greater Ethiopia: The Evolution of a Multicultural Society.* Chicago: University of Chicago Press, 1974.
Levine, Donald. *Wax and Gold: Tradition and Innovation in Ethiopian Culture.* Chicago: University of Chicago Press, 1965.

Lewis, Herbert. *A Galla Monarchy: Jimma Abba Jifar, Ethiopia 1830–1932.* Madison, Wisconsin: University of Wisconsin Press, 1965.
Marcus, Harold. *The Life and Times of Menelik II.* London: Clarendon Press, 1975.
Marcus, Harold. *Ethiopia, Great Britain and the United States: The Politics of Empire.* Berkeley: University of California Press, 1983.
Markakis, John. *Ethiopia: Anatomy of a Traditional Polity.* London: Oxford University Press, 1974.
Ottaway, David and Marina. *Ethiopia: Empire in Revolution.* New York: Africana Publishing Company, 1978.
Pankhurst, Richard. *An Economic History of Ethiopia.* Addis Ababa: Haile Selassie I University Press, 1968.
Perham, Margery F. *The Government of Ethiopia.* Evanston: Northwestern University Press, 1969.
Rahmato, Dessalegn. *Agrarian Reform in Ethiopia.* Trenton, N.J.: Red Sea Press, 1984.
Rubenson, Sven. *The Survival of Ethiopian Independence.* London: Heinemann, 1976.
Selassie, Berekhet. *Conflict and Intervention in the Horn of Africa.* London: Monthly Review Press, 1980.
Selassie, Zewde G. *Johannes IV of Ethiopia: A Political Biography.* London: Clarendon Press, 1975.
Shepherd, Jack. *The Politics of Starvation.* New York: Carnegie Endowment for International Peace, 1975.
Sherman, Richard. *Eritrea: The Unfinished Revolution.* New York: Praeger, 1960.

Articles

Ayele, Negussay, "The 1952–1957 Ethio-Italian Boundary Negotiations: An Exercise in Diplomatic Futility," *Journal of Ethiopian Studies,* July, 1971, pp. 127–148.
Bondestam, L., "People and Capitalism in the North-Eastern Lowlands," 12 *Journal of Modern African Studies,* 3, 1974, pp. 413–41.
Brietkze, Paul, "Land Reform in Revolutionary Ethiopia," 14 *Journal of Modern African Studies,* 2, Summer 1978, pp. 249–67.
Caulk, Richard, "The Army and Society in Ethiopia," 1 *Ethiopianist Notes,* 3, Spring 1978, pp. 17–24.
Chege, Michael, "The Revolution Betrayed: Ethiopia 1974–9," 14 *Journal of Modern African Studies,* 3, 1979, pp. 359–68.
Clapham, Christopher, "The December 1960 Ethiopian Coup d'Etat," 6 *Journal of Modern African Studies,* 4, 1968, pp. 495–507.
Cohen, John M., "Effects of Green Revolution Strategies on Tenants and Smallholders in the Chilalo Region of Ethiopia," 9 *Journal of Developing Areas,* April 1975, pp. 335–58.
Cohen, John M., and Peter Koehn, "Rural and Urban Land Reform in Ethiopia," 14 *African Law Studies,* 1, 1977, pp. 3–62.

Dunning, Harrison, "Land Reform in Ethiopia: A Case Study in Non-Development," 18 *U.C.L.A. Law Review,* 2, 1970, pp. 271–307.

Harbeson, John W., "Socialist Politics in Revolutionary Ethiopia," in Rosberg, Carl, and Callaghy, Thomas (eds.), *Socialism in Sub-Saharan Africa: A New Assessment.* Berkeley: Institute for International Studies, University of California, 1979.

Harbeson, John W., "Multilateral Approaches to Multidimensional Conflict Resolution: Lesson from the Horn of Africa," in Day, Arthur, and Doyle, Michael W. (eds.), *Escalation and Intervention: Multilateral Security and Its Alternatives.* Boulder, Colorado: Westview, 1986.

Harbeson, John W., "Afar Pastoralists and Ethiopian Rural Development," 28 *Rural Africana,* 1975, pp. 71–87.

Harbeson, John W., "Territorial and Development Politics Among the Afar of Ethiopia," *African Affairs,* 1979, pp. 479–98.

Keller, Edmond J., "State, Party and Revolution in Ethiopia," 38 *African Studies Review,* 1, March, 1985, pp.1–19.

Levine, Donald, "The Military in Ethiopian Politics: Capabilities and Constraints," in Bienen, Henry. *The Military Intervenes: Case Studies in Political Development.* New York: Russell Sage, 1968.

Markakis, John and Asmelash Beyene, "Representative Institutions in Ethiopia," 5 *Journal of Modern African Studies,* 2, 1967, pp. 193–219.

Ottaway, Marina, "Democracy and New Democracy: The Ideological Debate in the Ethiopian Revolution," 21 *African Studies Review,* 1, April 1978, pp. 19–31.

Ottaway, Marina, "Land Reform in Ethiopia, 1974–77," 20 *African Studies Review,* 3, 1977, pp. 79–90.

Ottaway, Marina, "State Power Consolidation in Ethiopia," in Keller, Edmond, and Donald Rothchild (eds.), *Afro-Marxist Regimes: Ideology and Public Policy.* Boulder, Colorado: Lynne Rienner, 1987, pp. 43–67.

Pliny the Middle-Aged (pseudonym), "The PMAC: Origins and Structure, Part One," 2 *Ethiopianist Notes,* 3, 1978–79 pp. 1–18.

Rahmato, Dessalegn, "The Political Economy of Development in Ethiopia," in Keller, Edmond, and Donald Rothchild (eds.), *Afro-Marxist Regimes: Ideology and Public Policy.* Boulder, Colorado: Lynne Rienner, 1987, pp. 15–81.

Spencer, John, "Haile Selassie: Triumph and Tragedy," 18 *Orbis,* No. 4, 1975, pp. 1129–52.

Index

Abebe Retta, 109
Abiy Abebe, General, 93, 95, 113–114
Abraha, Gedamu, 28
Abyot Seded (revolutionary flame), 159, 171
Ada, 63(n91)
Addis Ababa, 36, 74–76, 96, 100
Addis Zemen, 149–150
Adwa, battle of, 35–36, 42, 105
Afars, 49, 55–56
Agency for International Development (USAID), 21(n31), 55
Agricultural Marketing Corporation (AMC), 200, 209
Agriculture, 47
Ahadu Sabure, 106
Akala-worq Habte Wold, 95
Aklilu Habte Wold, Prime Minister, 45, 86–88, 92
 resignation (1974), 95–96
Alam-Zawd Tessema, Colonel, 108–112
Alemayehu Haile, Captain, 158
Ali, Ras, 31
All-Ethiopian Peasants Association, 159, 173, 183
All-Ethiopia Trade Union, 159, 173, 183
Aman Andom, General, 3, 114, 158
 in Eritrea, 123
 head of state, 120–123
 killed, 124–125
Ambas (mountains), 67
AMC. *See* Agricultural Marketing Corporation

Amharic, 4
Amibara Irrigation Project, 56
Ark of the Covenant, 24
Arusi highlands, 68, 194
Asfa Wossen, 91–92, 107, 114, 120
Asmara, 56–57, 68, 93–94, 109
Asrata Kassa, Ras, 93–96, 98, 110
Assab, Port of, 8
Assefa Ayene, General, 96, 110, 113
Atnafu Abate, Lt. Colonel, 111, 158–159
AVA. *See* Awash Valley Authority
Awash Valley Authority (AVA), 50, 55, 68
Awraja (district council), 54
Awraja self-administration proposal, 91

Bahr Das, 67
BBC. *See* British Broadcasting Corporation
Begemdir, 46
Bete Israel (Falasha), 8, 70, 81(n7)
British Broadcasting Corporation (BBC), 85
Bruce, John, 131–135

Cabinet of 1974, 96–98. *See also* Endalkachew Makonnen
CADU. *See* Chilalo Agricultural Development Unit
Caulk, Richard, 25
CELU. *See* Confederation of Ethiopian Labor Unions
Central Planning Supreme Council (CPSC), 173–174

Index

Chamber of Deputies, 53, 89, 106–107
Chilalo Agricultural Development Unit (CADU), 47–48, 50, 55–56, 63(n91)
Chilot (private court), 13, 113
Christianity, 24–25
Church, Ethiopian Orthodox, 29–31, 36, 70–73, 94
 split with *derg*, 147
 threat to *derg*, 106
Civilian socialism, 2
Clapham, Christopher, 15, 45–46
Class, 11, 74–76, 153
Cohen, John M., 73, 132, 198
Collectivization of agriculture, 169, 172, 175–176, 194, 204
Commission for Organizing the Party of the Working People of Ethiopia (COPWE), 180–186
Confederation of Ethiopian Labor Unions (CELU), 77, 105, 121, 154
 opposition to the *derg*, 145–147
Congo, 79
Constitution of 1931, 119
Constitution of 1955, 53, 90–91, 119
Constitution of 1987, 7, 168, 190–191
COPWE. *See* Commission for Organizing the Party of the Working People of Ethiopia
Council of Ministers, 44–45, 95
 under the *derg*, 158–159, 176
Coup attempt of 1960, 52–53, 77, 94, 97
CPSC. *See* Central Planning Supreme Council
Crown Council, 93, 113
Crummey, Donald, 31
Cuba, 6

Debra Zeit, 93, 109
Dejazmach Berhane Meskel, 67
Dejazmach Zewde Gebre Selassie, 97

Deresse, General, 92–93
Derg (committee), 4, 108–109
 class formation, 153–154
 "creeping coup," 125
 dissension within, 156–157
 and interest groups, 122
 origins, 111–112
 party formation, 149–150
Dessalegn Rahmato, 196, 203
Dessie, 40
Dimbleby, Jonathan, 85
Dire Dawa, 93
Djibouti, 36

Economic aims, 170–179
Economic comparisons, 72(table 3.1), 88–91, 207, 211–212
Economic policy, 128
EDU. *See* Ethiopian Democratic Union
Educational system, 77–78
Education Sector Review (1974), 86–88, 93, 103, 108
Egypt, 29, 33, 68
ELF. *See* Eritrean Liberation Front
Endalkachew Makonnen, 95–104
ENDF. *See* Ethiopian National Democratic Front
English language, 68
EPRP. *See* Ethiopian People's Revolutionary Party
Eritrea, 4, 52–53, 56–57, 71–73
 derg plan for, 155
 rebellion, 167(n82)
Eritrean Liberation Front (ELF), 57, 155
Eritrean People's Liberation Front, 57, 155, 184
Erlich, Haggai, 111–112
Eskinder Desta, Rear Admiral, 94, 109
Ethiopian Democratic Union (EDU), 5, 18(n7), 157, 184
Ethiopian Grain Corporation, 90
Ethiopian Herald, 106
Ethiopian National Democratic Front (ENDF), 184

Ethiopian People's Revolutionary
    Party (EPRP), 5, 147, 150–157
Ethiopian University Service (EUS),
    54
Ethiopia Tikdem (Ethiopia First),
    18(n5), 113, 119–120, 128
EUS. *See* Ethiopian University
    Service
Executions, 4, 124–125
    of *derg* members, 156–157
    by Mengistu, 158–159
    of merchants, 154–155

Famine, 3, 7, 26–27, 67, 83–86,
    163, 207–208
FAO. *See* Food and Agriculture
    Organization
February Revolution, ix
Feudalism, 26
Fikre Merid, 157
Food and Agriculture Organization
    (FAO), 55
Fourth Five-Year Plan (1973), 84
France, 36

Galla, 25
Gamst, Frederick, 28
Geography, 66–68
Getachew Nadew, Brig. General, 156
Girma Fisseha, 109
Gojjam, 32, 39, 46, 57
Gondor, 31
Gran, 29
Great Britain, 32–33
Greenfield, Richard, 34
Gult (Land tenure), 35, 73

Haile Fida, 158
Haile Selassie I, Emperor, 1, 23, 30,
    35–37, 39–47, 51–52, 57–59
    attempted reforms (1974), 102–
    103
    famine, 83–85
    house arrest, 113–114
    legacy, 118–119
    succession, 91–92

Harar highlands, 68, 93
Hess, Robert, 50
Hoare-Laval Plan, 40
Horn of Africa, 8, 161–164
House of David, 24
Housing, 211
Huntington, Samuel, 13
Hyden, Goren, 11–13, 202, 228

ICFTU. *See* International
    Confederation of Free Trade
    Unions
Imru, Michael, 97, 113–114
Imru Haile-Selassie, "Red Ras," 5,
    97, 114
Infant mortality, 212
Institute for Agricultural Research,
    213
Insurgencies. *See* Eritrea;
    Nationalities; Oromo; Tigre
International Confederation of Free
    Trade Unions (ICFTU), 77
International Labor Organization,
    199, 209
International relief efforts, 8
Isakson, Nils-Ivar, 198
Islam, 27–28, 38–39, 70, 107
Israel, 8, 70
Italy, 23, 33–35, 40, 68, 162
Iyasu, Emperor, 38–39, 42

Johannes, Emperor, 23, 30–35, 42

Kagnew, 56, 162
Kasfir, Nelson, 23
Kassa Wolde Mariam, 109
Kebelles (cooperatives), 137–139,
    143, 171–174, 183, 205
Kenya, 67
Kifle Hagas, 91
Kiros Alemayeheu, Captain, 156
Kitema Yefru, 89–90
Kohen, Peter, 132
Korea, 79

Land reform, 4, 16, 35, 223–224

Index 237

under the *derg,* 127–128, 178
  in rural areas, 130–136, 202–204
  in urban areas, 136–139
Land tenure system, 26, 27, 71–74
Language groups, 68–70
League of Nations, 40, 162
Legesse Asfaw, Master Sergeant, 159
Levine, Donald, 26–29, 42, 70
Literacy, 200–201, 212
Local Self-Administration Order of 1966, 54

Mahdist actions, 33, 36
Maleride, 160
Management theory, 15–17
Maria Theresa thalers, 36
Markakis, John, 24, 46
Marxism-Leninism. *See* Socialism
Massawa, 33, 93–94
Meison, 147, 150–159, 184
Mekele, 67
Melba (first stage cooperative), 176
Mendez, Alphonozo, 28
Menelik II, Emperor, 23, 27–30, 32–38, 42–44, 73–74
Mengistu Haile Mariam, 4–9, 15, 111, 148, 157–158, 172–185
Mesfin Sileshi, Ras, 109
Mesfin Wolde Mariam, 136
Mikael, Ras, 39
Military, 78–79
  insurgency, 92–94
  leaflets of, 100–102
  origins of rule, 108–114, 116(n25)
Military-led socialism, 2
Minasse Haile, 98, 113
Minimum Package Program (MPP), 55–56
Ministry for Commerce, Industry and Tourism, 89–90
Ministry of Agriculture, 84
Ministry of Education, 54
Ministry of Interior, 54, 91, 97
Ministry of Land Reform and Administration, 134
Ministry of National Community Development, 85

Ministry of Public Works, 137
Ministry of State Farms, 199
Missionaries, 33
Moges Woldemichael, Captain, 158
MPP. *See* Minimum Package Program
Mussolini, Benito, 40

National Committee for Central Planning (NCCP), 178–180
National Defense and Security Council (NDSC), 185
National Democratic Revolutionary Program (NDRP), 6, 147–155, 159–160, 179–186
National Emergency Relief Committee (NERC), 84
Nationalities, 151
National Literacy Campaign, 200–201
National Military Service Proclamation (No. 236, 1983), 185
National Revolutionary Development Campaign (NRDC), 172–174, 180
National Revolutionary Operations Command (NROC), 171, 180
National Security Commission, 110–111
Natural disasters, 26
NCCP. *See* National Committee for Central Planning
NDRP. *See* National Democratic Revolutionary Program
NDSC. *See* National Defense and Security Council
Nega Tegegne, Major General, 110
Neghelli, 92
Negus (king), 35
Negusa negast (king of kings), 39
NERC. *See* National Emergency Relief Committee
Nile, 68
Nobility, 25
NRDC. *See* National Revolutionary Development Campaign

NROC. *See* National Revolutionary Operations Command

Ogaden. *See* Somalia
OLF. *See* Oromo Liberation Front
Organization of African Unity, 52, 84
Oromo, 25, 29, 42
Oromo Liberation Front (OLF), 163, 184
Ottaway, Marina, 141

Pankhurst, Richard, 36–38
Parliament, 53–54, 90
Pastoralists, 49, 67–68, 213. *See also* Afars
Peasantry, 26–27, 191–214, 229
  associations, 139–142, 171, 178–179, 204–207
People's Democratic Republic, 149, 190, 208–209, 222
People's Organizing Provisional Office (POPO), 149
Petroleum, 88–90
PMAC. *See* Provisional Military Administrative Council
POMOA. *See* Provincial Office of Mass Organizational Affairs
POPO. *See* People's Organizing Provisional Office
Portugal, 29
Proclamation No. 1 (1974), 122
Proclamation No. 31 (1975), 130–136, 142, 203
Proclamation No. 47 (1975), 137–139
Proclamation No. 71 (1975), 142–143
Proclamation No. 77 (1976), 143
Proclamation No. 104 (1976), 143
Proclamation No. 174 (1979), 181
Producer cooperatives, 175–176, 194–199, 205–207
Provincial Office of Mass Organizational Affairs (POMOA), 141, 149, 157

Provisional Military Administrative Council (PMAC), 120–122, 173, 182–186

Railroads, 369
Ras (prince), 5
Red March, 155–156
Red Terror, 157–159
Relief and Rehabilitation Commission, 84
Resettlement, 175–178, 196–198, 206
Revolutionary Ethiopian Women's Association, 173, 183
Revolutionary Ethiopian Youth Association, 173, 183
Rothchild, Donald, 14
Rubenson, Sven, 23–24, 29, 37, 41

Sahle Selassie, 32
Saint Cyr, 40
Separatist nationalism, 2
Setit Humera, 158
Sheba, 24
Shengoes (assemblies), 187
Shepherd, Jack, 85–86
Shoa, 32
Shum shir (divide and rule), 92
Siad Barre, 161, 170
SIDA. *See* Swedish International Development Authority
Sidamo, 106
Sissay Habte, Captain, 156
Skocpol, Theda, 9–11, 14, 228
Slavery, 51
Socialism. *See also* COPWE; Ethiopia Tikdem; WPE
  democratic centralism, 174
  goals, 126–129, 169
  Marxism-Leninism, 100, 230(n1)
  parties, 160
Solomon, 24
Somalia, 6, 19(n9), 39, 52, 163–164, 170
Somali-Abo Liberation Front, 184
Soviet Union, 6, 68, 162, 180

Index

State, 11
State farms, 174–175, 199–200, 207
State transformation, 14
Strikes, 105–108
Students, 77–78, 96, 99–100, 121.
  See also Zemechas
Sudan, 8
Swedish International Development
  Authority (SIDA), 47–48, 55

Tafari, Ras, 39, 42
Tamrat, Taddesse, 26
Tanzania, 11, 16, 128, 202, 209. See
  also Hyden, Goren
Teachers, 77–78
Tef (local grain), 137
Teferri Bente, General, 158
Tej (local beer), 37
Tekalign Gedamu, 98
Tekla Wolde Hawariat, 41
Teklehaimanot, 32–33, 39
Tendaho plantation, 49
Ten Year Plan of 1984 (TYP), 175, 189, 193
Tessema, 38
Tewodros, Emperor, 23–25, 30–35, 42
Tigre, 8, 46, 71–73
Tigrean People's Liberation Front
  (TPLF), 156, 184
Toynbee, Arnold, 23
Trade unions, 53, 74, 76–77, 90, 99–100, 183
Turkey, 29, 68
TYP. *See* Ten Year Plan of 1984

UNDP. *See* United Nations
  Development Program
UNICEF. *See* United Nations
  Children's Emergency Fund
United Nations, 52, 79, 125
United Nations Children's Emergency
  Fund (UNICEF), 85

United Nations Development
  Program (UNDP), 55
United States, 56, 79, 125, 162
University Teachers Association, 100
USAID. *See* Agency for International
  Development

Villagization, 175–177, 197–198, 205–206

Wabe Shebelle, 68
Waldheim, Kurt, 125
Wasleague, 160
Weber, Max, 14
Weintraub, 73
Weland (commune), 176
Welba (second stage cooperative), 176
Welo, 39, 84–86
Western Somalia Liberation Front
  (WSLF), 163, 184
White Terror, 157–159
Wichale, Treaty of (1889), 35
Wolamo, 63(n91)
Wolde-Ghiorgis Wolde-Johannes, 45
Wolde Selassie Bereket, General, 95
Workers National Control
  Committee, 185
Workers' Party of Ethiopia (WPE), 169, 186–191, 201
World Bank, 55–56, 198, 203–208
WPE. *See* Worker's Party of Ethiopia
WSLF. *See* Western Somalia
  Liberation Front

Zamena mesafint (the era of princes), 23–24, 30, 38
Zara Yacob, Prince, 92, 107
Zauditu, Empress, 39
Zemechas (campaigns), 4, 123–130
  failures of, 156
  land reform and, 132–134, 140–141
  opposition to the *derg*, 144
Zimbabwe, 140